THE ART of DISSENT

EDITORS
Hilary Powell
Isaac Marrero-Guillamón

COVER IMAGE
Stephen Gill, from *Buried* series

PUBLISHED BY
Marshgate Press
Unit 9E, Mother Studios
Queens Yard, White Post Lane
Hackney Wick
London E9 5EN

First published, 2012

ISBN 978-0-9572943-0-1

DESIGN
See Studio
13 Prince Edward Rd.
Hackney Wick
London E9 5LX

PRINTED AT
Calverts Co-operative
9-10 The Oval
London E2 9DT

THANKS TO
The Bartlett School of Architecture Research Fund, UCL
The Art and Design Research Institute, Middlesex University
Arts and Humanities Research Council
Spanish Ministry of Education

THE ART of DISSENT

ADVENTURES IN LONDON'S OLYMPIC STATE

EDITED BY HILARY POWELL & ISAAC MARRERO-GUILLAMÓN

MARSHGATE
PRESS

Table of Contents

Timeline

London Olympics	**1908**	
London Olympics	**1948**	
Cedric Price and Joan Littlewood's Fun Palace plan for the Lea Valley	**1964**	
Olympic Symbol (Protection) Act is passed	**1995**	
16 January. London's Olympic bid is launched	**2004**	Braden and Campany begin Adventures in the Valley (p. 160)
6 July. London wins Bid 7 July. London bombings The London Development Agency serves Compulsory Purchase Orders Museum of London Archaeological services on site	**2005**	SPACE begins Legacy Now series and the Olympic Artist Forum (p. 264) Saint Etienne film What Have You Done Today Mervyn Day
London Olympic and Paralympic Games Act is passed Public Consultation begins (p. 214)	**2006**	Stephen Gill's Buried book is published (p. 110) Gesche Würfel begins Go for Gold! (p. 136) Stephen Cornford begins trespassing the Olympic site (p. 35) Juliet Adair takes a plot at the Manor Garden Allotments (p. 220)
12 July. The Olympic Delivery Authority aquires the Olympic site Manor Garden Allotments eviction Clays Lane Estate eviction The blue fence is erected Demolish Dig Design phase begins Soil cleaning 2012 Logo launched	**2007**	Thomas Pausz's Revisiting the Community shed (p. 228) Alessandra Chilá's Olympian Visions (p. 184) Mark Wayman performs an East London Border (p. 78) Hilary Powell films The Games (p. 100) Pudding Mill River begin harvesting in the Olympic fringelands (p. 124) Jean-François Prost begins his "residency" and interventions around the blue fence (p. 72)

2008

The Cultural Olympiad is launched
Beijing Olympics Torch Handover
First Adizones are installed in the Olympic boroughs (p. 56)

Susan Pui San Lok's Faster, Higher is shown at the BFI (p. 90)
Richard DeDomenici is a torch handover imposter (p. 40)
Kirscher and Panos' Trail of the Spider is premiered in Hackney (p. 164)
Soundproof project begins (p. 82)
Salon de Refuse Olympique begins
OSA's Point of View is built (p. 68)

2009

Blue fence replaced by electric fence
The Olympic Park Legacy Company (OPLC) is established

Lara Almarcegui's Guide to the Wastelands of the Valley is published (p. 126)
David George Dissolution Series (p. 178)

2010

Vancouver Winter Olympics
ArcelorMittal Orbit Tower is announced
Olympic Park Big Build phase
Olympic Park Artist in Residence Neville Gabie is appointed.

Fantich & Young show Double Games Red in Tooth and Claw during the Hackney WickED Festival (p. 105)
Jim Woodall's Olympic State (p. 30)
Giles Price's Amber Alert (p. 21)
SPACE commission The Cut

2011

13 September. Westfield Stratford City Shopping Centre opens
British Waterways announces changes to the mooring policy on the canals and restrictions during the Games
Official art commissions are installed on the Olympic Park

Iain Sinclair's Ghost Milk is published (p. 136)
Alex Sprogis casts a Stratford Façade (p. 278)

2012

The London Legacy Development Corporation (LLDC) is established
London 2012 Games

The Art of Dissent

Introduction
Intervening in London 2012

ISAAC MARRERO-GUILLAMÓN AND HILARY POWELL

This book is a monument to dissent. Not a celebration, not a commemoration of past events, but a monument – it preserves, for the eyes and ears of the future, the enduring vibration of a series of dissenting percepts and affects, landscapes and faces, visions and becomings.[1] We have brought together a collection of works that shake up the cartography of the sensible and the thinkable enacted by the Olympics.[2] The contributors gathered in this volume have refused their role as recipients and spectators of the Olympic-led transformation and acted in myriad ways – subtle, militant, analytical, passionate – upon the arrival of the Olympic machine in the East End of London. In doing so, they have challenged a key element in the production of consensus around the Games: the division between those who may speak and those who may not, between that which can be discussed and that which cannot.[3] This is a book made of words that were not meant to be heard, images that were not supposed to be seen – a slit in the consensual space of London 2012.

The Art of Dissent: Adventures in London's Olympic State is a heterogeneous assemblage. We have attempted to form a dissenting coalition, but one without a unified form. First, we have ignored disciplinary or reputational distinctions and "artistic", "academic", "poetic", or "amateur" contributions, by known and unknown authors, coexist next to one another. Second, the singularity of each contribution is preserved as such and not subsumed into a wider commonality, be it narrative or political.[4] We have been careful to let these works "be together apart",[5] considering that this form of decentralised multiplicity, defined by the lack of a unified position, is productive in the generation of platforms that cut across more traditional forms of belonging. In doing this we are also mirroring the wider unfolding of the resistance and critique to the London Games, which has been characterised by the lack of a coordinated, centralised organisation. The absence of such a structure, we would argue, has created an inclusive space for dissent in which no *proper* course of action could be defined and in which a variety of *improprieties* could indeed be tested.[6]

It is fair to say that the only common characteristic shared by the works that make up this book is *to be in disagreement* over one aspect or another of the mega-event and its imprint. "Dissent" comes from the Latin verb "dissentire", or "differ in sentiment", and the *Oxford Dictionary* defines it as "the expression or holding of opinions at variance with those previously, commonly, or officially held" and the "refusal to accept the doctrines of an established or orthodox church; nonconformity". Inspired by its etymology, its literal meaning and the work of Jacques Rancière, this book takes dissent as the driving force in a series of incursions and excursions designed to crack (wide) open London's Olympic state.

We have divided *The Art of Dissent* in four parts: "Incursions" explores the political economy of the mega-event, including its legal foundations, physical footprint and symbolic dimension. "Excavations" looks at the recent past of the Lower Lee Valley – a past already effaced by development. The area where the Olympic park now sits was until recently host to a wide array of unregulated and unpoliced activities whose ghosts are summoned by the works in this section. "Displacements" engages specifically with those who were evicted to make way for the Olympics. Clays Lane residents, Manor Garden Allotments users and members of the boating community are here heard in their own words and through the work of others. "Aftermaths" considers the question of the Olympic legacy. Below, each of these four sections and the works featured in them are introduced with greater detail.

Incursions

This section explores the legal, economic and physical "architecture" of the London Olympics. Isaac Marrero-Guillamón's text discusses the unofficial declaration of a "state of exception" to "protect" the Games and its sponsors – and the concomitant militarisation of urban space (p. 20). Julian Walker studies the draconian legislation passed to prevent "ambush marketing", including the "protection" of words such as "Summer", "London" or "Gold" (p. 41), while Alistair Siddons fully adopts this logic and takes it to its absurdity (p. 51). The main beneficiaries of this exceptional state within a state, besides the organisers of the Games themselves, are of course the official "partners": among others, Coca-Cola, Dow, McDonald's, Omega, Visa, BP, BMW, EDF and British Airways. Alberto Duman's photo-essay studies the way one of those sponsorship deals became integrated in urban planning through a case study of AdiZones, branded outdoor gyms produced by Adidas (p. 56).

The regulation and control over public space enforced by the Olympic authorities is the target of several of the projects featured in this section. Giles Price's pictures of the Olympic Park's electric fence deploy a visual language that generates dark resonances with other well-known spaces of seclusion and brutality (p. 21). Jim Woodall's self-made hut is effectively a counter-surveillance control room aimed at the Olympic border (p. 30). Woodall's response to the prevalence of CCTV in the area was to add a new layer to it creating a sort of infinite loop, with two sets of cameras watching each other, showing nothing much – but a nothingness that was not supposed to be seen. Stephen Cornford's repeated trespassing of the site literally challenged the regime of invisibility imposed by Olympic Delivery Agency, that had not only fenced up and closed to the public an 11-mile perimeter, but also prohibited any image-making in the surroundings (p. 35). The images and narratives Cornford produced are a testament to the fact that the prohibition was not so much aimed at preventing people from recording something particularly controversial or secret – but to regulate the visible and to establish a clear distinction between image-producers and image-consumers. Similarly, the iconic blue plywood fence that enclosed the area (p. 66) until it was substituted by an electric version was kept spotless by an army of painters working around the clock. This made graffiti and other interventions particularly ephemeral – it did not matter *what* was written on the wall, but the fact that somebody had done it.

Nonetheless, critical interventions flourished. Jean-François Prost managed to trace the exact colour used and responded to the lack of duration of inscriptions of dissent on the wall by painting blue "extensions" to it instead (p. 72). The Office for Subversive Architecture built a viewing platform and attached it to the fence so that anybody could peek into the construction site (p. 68). Studio Superniche got hold of some discarded bits of the wall and recycled them into pavilions designed to reclaim other uses for the site (p. 74).

Those who trespassed or peeked onto the site have revealed something important: there was nothing to hide in it. Behind the wall there was only a *void*, an empty centre – as in Michael Ende's *The Neverending Story*, where diverse landscapes and populations are threatened with horrible extinction by the encroachment of "The Great Nothingness". Mark Wayman's *An East London Border* performance navigates the perimeter of this nothingness without ever looking into it, its absence becoming increasingly conspicuous through its effect in the neighbouring landscapes (p. 78).

The iconography of the Games, supposedly the most widely recognised brand in the world, is a major component in the production of the consensus (and profit) around the Olympics. As John Wynne and Helen Lenksyj discuss in conversation (p. 86), its very universality makes it "ripe for détournement". Wynne's work with subverted Olympic rings and audio messages was part of Monica Biagioli's Sound Proof commissions, a yearly series that among other things examined the myths, rites and symbols of the Games (p. 82).

Fantich & Young's sculptures unleash the violence of competition embedded in Gymnasium apparatus, relating sport and physical education to the project of eugenics (p. 105). Hilary Powell discusses with Ali McGlip her film *The Games* (p. 100), where the grandiose spectacle of the Olympics is given an anti-heroic, gritty rendition, with non-athletes competing among the future ruins of the Lower Lea Valley. The deconstruction of the Olympic "spirit" is here accompanied by the geography of Olympic cleansing. Susan Pui San Lok has adapted her five-screen installation *Faster, Higher* into a visual essay where the resonances between sport, nationalism, patriotism and physical achievements are investigated (p. 90). The ritualistic aspect of the Olympic spectacle is here put in relation with other ceremonies and national celebrations in a multi-layered, non-linear way.

These disturbances and interruptions of the Olympic symbols and properties attempt to taint the benign, harmless image the Games rely on. Far from a mere semiotic exercise, tarnishing the so-called purity of the Olympic brand is a strategy to undermine the cornerstone of its economic architecture. By associating these symbols with the violence of land-grab, competition, urban renewal or nationalism, we hope to crack the impunity they enjoy.

Excavations

In the alchemical rhetoric of renewal and regeneration the Lower Lee Valley was consistently described as dirty, an undeniable site of noxious dumping with a history of heavy industry, ripe for deep cleansing and transformation. The archival urge present in many of the works in this section stands in direct opposition to the amnesia of development and its "palimpsest of erasures".[7] These projects make an argument against a notion of memory as passive and invoke an active past in which remembering (and even nostalgia) takes on new form and meaning as protest, monument, and at times revenge.

It is apt that this section begins quite literally in the dirt with a process of unearthing as Ben Campkin (p. 112) examines Stephen Gill's *Buried* photo-works – a collaboration between image and matter, a double chemical exposure to light and soil, to the effects of time and decay, as photographs were buried and later exhumed from east London's earth (p. 110). As seen in Victoria Lenzoi Lee's *Olympic Terra* (p. 108), this soil tells a story of contaminated land and vision, a layered history of an area sampled and surveyed.

An expanded poetic and archaeological investigation of this delicately poised pre-Olympic site emerges through these works. In the beginnings of archaeology the "artist's impression" was a core element of a site's "uncovering", and in their own permutations of this process and variant "field studies"[8] the artists here assembled draw on a diverse range of "data" and "finds" exposing and piecing together a multifaceted counter-history and story of a site under duress. Mining the mundane and everyday visions and experiences of place they dig deep and lay bare the easily buried and forgotten narratives and fictions of the area - both uncovering and creating the intertwined texts and textures that make up a place and a "narrative subjected to the city, in its endless process of splits, multiplications, openings, abandonment."[9] An excerpt from Lara Almarcegui's *Guide to the Wastelands of the Lea Valley* (p. 126) reveals a history of literal waste management inscribed in the invisible pipes running beneath the pastoral landscapes of the Greenway. Another excerpt, from Iain Sinclair's *Ghost Milk*, summons the radioactive ghosts and the toxic spectres disturbed by the Olympic Delivery Authority's diggers (p. 131).

As newspaper headlines urged the area to "Go For Gold!" early on, Gesche Würfel adopted the same title for an on-going series of pictures depicting the spaces of the future Olympic venues starting before the transformation had begun (p. 136). While the captions described Hockey Arenas, Olympic Stadiums, Media Centres and Velodromes, the photographs portrayed industrial estates, dense vegetation or car repair garages – with the gap between image and text closing in as the project progressed. The interplay between presence and absence, appearances and disappearances is explored by Chris Dorley-Brown in his *Re-shoots* series (p. 140). By systematically pairing pictures in a classic "before and after" fashion, the mapping of the changes in the territory becomes an essay on time and the city. In *Adventures in the Lea Valley*, Polly Braden and David Campany occupy the spaces about to be transformed, constructing cinematic scenes of social, animal and vegetal life in the valley filled with affection (p. 160). More than a lament or anticipation of loss, these images are a celebration, at times epic, of the hidden life of the canals and the marshes. Leigh Niland, in conversation with Sally Mumby-Croft (p. 170), explains how she exploited the relative slowness of drawing and painting to embed these records of the quick changes in Hackney Wick with personal and social intensity.

The love of place, or "topophilia",[10] is also an important part of David George's *Dissolution Series*, in which he set out to capture the disappearance of the marshes as he knew them; these haunting, pictorial images portray the Lower Lea Valley teetering on the brink of a vanishing point (p. 178). Reviewing Anja Kirshner and David Panos' *Trail of the Spider*, Neil Gray explains how the filmmakers made sense of the massive land-grab operation on the marshes via a subversion of the spaghetti western genre (p. 164). A similarly unsettling effect is provoked by Anthony Iles in his exploration of the continuities between previous development plans for the area, including Cedric Price's Fun Palace, and the Olympic-led regeneration masterplan (p. 150).

Displacements

From 2005 to 2007 the London Development Agency managed the largest Compulsory Purchase Order in British history: 1,500 residents, 200 businesses and 5,000 jobs were displaced in order to assemble the land needed to build the Olympic park. This section analyses this process and presents some of the counter-narratives it triggered.

It opens with an image from Rebecca Court's *Olympic Site CPO*, a project examining the politics of language, law and land-acquisition with typeset soil "text interventions" in the vicinity of the Olympic site - with the words "compulsory purchase order" as a literal writ on the land (p. 182). Alessandra Chilá's *Olympian Visions* follows: an image-text project in which militant captions discussing the violence of Olympic-led transformation offset the beauty of a series of pictures of the Valley on the verge of transformation, but without a trace of the Olympics (p. 184).

The link between the land assembly process and the discourse and visualisations of "regeneration" is explored in detail by Juliet Davis (p. 188), while Craig Hatcher's detailed study of the use of Compulsory Purchase Order in the case of Clays Lane unpacks the legal devices of displacement (p. 197). Operating against the politics of erasure enacted by the ODA, Benjamin Beach's gobo projection "Clays Lane Was Here" (p. 199) inscribes the disappearance of the estate onto the new surfaces of the Olympic site, while Adelita Husni-Bey's *Clays Lane Live Archive*, made in collaboration with evicted residents, provides a cacophonic platform for their memories, images, documents, desires – reassembling a common space that has been dismantled by "regeneration" (p. 207).

Cultivated for over 100 years, the Manor Garden Allotments held a plethora of stories and variegated experiences – an abundance in stark contrast to a hard-fought but eventually fruitless campaign against eviction. Fragments of this narrative are uncovered and celebrated in Juliet Adair's *Athletes to Zuchinis: An A-Z for Manor Garden Allotments* (p. 220) and photographer Mimi Mollica's portraits of stoic long-time occupants (p. 223). This portent of imminent disappearance is made both tangible and spectral in Jan Stradtmann's photographic series of the makeshift allotment sheds illuminated by night - vernacular ruins made temporary monuments by their forced obsolescence (p. 231). Thomas

Pausz's *Revisiting the Community Shed* (p. 228) project appropriates and subverts the box-ticking exercises of community consultation – a procedure explored as tragic farce in Martin Slavin's revealing photographs of the Olympic consultation process (p. 214).

The boaters community has also been dislocated by the Games, the canals being taken over by security and landscaping concerns. Jessie Brennan's large-scale drawing *The Cut* alludes to a filmstrip montage of the area in its intricately constructed cross-section of a community/place/history on the move, a multiple narrative appropriately drawn within the contours of a canal boat (p. 232). The urge and need to collect and inscribe alternative histories and overlooked narratives is also present in Man Cheung's series of stories and portraits of boaters resident on the River Lea (p. 238). A boater himself, poet Andrew Bailes weaves in a dystopian fiction of displacement and future ruination intercut with the language of compulsory purchase orders collected and appropriated from their multiple locations, hidden in plain sight on fences, pylons, or telegraph posts (p. 243). This recovery of a fragmenting/fragmented language and landscape is also evident in the excerpts of Jude Rosen's long-form poem *Reclamations: Voices and Narratives from the Olympic Zone* (p. 65, 181, 230).

Aftermaths

The restrictions on independent image-making around the Olympic site have had their counterpoint in a constant procession of happy, hygienic images of the future. In this section, these visions and visuals are contested through various dystopian exercises and reality checks. Rowena and Duncan Hay combine fictional prose segments written in an alternative future with a critical analysis of the Olympic regeneration promise and model (p. 254). A similar effect is achieved by Benedict Seymour in *OlympicField*, a short film that re-samples an official advertisement campaign[11] as future found footage to create a dystopian, apocalyptic science fiction tale in the best John Carpenter tradition (p. 284).

If there is one promise that has been relentlessly announced it is without a doubt the outstanding "legacy" that the Games will leave for east London. Anna Harding from SPACE (p. 264) discusses *Legacy Now*, the organisation's attempt to facilitate a sustained dialogue between local artists, politicians and developers, rejecting the idea of legacy as something bestowed or bequeathed and reclaiming the role for local actors in defining it. Oliver Wainwright investigates one of the first tangible materializations of the Olympic legacy – the rising development strip that is Stratford High Street, and its pastiche architecture (p. 272). In the same street, Alex Sprogis casts the surface of a façade recovering "the density of the city through a scavenging poetic, which works like an inverted parody of future-orientated urban planning"[12] (p. 278). The contrast between the ostentatious new structures and the general state of neglect of their surroundings is encapsulated in two distinct registries: Henrietta Williams' new topographics-style images of the Olympic Village (p. 252) and the vernacular style of the photo-essay produced by local Stratford youth who participated in Paul Watt and Jacqueline Kennelly's research project, in which the Olympic legacy promises are filtered through the experiences and expectations of those living under its very shadow (p. 281). Also operating in this area, Laura Oldfield Ford's *Savage Messiah* posters stand against the rising capitalist- and debt-fuelled architecture of Stratford, short-circuiting the anodyne visions of official images with violent strokes: suppressed memories, forbidden desires and dystopian renderings are all summoned in her drawings (p. 260).

Working both on demolition sites on the edges of the Olympic Park and with the archaeological archives of the Olympic site itself, Hilary Powell's *Structures of Enchantment* is a vast archive of all the buildings once standing reconstructed as pop-up books (p. 286). In this archaeology or "ruins in reverse", collapse and progress occur simultaneously and large-scale building works seem to "cast the shadow of their own destruction before them and are designated from the first with an eye to their later existence as ruins."[13]

About the origins of this book

This book is the result of the encounter between Hilary's continuous and continually changing relationship with the area surrounding the London 2012 Olympic Park since 2001 and Isaac's involvement in the subject of critical art and the Olympics a decade later. *The Art of Dissent* grows out of this collaboration, as well as a series of relationships built over time, through a range of events, with the many others who have also been possessed with a need to intervene in, document, create and critique the processes, politics and poetics that surround the Lower Lea Valley and its takeover by the Olympic "machine". What follows is a necessarily partial account of the events that led to this book.

Soon after London won the right to host the 2012 Olympics in July 2005, SPACE established the Olympic Artist Forum alongside their *Legacy Now* series, aiming to bring together artists whose work engaged with or critiqued the Olympic development. Living and working on the future Olympic Park's borders and focusing both her artistic practice and research in and about this changing place, Hilary later took on the organisation of the Artist Forum. This began with a "pecha kucha" debate hosted by SPACE, chaired by performance artist Richard DeDomenici (p. 40) and introducing the work of artists Alberto Duman (p. 56), Grunts for the Arts, Thomas Pausz (p. 228) and the "I Love the Olympics" tour initiated by Ana Méndez de Andés. By 2008 the Forum had become the "Salon de Refuse Olympique" – the new name responding to over-zealous Olympic copyright laws regulating the use of "protected" words, as well as the appeal of the reference to the 19th Century Parisian Salon des Refusés where the exhibition of "rejects" became an avant-garde of sorts. The idea of providing a platform for counter exhibition and a site of experimentation and innovation was indeed integral to the project. One such salon was held at Café Oto in Dalston as part of This Is Not A Gateway Festival, and included artists Stephen Cornford (p. 35), Tessa Garland, Julika Gittner and Jon Purnell, Gesche Würfel (p. 136), Jim Thorp and Andreas Lang, alongside Emma Dwyer of the Museum of London Archaeological Services and Fiona Fieber of SPACE.

In February 2009 Hilary was invited by muf architecture/art to reconvene the Salon de Refuse Olympique for Yale students and a public audience at the Elevator Gallery in Hackney Wick, with a focus on "Alternative Olympic Legacy". In collaboration with Arcola Green Sundays and the Festival of European Alternatives, May 2009 saw these events move outside to the borders of the Olympic Park with a guerrilla screening evening called "Blue Movies on the Greenway". Films including David Knight's *Outfall*, Jean-François Prost's *All Aboard*, Jem Finer's *Rise and Fall of the Olympic State* (p. 83), Tessa Garland's *Parklife*, Hilary Powell's *The Games* (p. 100) and shorts from "Pudding Mill River: Purveyors of Sporting Spirits and Foodstuffs" (p. 124) were projected on the remaining sections of the blue fence that surrounded the site to mark its dismantling and replacement by a high-voltage electric version.

In June 2009 the model of debate followed by outdoor screenings continued with "Fringe in the Fringelands". A discussion on artists' responses to the Olympics was held at the Counter Café in Hackney Wick, incorporating the launch of Jean-François Prost's *Adaptive Actions* publication (p. 72) and the making of boats out of the remains of the Olympic blue fence with a group of then Royal College of Arts students. "Blue Movies" (films made on, about, around the Olympic Park and its blue borders) were then projected onto the sails of these craft as they drifted past the growing Olympic Stadium.

In January 2011, Hilary received a three-year Arts and Humanities Research Council postdoctoral fellowship in the creative and performing arts at the Bartlett School of Architecture (UCL) for her project *Structures of Enchantment* (p. 278) focusing specifically on the past, present, and future of the London 2012 Olympic site. The same month, Isaac got funding from the Spanish Ministry of Education for a two-year postdoctoral fellowship at Birkbeck, University of London, with the project *Looking at/for the militant city: political space and art in the post-industrial Olympic city*. The project kicked off with an event organised in Stratford by Birkbeck and Gasworks Gallery entitled "Learning From Barcelona: Art, Real Estate and the Pre-Olympic City". A dialogue between London and Barcelona practitioners was established around the impact of the Olympics on the political space of the host city. Representing London were Peter Coles, Adelita Husni-Bey (p. 207), Ben Seymour (p. 284), Iain Sinclair (p. 131), Martin Slavin (p. 214) and Jim Woodall (p. 30).

The event led to the organisation in May 2011 of *24-hour Olympic State*, a collaboration between Jim Woodall, Cristina Garrido, See Studio and Isaac, which took the form of a day-long event featuring works and presentations by Hilary Powell, Monica Biagioli (p. 82), Giles Price (p. 21), Charlie Hope, Adnan Hazdi, Alyssa Moxley (p. 30), let_them_eat_coal & Hamilton Industry, public works, muf architecture/art, Francesca Weber-Newth, Martin Slavin (p. 214), Fiona Fieber, Chris Dorley-Brown (p. 140) and Daniel Lehan.

By this point, Hilary's and Isaac's projects and networks were starting to overlap, a fact later ratified by the joint organisation of "An Olympian marathon" of five "Salon de Refuse Olympique" debates in September and October 2011. This collaboration planted the seed to the co-editing of this book – itself an attempt to bring together these trajectories into a manageable assemblage.

We hope that the debates that structure this book and the trajectories it draws from provide the elements to articulate an alternative narrative of London 2012. With the works here assembled we have attempted to rethink the legacy of the Olympics by way of a history of the antagonisms it has triggered - a counter-legacy written against the grain of the hegemonic "regeneration" narrative. Humans, plants, buildings, spirits, toxic residues, façades, memories have all taken the stage and spoken. We have heard and seen stories of displacement and effacement, critical analyses, images of abandoned pasts and futures, daring interventions, playful narratives - all co-existing in a heterogeneous assemblage of dissenting voices. Perhaps their enduring vibrations can inspire and awake the desire and belief to dissent in other places and times as well.

Gustavo Murillo,
Blue Fence, 2012

INCURSIONS

THE LONDON 2012 OLYMPICS HAVE ESTABLISHED WHAT PHILOSOPHER JACQUES RANCIÈRE CALLS A "POLICE ORDER" – A REGULATION OF WHAT IS VISIBLE, SAYABLE AND KNOWABLE ABOUT THE MEGA-EVENT, AND BY WHOM. THIS SMOOTH SPACE OF CONSENSUS RESTS ON A SERIES OF PHYSICAL, LEGAL, ECONOMIC AND SYMBOLIC STRUCTURES, ALL OF WHICH ARE CHALLENGED IN THIS SECTION. THE WORDS AND IMAGES HERE SUMMONED UNPACK SOME OF THE ARRANGEMENTS THAT SUSTAIN AND FUEL THE OLYMPIC MACHINE, ENGAGE WITH THEIR PHYSICAL MANIFESTATION IN THE FORM OF FENCES AND RESTRICTIONS, AND ACTIVELY RESIST THE ATTRACTION OF ITS CONSENSUAL ICONS AND LANGUAGE.

Olympic State of Exception

ISAAC MARRERO-GUILLAMÓN*

Every other year the Olympic machine lands at a different city, where it nonetheless encounters a familiar scenario: by the night of the opening ceremony all the necessary infrastructures will have been built, free of charge, by the host; all of the city's advertising space will have been occupied by the official sponsors of the event; state of the art security and military measures will have been deployed to protect the event; high-speed lanes connecting the venues with certain hotels will have been made exclusively available to the convenience of the members of the International Olympic Committee (IOC); and, if everything has gone according to plan, tickets will be long gone and an army of eager volunteers will be at the disposal of the organisers.

The Summer and Winter Olympics, like the FIFA World Cup or the Formula 1, are travelling mega-events which far exceed the realm of organised sports. They are global multi-billion businesses, as well as powerful instruments of local urban policy, usually linked to vast regeneration schemes.[1] Cities compete for hosting these events, offering favourable fiscal conditions and large infrastructure investments, as a unique opportunity for place marketing and international attention. They are also increasingly legitimised on the basis of their positive legacy for the city. This chapter explores some of the tensions these arrangements have generated in the case of the London 2012 Olympics. More specifically, I will discuss how the smooth (and profitable) operation of the Games requires a "state of exception", regulated by exceptional laws and protected by extraordinary measures. My goal in this text is to analyse the interface between the exceptionality of the "legal architecture" of the Olympics (the laws and contracts that regulate the mega-event) and its spatial manifestation in the form of a military urbanism.

Drawing from Giorgio Agamben's work,[2] I will argue that the colossal transformation of the legal and spatial landscape brought about by the 2012 Games effectively relies on the unofficial declaration of a state of exception, that is, the suspension of the ordinary juridical order. Agamben's study of the deployment of the state of exception shows how rather than a provisional and exceptional *measure* it has become a *technique* of government, increasingly used in a range of non-war situations, such as financial crises, general strikes[3] or, more recently and infamously, the USA Patriot Act and Guantánamo. Defined as the suspension of law by law, the state of exception produces an empty

Giles Price,
Amber Alert, 2010

space, a zone of indeterminacy in which bare life (the human being stripped of political and legal attributes) is encompassed by naked power (a limitless power, which is not tied to the legal system). However void, this legal no-man's-land has proved to be highly effective, to the extent that "the voluntary creation of a permanent state of emergency (though perhaps not declared in the technical sense) has become one of the essential practices of contemporary states, including so-called 'democratic' ones."[4] The state of exception is legitimised on the grounds of exceptional necessity, and sustained through military metaphors: "a vocabulary of war is maintained metaphorically to justify recourse to extensive government powers".[5]

The state of exception, as a legal phenomenon, is linked in Agamben's theory to the "camp", "the space that is opened when the state of exception begins to become the rule".[6] Although concentration camps or detainee centres would be clear examples, the concept of the "camp" refers to *any* space in which the normal order is *de facto* suspended: "To an order without localization (the state of exception, in which law is suspended) there now corresponds a localization without order (the camp as permanent space of exception)."[7] My goal in this text is to establish a series of analogies between Agamben's concepts and the legal and physical architecture of London 2012.

The legal architecture of the Games

The IOC is the supreme authority of the Olympic Movement, responsible among other things for promoting Olympism worldwide and ensuring the regular celebration of Olympic Games. The Games are the IOC's exclusive property; they own "all rights and data relating thereto, in particular, and without limitation, all rights relating to their organisation, exploitation, broadcasting, recording, representation, reproduction, access and dissemination in any form and by any means or mechanism whatsoever, whether now existing or developed in the future".[8] This includes control over all the "Olympic properties": the Olympic symbol, the flag, the motto, the anthem, the emblems, the flame, the torches, and so on. The exploitation of these rights and properties allowed the IOC – a not-for-profit international non-governmental organisation with circa 300 employees – to make an estimated $2,300 million between 2001 and 2004[9] and a profit of $383 million on the Beijing 2008 Summer Olympics alone.[10] Based in Lausanne, the IOC is not subject to income or wealth tax by virtue of an agreement with the Swiss Government.[11]

When London won the right to organise the 2012 Olympics in July 2005, the city signed the Host City Contract with the IOC.[12] Following the agreement, a limited company, the London Organising Committee of the Olympic and Paralympic Games (LOCOG), was established in order to organise the Games with "maximum benefit and efficiency".[13] Shortly after, the London Olympic and Paralympic Games Act 2006 (LOPGA) was passed. Among other things, the Act established the creation of a public body responsible for building the infrastructures needed for the Games, the Olympic Delivery Agency (ODA).

The ODA has extraordinarily wide-ranging powers: the capacity to design and implement urban plans, the development of the sporting and transport infrastructure, the control of the advertising space and street trading licences around Olympic venues, and the power to investigate and prosecute breaches of Olympic brand related rights. As James and Osborn have observed: "No other public body combines the functions of a local council, planning authority, transport executive, trading standards office and police service, yet the ODA has been granted powers similar to those exercised by each of these bodies."[14] *First measure of exception: the abolition of the distinction between legislative, executive and judicial powers.*

According to the Host City Contract, any profit resulting from the organisation of the Games is to be divided between the British Olympic Association (20%), the promotion of sport in the host country (60%) and the IOC (20%). Were there to be losses, however, the public bodies are liable.[15] In addition, all payments made by or to the IOC regarding revenues generated in relation to the Games are tax-exempt. Article 49 establishes that the city and/or LOCOG "shall bear all taxes, including direct and indirect taxes, whether they be withholding taxes, customs duties, value added taxes or any other indirect taxes, whether present or future, due in any jurisdiction".[16] The amounts involved are not insignificant. LOCOG's budget, self-funded by ticket sales, a percentage of the IOC's revenue, and its own exploitation of the Olympic brand, is £2,000 million; meanwhile, the ODA's budget, 98.2% public-funded, is £9,325 million.[17] In other words, £9 billion of public funds have been allocated to set the scene for a £2 billion privately owned and tax-free event, whose owner is also rendered non-liable for any hypothetical losses. *Second measure of exception: the creation of a tax haven in East London.*

These exceptionally generous fiscal conditions secured by the IOC rest on the generation of substantial surplus value in the first place. In relation to this, the city has to obtain "control over all city advertising opportunities: airport, train, bus, and other transport advertising, as well as billboard advertising"[18] for the period of the Games and the previous month, and hand it over to the official sponsors. Most of the Olympic revenue comes from exclusive broadcasting (47%) and sponsorships (45%) contracts.[19] The IOC oversees all broadcasting contracts and the worldwide "The Olympic Partners" (TOP) sponsorship programme, while allowing local organising committees to manage ticket sales and sign local sponsorship deals. These contracts exploit the value of the exclusive association with the Olympic brand, which is the reason why the latter must be "adequately and permanently" protected.[20]

In the case of London 2012, this protection is granted by the Olympic Symbol etc. (Protection) Act 1995 and the LOPGA 2006, cited above. As Julian Walker explains in more detail in this volume, words such as "Olympiad", "Olympian", "Olympic", "Summer", "2012", "Twenty-Twelve" or "Gold", as well as all the iconography associated with the London Games, have their use restricted to official sponsors. In fact, "any representation (of any kind) in a manner likely to suggest to the public that there is an association between the London Olympics and (a) goods or services, or (b) a person who provides goods or services"[21] will be deemed an instance of "ambush marketing" and hence subject to legal and police action:

> Ambush marketing occurs when an unauthorised commercial entity implies an association with the Olympic Movement without a marketing agreement with an appropriate Olympic party… The value of the rights granted to the Olympic marketing partners is directly related to the Olympic Family's ability to protect that exclusivity. Ambush marketing occurs when this exclusivity is violated by any entity… [It] poses a serious potential threat to the Olympic Movement, because: (a) it could destroy the overall revenue base of the Olympic Movement, and (b) it undermines corporate confidence in Olympic partnership investments.[22]

The notion of financial threat, or even catastrophe, becomes the legitimating force that justifies the draconian measures established by the LOPGA 2006, discussed below. *Third instance of exceptionality: the use of the vocabulary of war to justify resort to exceptional forms of penality.*

Sections 19–31 of the Act regulate advertising and street trade in the vicinity of the events, as well as the powers of enforcement. Any form of unsanctioned advertising of goods or services or street trading is strictly forbidden, with fines up to £20,000 on conviction being established. The Act also grants the police the right to "enter land or premises on which they reasonably believe a contravention of regulations" is occurring; "remove, destroy, conceal or erase any infringing article" and "use, or authorise the use of, reasonable force for the purpose of taking action under this subsection".[23] This framework grants the IOC an "extreme and unprecedented"[24] protection over their properties. It is hard to exaggerate the extraordinariness of the situation: anti-terrorist-like powers have been approved by Parliament in order to "protect" a set of words, signs and symbols so they can be commercially exploited by the IOC and LOCOG. Moreover, the Act rests on the reversal of onus: it requires the accused to prove the elements of the defence as opposed to being presumed innocent.

The Act controversially considers non-commercial communication as advertising, too, effectively criminalising political demonstrations, religious manifestations, and so on. More recent regulations have however taken a step back in this regard, creating a specific exception for "advertising activity intended to: (a) demonstrate support for or opposition to the views or actions of any person or body of persons, (b) publicise a belief, cause or campaign, or (c) mark or commemorate an event".[25] While this "exception" in theory re-establishes the legality of protest in the vicinity of the Olympic venues, critics like Kevin Blowe[26] are cautious, as other pieces of legislation such as the Public Order Act may be used to block protest – or new legislation introduced, like the recent ban on "encampment style protest" around Olympic venues.[27] Needless to say, this is also the case inside the Olympic venues. Rule 61 of the Olympic Charter establishes that "no kind of demonstration or political, religious, or racial propaganda is permitted in the Olympic areas".

Entering the Olympic "camp" implies surrendering the right to express oneself freely or, more exactly, accepting that it has been "suspended by law". *Fourth instance of exceptionality: the creation of a no-man's-land where exceptional measures are in place, and which are legitimised by the extraordinariness of the situation and its threats.* The tautological nature of the argument is now apparent: the exceptionality of the Olympics is both its legal status and the alibi that justifies it.

Military urbanism and the architecture of fear

The legal structures described above are complemented by an equally exceptional security design. The legal engineering of the Games has indeed a spatial counterpart, the architecture of fear.[28] Also drawing from Agamben's work, Fussey et al. argue that "conceptions of terrorist threat have stimulated 'total security' 'Olympic spaces of exception'."[29] After 9/11 in particular, the security of the Games has been tied inexorably to the fear of a terrorist attack, and a

Giles Price,
Amber Alert, 2010

concomitant security paradigm, legitimated on the basis of "necessity, atypicality and ephemerality", has been produced and exported to the different sites:

> These strategies... comprise "exceptional" (temporary, plural and refocused) policing models that draw heavily on zero-tolerance orthodoxies, the militarization of urban space, extensive private policing, architectural and environmental designs to harden targets and deter transgressive behaviour and heavy reliance on intensive technological surveillance measures.[30]

In the case of London 2012, the fact that the 7/7 bombings took place the day after the city won the right to host the Games further cemented the links between fear of terrorism and the Olympics. Not surprisingly, then, the security operation is closely linked to the Home Office counter-terrorism strategy, CONTEST. The operation has five main components: "protect", "prepare", "identify and disrupt", "command, control, plan and resource" and "engage". These principles of action have a number or ramifications, from intelligence work to border agency co-ordination. I will focus briefly on the three aspects more closely related to the militarisation of urban space: architecture, surveillance and policing.

The architecture of security (or fear) is the most visible aspect. A 16-kilometre electrified fence surrounds London's Olympic Park. Access to this "sterile zone" is strictly restricted to authorised personnel, controlled by airport-like checkpoints, and protected by "hostile vehicle mitigation" (HVM) devices. Immediately adjacent to it there is a "peripheral buffer" zone, in which large-scale access restrictions, including a traffic exclusion zone, operate. A wide array of technologies of surveillance is in place around this area: a dense network of CCTV and face recognition CCTV cameras; the use of existing automatic number plate recognition (ANPR) infrastructure; and unmanned aerial vehicles (UAVs) like the GA22, which being under 7 kilos is not subject to the Civil Aviation Authority oversight. Policing will obviously be a complementary element to these infrastructures of surveillance and control. The latest figures available at the time of writing[31] state that up to 12,000 police officers, 16,000 private security guards (from G4S) and 13,500 military personal will be deployed to secure the Games. It has also been made public that ground-to-air missiles will protect the event.[32]

Fussey et al. argue that these security operations and the bordered spaces they generate, once established, engender a particular vision of order, which tends to become permanent. There are numerous examples: ANPR, first installed in the City of London as a response to the IRA's bombings, was then rolled out city-wide for its use in relation to the Congestion Charge, and later expanded again to cover the Greater London's Low Emission Zone; "extraordinary" zero-tolerance municipal by-laws to regulate behaviour and assembly during Sydney 2000 were retained after the Olympics; a legacy of private policing followed both Tokyo 1964 and Seoul 1988.[33]

In the case of London 2012, many of the security infrastructures that are built into the design of the Olympic Park and its surroundings will most likely become part of the legacy of the Games; it is not for nothing that the ODA was given an award by the Association of Chief Police Officers for its implementation of "Secure by Design" (SBD). As the Association put it, "the application of the SBD project ensures that the general public, residents and retailers will enjoy the benefit of a prestigious and safe environment long after the Games have concluded."[34] *Fifth measure of exceptionality: provisional and exceptional measures are transformed into techniques of government. These techniques, in turn, are incorporated into the design and management of these spaces, producing norms and practices of control that also become installed in a more permanent sense.*

Necessity, temporality, atypicality or threat are some of the notions used to legitimise the extraordinary set of exceptions and exemptions that give form and make possible the London 2012 Games. The Olympic Park, isolated legally and physically from its urban surroundings, is the "camp" where the rule of law has been displaced by the power of exceptional regulation. Within this legal no-man's-land, subjects are divested of their rights and power deprived of its habitual limitations – while a few corporate entities are allowed to operate freely. It should not be forgotten that the production of this space has required an unprecedented alignment of fiscal, planning, commercial and security public policies. The analysis here provided of the legal mechanisms, physical manifestations and legitimating devices that have made this possible may shed some light (or shadows!) on important dynamics of the contemporary neo-liberal city. In particular, it raises the question whether the "exceptional legacy" that London was promised when bidding for the Games will not instead be a *legacy of exception.*

* A first version of this text was published as "London 2012: Espacio de Excepcion", *Urbe, Revista Brasileira de Gestão Urbana (Brazilian Journal of Urban Management)* 3, no. 2 (2011): 179-190.

Jim Woodall's Olympic State:
An Observation Story

ALYSSA MOXLEY*

Hackney Wick, November 2010

The day after filling cardboard boxes from the factory downstairs with foam for insulation, he stacked them neatly around the wooden frame of his bungalow. The first night he films himself looking into the camera's eye before turning it on the site of the Olympics, on the fences and buildings, and arrays of security cameras that guarded it. They look into each other again and again, an optical illusion of an eternal refraction, a profoundly empty stare.

Despite the fresh snow and the November cold snap, he wakes up sweating from the heat of the screens. Their steady exhale at 50Hz moves the air inside on a frequency parallel to the flickering hum of his unconscious mind. At 8am, he wakes inside the hut for the first time, elated yet meditatively still. A whiskey warmed by coffee and a puff of cigarette smoke incense the muggy atmosphere, saturated with an evening's sleeping breath. Eyes dry, he peers into the distance, at simultaneous multiple locations. Images of camera set upon camera, upon empty roadways, scanning the perimeter like reverse binoculars, make everything smaller and farther away.

Pushing aside the stack of boxes that serve as the door, he attends to the array of lenses set up outside on the roof top edge. He steps over the long fluorescent bulbs alongside the makeshift hideaway, installed to emulate the lighting systems of the stadium, only at a much more modest scale. Is it possible that his Davidian minute gaze could impact the Goliath opposite? When he steps outside, the distant scene he observed is revealed to be much closer. Like a constantly recurring dream, memories of the present, seen from multiple perspectives by some omniscient being, cycle him. Inside the hut he feels higher than the roof, looking down on the proceedings. While performing maintenance and choosing his view, his own smallness is amplified.

He remembers reading about a group of Amazonian tribesmen who had never been out of the jungle, being taken by aircraft to a small town where all the jungle had been cleared for miles around. They were reaching out, trying to pick up the tiny cows that were a quarter of a mile away, because for their entire lives they had been surrounded by trees and had never seen anything in the distance. He thought, this must mean that our brains have been programmed to see the nearby as big and the far away as small, only because of the way we

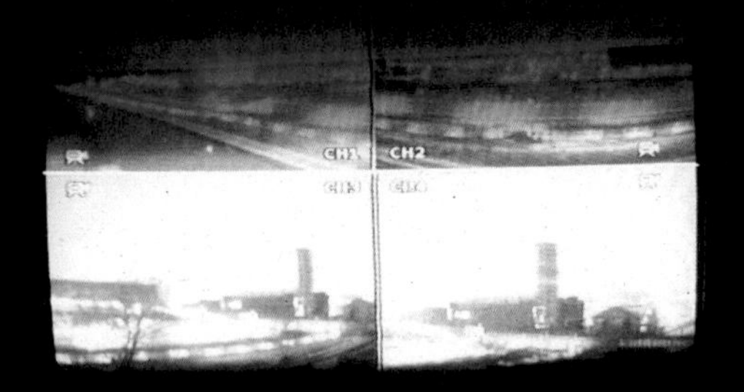

REC ●

Daren Ellis,
Jim's Hut, 2010

experience these perspectives in our environment.

So what happens when you no longer imagine these angles? When you multiply the possibilities and the perspectives into a widespread reality? Do near and far disappear? Does the relevance of your little viewing platform within a body in time and space dissolve?

Two police officers stopped by the next morning and asked him, "What are you doing? What are you looking at? There's nothing to see here. If you want to get a better look, images are provided online." They are obliged to intervene, to notice who else is taking notice and collecting data; they may even be part of the dedicated police intelligence service set up by the Home Office as one of the cooperating security bodies working under the remit of the Olympic and Paralympic Safety and Security Strategy. In the end, they don't consider him a "domestic extremist" intent on maliciously attacking anybody's safety, just a little eccentric. Bemused, they leave the structure and its occupant to their idiosyncratic action. The knowledge too is left with him that they know where he is.

Some events are unwanted, cruel and dangerous. When everyone is looking, someone will want to use the chance to showcase destruction. This calls for precautions: the Olympic Security Directorate within the Home Office, a dedicated intelligence unit within the police service, a dedicated team to police the Olympic Park construction site and another within the British Security Industry Association and the Government to qualify and provide reliable staff.

For two weeks, he watches this space mostly in isolation, observing construction, and the devices set up to safeguard its completion, as the workers trolley in and out, preparing the site for real spectatorship, for something worth paying attention to. The builders are the most bountiful living creatures in the area – like roaming herds shepherded by pastoral caterpillar cranes.

The new city is built to temporarily house men and women of exceptional ability to perform tasks of monumental consequence. Their actions would leave a mark upon humanity, and pave a vision of future obstacles to overcome. Their bodies would demonstrate the potential of the species to tighten, bind, release and leap, to withdraw from temptation and expand the frontiers of achievement. Only the most well-trained animals would be on show in this arena.

The next phase is a bridge to the outside world. The bridge is planned to take down half of the building that the hut is built upon. The side that's exposed for having had its other half torn away will be lined with flowing ivy. The leaves of romantic neglect will be sown at its base, perhaps only truly reaching the height of the facade after the Olympics has finished, and left the facilities empty again. A little like the quiet sadness when the circus leaves

Giles Price, Jim Woodall's Olympic State, 2010

town, and the diversion of oddity and unthinkable confounding contortions recedes into another impossible dream.

All the buildings were excessively huge, to hold the surge of world citizens that would flow in, on a spectral river of money and expectation. The grey-checkered handball court, the waving back of the aquatic centre, the velodrome, and the stadium buzzing with workers. The immenseness of the buildings was deflected inside the hide by the camera's slight fisheye lens and the angle subtended by the render window on the screen.

The land was supposed to be beautiful in a year. The saplings that stand leaning against each other in forgotten dead ends would be fork lifted into place. Reeds would emulate a more beautiful version of the natural habitat of weeds, and manicured gardens would grow in place of the 80-year-old allotments that had been removed. The buildings would be unwrapped, and the blue plastic sheets that had concealed them would be balled up and chucked away. Sports stadiums await spectators and sportsmen. Schools await children. Flats await residents. Vegetable patches await growers and eaters. Construction workers lay pipes, push dirt, stack the frames of homes and arenas, until completion. Cameras await disturbance and vandalism. He wondered what he was waiting for. Another day passed. Fog, heavy snow. The cameras need to be maintained, angles adjusted, snow wiped from the lenses. A heavy fog blows up from the canal. The fog remains all day and clears at night. The next day the morning radiates glorious sunshine.

Camera Right, watching a stack of the future Westfield shopping centre's cameras, is obscured by a heavy snow-fall during the night. The silhouette of a white transit van breaks the symmetry of the tall grey link fence next to the canal. A few cyclists and pedestrians occupy the waterside path on the bank opposite the Olympic Park throughout the day.

A journalist from the BBC wandering around the Olympic Park, looking for significance and embedded community reaction, spots the hideaway from the ground. Inconspicuous and local as the materials may be, they are arranged in an out-of-the-ordinary way. Foam-filled boxes stacked into a hide-away shape like a Maltese bird-hunter's shack stand out on a rooftop in Hackney Wick. Curiosity impels him to search for the building's entrance and make his way up the stairs of the Wallis Road warehouse. He shelters from the blustering wind within the cardboard and joins the artist in watching nothing.

Some day it might be significant, if something were to happen... This evidence allows the chance to write an alternative history constructed from the memorabilia outside the sanctioned monuments of legacy. Camera Left caught green and yellow tipper trucks, white vans, blue buses, and a silver jeep on their daily journeys – travelling from left to right in the morning and right to left in the late afternoon. Fog envelops the proto-city scape. A lonely industrial spire spurts thick smoke into the sky, a dancing plume above the settled low clouds. He files the last 12 hours of data, to the previous 324, clicking USB sockets to external data drives.

* First published in *The Hackney Wick*, no. 1 (Summer 2011), 2-3.

Trespassing the Olympic Site

STEPHEN CORNFORD

Trespassing the Olympic Site was a performative project carried out between 2006 and 2008, initiated in response to the compulsory purchase of the 500 acres that now make up the Olympic Park. I appointed myself artist in residence two months before access to the area was restricted by the locally infamous blue fence; my intention was simply to perform regularly the action of trespass across its length and breadth. The project questioned the reality of public ownership in a privatised world by repeatedly attempting to traverse this patrolled enclosure alone and on foot, treating literally the notion of it as London's newest public park.

Performances, which took place at night – unannounced – every month throughout the two-year period, were conceived not as actions to be watched but tasks to be carried out, the aim being to remain hidden from my potential audience of security guards, demolition workers and dog patrols. I documented the work in a series of staged digital stills, using the camera's built-in shutter delay and exposures of up to a minute. Initially these images were simply a means of recording my presence, but as the project wore on they became spaces to pit myself against the increasingly dehumanised landscape, chances to comment, albeit silently, on the transformations that took place between my visits.

I retrospectively wrote a diary of my actions, publishing the entries online as a means of answering the questions that I was repeatedly asked, and returning the project and its archive to the public domain.

Good Friday, 2008

So this was the end. I didn't know it at the time, but the moment had passed and even if it weren't for the 5,000 volt electric fence constructed as a replacement to the blue hoardings, the project would still have finished on that night. The change of fences marked a change of process: from demolition to construction. The enclosure of that which was earmarked for removal, which at the time seemed so shocking in its disregard for existing public rights of way, bore no comparison to the extent of the fortifications required to protect the new. But with this shift – the point at which all evidence of previous use had been eradicated, my interest in it also ceased.

By now I had given up hope of ever reaching the stadium. I had tried in earnest twice, once following the canal towpath that leads into the site from the edge of Fish Island, alongside the abandoned Big Breakfast house: that tiny premonition of what the entire park might become. I had easily slipped through the first fence, but found a further towpath barricade impassable. The second attempt was also thwarted, by the ominous barking of a dog, which started up as soon as I got within scent-range. But even if the finishing line was well and truly out of reach I was convinced I could easily get deeper in, further from the safety of the fence than I was used to going. To ground that I would not have trodden since the heady days of wandering with cautious abandon across an evacuated landscape before the fence went up.

On a drizzly Good Friday evening I was once again perched on the Greenway. The new, temporary bridge over the Channelsea River was my target, having failed to reach it three months before when the lure of short, floodlit exposures had left me in view too long and had me scampering at full pelt back to the fence just seconds from being cut off by security. I looked down on a completely deserted site. I had picked a good night.

In spite of the silence I stuck to the now customary wait for the security patrol. Eventually they swung past, beacon revolving, and I immediately dropped over the fence and scurried along the familiar mote edge, across ex-Marshgate Lane, and straight for the near side of the bridge. Over the past couple of weeks I had been working on a new addition to the project, stitching the words ARTIST IN RESIDENCE in white caps onto the back of the black snowboard jacket that had become my trespass top. The letters were covered by a black Velcro patch, which could be easily torn off once out of sight of the security patrols who stuck largely to an unadventurous circuit of the site. I stopped before crossing the bridge, ducked behind a barrel and decided to relax a while into the uncanny calm. I tried a shot using the jacket, but with the long exposure the letters came out blurred.

I folded the tripod and strolled across the bridge, unprepared for the transformation that awaited me. The space opened out into a landscape laid bare: hundreds of tons of topsoil had been shunted about into several heaps and at the side of each lay a dormant yellow sorter, their diplodocan necks stretching skyward. The place was unbelievably peaceful that night; even the traffic and trains seemed a very distant rumble. Two ducks squawked low overhead, discussing how much the place had changed and how muddy the waterways in the area now were. It was unrecognisable by comparison with my last visit. The extent of the earthworks ensured that even the ground beneath my feet was not the same ground on which I had stood when last here. That was early on, before even the scope of my 'residency' had been finalised. I had flung my arms around

Stephen Cornford,
Trespassing the Olympic Site, 5 Sep 2007

a JCB's neck, trying to embrace the ubiquitous vehicle of urban regeneration, the first of many such grubby hugs.

All signs of previous inhabitation – the BOC gas bottling plant, the artist's studio block – had been sorted and swept into neat piles, most of it long ago removed. It now resembled a colossal recycling centre. Even the trees had all gone, and near the railway sidings was a mountain of chain-sawed trunks and boughs, isolated from the other debris. I tried a couple of shots, nothing dramatic or strenuous tonight – the melancholy of desolation and intermittent drizzle forbade it – just standing among the sorters, looking out into the distance, peering curiously into their guts, or trying to scale the massed tree graves.

The rain gained some force, slowly adding to the silty layer forming on the meticulously flattened ground. I trudged about in search of shelter, happy to take my time, to take advantage of the quiet, to not be nervously checking my back every minute. The security patrol would not come through here – this was digger territory: no tyre marks, only caterpillar tracks, and inhospitable as hell to my trainered feet. I found a container and squatted down next to it, rolled and smoked a cigarette, contemplating the unruly stack of galvanised fencing and knotted steel rods to my right. On my last visit an impressive electricity substation had stood on the same spot and next to it a pile of railway fixings. I had stood among them and held one aloft trophy-like in a crass attempt to ape Olympian heroism. Tonight I tried to stand in what I hoped was the same spot, this time keeping it simple. It was hard enough just to stand safely in these bundled rods and spikes. I perched awkwardly, hand outstretched for support, and tried to maintain stillness for the full 60 seconds in spite of the horrific images of impaling accidents that ran through my mind.

Beyond the next mound my path was blocked, not with the scaleable obstacles I was used to but a stagnant stream of churned slurry, stretched out over the next hundred or so metres, flanking the railway sidings and beautifully reflecting their bright sodium lighting. I was determined to capture the scene, though it was impossible to tell how thick the sludge was before solid ground began. I set up the camera, pressed the shutter and splashed forward ankle deep in the ooze, coming to rest after the ten second mental count and freeze. Mud seeped into socks; I had chosen the wrong route and on the way back managed to negotiate a dry path with ease.

With sodden feet I decided to start retracing my steps back towards the fence. It had been a lacklustre evening's trespass, which I had no appetite to prolong. Perhaps on an evening of such easy pickings the adrenalin rush I sought wasn't here; the sprinting for cover, the scaring myself with the sound of a fox's footsteps, the ducking behind pillars; but I felt as if I was running out of material, going through the motions, re-enacting past feats. As time has told, this moment's inkling, these minutes of doubt, proved enough to halt the project in its tracks. I just never felt the need to return inside the fence after that evening.

In retrospect I realise that it was the process of clearing the site, the gradual erasure of its history, that I felt the need to be a part of. Once building began it just didn't retain its magnetic attraction. The documentation of the construction process would no doubt be captured in myriad time-lapses and aerial swoops and I had no wish to add to this clamour of the forthcoming circus and the much heralded legacy of a brave new Dagenham.

Before departing, still searching for a way out of the creative dead end I had felt myself occupying that night, I tried something new: comedy. A spool of blue cable ducting was slung onto a protruding scaffold pole. I jumped up and lounged back in it, a seat from which to look out towards the bright lights of Canary Wharf. Off the back of that, I tried another visual joke, jumping into the cab of a steamroller that had been left at the end of a wide strip of fresh tarmac, a road not yet listed in the *A to Z*, hands on the wheel, going nowhere fast. And that was that, my final exit from the site was uneventful. I climbed down that familiar tree and have never returned.

Richard DeDomenici, Olympic Torch Relay, 6 April 2008 (picture by Tanya Nagar)

Taking advantage of the inexact schedule of the Torch Relay, I made my own torch and ran approximately five minutes ahead of the official parade. The performance was designed to be primarily documented by the public.

Blogger Robert writes: "A rogue participant, complete with home-made torch, eagerly awaits Trevor McDonald, hoping to intercept the proceedings. The real runner waits a little further along the road. Trev' makes it past the rogue runner to Denise."

The Implications of Linguistic and Other Associations with Certain Physical Events Happening Somewhere at Some Time

JULIAN WALKER

One of the most widely reported events at the FIFA World Cup in South Africa in 2010 was not to do with the football, but concerned 36 young women wearing orange dresses. Having managed to get hold of a block of tickets for a game between the Netherlands and Denmark, they entered the stadium dressed as Danish fans but stripped off their red and white clothes to reveal orange dresses, of a design which had been used as a marketing tool in a brewery company's advertising campaign. Despite being seen waving officially acceptable flags, when they stood up and waved their arms at times when the action on the field was such that television cameras were more likely to pick them out, they were deemed to be engaging in "guerrilla marketing". At length they were ejected from the ground, and two of them were arrested for allegedly organising "unlawful commercial activities";[1] it turned out that their travel tickets were allegedly paid for by a third party. FIFA lodged a criminal complaint against the brewer, Bavaria, claiming that it was obliged to protect the interests of the official supplier of beer to the World Cup, American brewer Budweiser.[2] The brewer meanwhile gave legal support to the two arrested women, though it is unclear whether the group as a whole was supported financially. In terms of the exercise of legal power this was clearly a victory for FIFA and its sponsors, but in terms of advertising, clearly a resounding win for Bavaria (though nobody seems to have questioned the propriety of a Dutch brewer calling itself "Bavaria").[3]

On 6 July 2005 London was awarded the right to host the top athletics meeting in the world for seven years hence. In March 2006 the British Parliament passed The London Olympic Games and Paralympic Games Act 2006. In 2010 LOCOG (the London Organising Committee of the Olympic and Paralympic Games – the "P" for Paralympics seems to have been dropped so as to avoid disturbing a catchy vending acronym, marketing being more important than precision) published *London 2012's UK Statutory Marketing Rights: Brand Protection* (henceforth called by its subtitle, *Brand Protection*), a report giving its interpretation of the content of the 2006 Act.[4] It had a disclaimer stating clearly that what the website contained was to be taken as

LOCOG's interpretation of its statutory rights, and not as a substitute for legal advice – with the statement, "If you think you may have infringed our rights, or you are proposing to do something which you think may infringe our rights, we recommend that you seek independent legal advice" repeated at the foot of every page. The document contains the following clauses:

> Examples are given for illustrative purposes only and do not indicate that an activity definitely will, or will not, infringe LOCOG's rights. A wide variety of factors, including content, context and presentation will be relevant when determining infringement and cases must be reviewed on an individual basis considering all the circumstances.
>
> The information provided is intended to help people stay within the law and LOCOG expects it to be used in good faith. In areas of doubt, please respect the spirit of the law and do not undertake any activity which is contrary to LOCOG's aims and objectives (see further point 1 below).[5]

A disclaimer states, "This document is for illustrative purposes only and reliance is at the reader's own risk." The document also refers to the London Olympic Association Right (OAR), a regulation within the Act which is intended to prevent anyone without authorisation from benefiting financially from association with the events in question.[6] As *Business Matters* magazine puts it:

> The London OAR has been created to deal with those who will inevitably try to get round the original OAR by making an association with the London Olympics without using any of the representations covered in the 1995 Act. It gives the London organisers the exclusive right to use any visual or verbal representation in a manner likely to create an association in the public mind between the London Olympics and goods or services or a trader in goods or services, with association having a very wide definition.[7]

To sum up, the 2006 Act controls who can use the brand and associated words and images for financial gain, and makes sure that payments are made for the rights to use these words and images, with an undefined sense of what constitutes an association between goods or services offered and the events planned.

The images in question are the five rings and the logos designed for the event. These are fairly clear, and would make an obvious association. LOCOG advises that the words will be managed as two lists. The "listed words" in List A are "Games", "Two Thousand and Twelve", "2012", "twenty twelve"; and in List B "Gold", "Silver", "Bronze", "London", "medals", "sponsors", "summer".

The use of two words from List A or one word from List A with one or more words from List B in such a way as to create an association with the planned events may be deemed to be an infringement of the Act. Lest we should be concerned that a school could not have a "summer 2012 fete", *Brand Protection* points out that an advert that creates no association (such as "Massive Summer Sale – Games, Toys, Gadgets") will be safe. But it seems likely from reading the report that only a court of law could determine whether association has occurred, or was intended. And if in doubt, "please respect the spirit of the law and do not undertake any activity which is contrary to LOCOG's aims and objectives".

"The spirit of the law" could be seen in a number of ways, ranging from common sense and "good faith" to an understanding that the authorities can keep their options open and decide what constitutes an infringement: "A wide variety of factors, including content, context and presentation will be relevant when determining infringement and cases must be reviewed on an individual basis considering all the circumstances." This appears to imply that the only way you can know that you have infringed the law is by being accused of having infringed it, and dealing with the judicial consequences.

What is going on here can be seen in a range of ways. At one end is the view that a democratically elected government should hand over to a properly vetted committee the control of selling the use of certain marketing tools to entities who should pay for such rights, and the money raised should go towards funding the Games. At the other end is a view of this as a deal sewn up behind closed doors, between government and the corporate world, to make sure that nobody but major companies should benefit financially from the ludic celebrations, while the rest of us spend, spend, spend. For those cynics who might lean towards the latter view it is worth reading the following reassuring words from *Brand Protection*:

> These laws will allow LOCOG to protect the integrity and value of the 2012 Games and the Olympic and Paralympic movements in general. By applying and enforcing these laws, LOCOG will stop people undermining the rights granted to the official broadcasters, sponsors, suppliers and licensees of the 2012 Games. These rights are acquired by companies who invest millions of pounds to help support the plan-

> ning, staging and organisation of the 2012 Games in an official capacity. People who seek the same benefits for free, without investing in the Games by paying for these rights – for example by engaging in "ambush marketing" or producing counterfeit goods – are effectively depriving the Games of key revenue. If the 2012 Games are to be the great success to which we all aspire LOCOG cannot allow such unlawful activity and will do everything to ensure it is stopped... LOCOG must raise money by selling rights of association to the 2012 Games to sponsors, by selling official merchandise and by selling tickets. In order to maximise sponsorship revenue it is essential that the association which can be granted to sponsors is exclusive. LOCOG must therefore be able to prevent others from creating an unauthorised association with the Games and thereby profiting from the Games for free to the detriment of those who have lawfully acquired such rights.[8]

Unfortunately the Act is rather vague as to what may constitute an association with the games. Schedule 3 of the 2006 Act amends The Olympic Symbol etc. (Protection) Act 1995 (the 2006 Act adds the words in italics):

> A person infringes the Olympics association right if in the course of trade he uses:
> (a) a representation of the Olympic symbol, the Olympic motto or a protected word, or
> (b) a representation of something so similar to the Olympic symbol or the Olympic motto as to be likely to create in the public mind an association with it, *or a word so similar to a protected word as to be likely to create in the public mind an association with the Olympic Games or the Olympic movement.*

How may we know, without testing the judiciary system, what constitutes an infringing degree of similarity in a word? Is "medallion" too close to "medal", "golden" too close to "gold"? Could you market "golden medallion drinks" without getting into trouble, or would only "shiny yellow disc drinks" keep the police from your door? To help us the following text appears in *Brand Protection*:

> LOCOG is NOT suggesting that use of the items listed below will immediately create an association with the 2012 Games, but they may well be relevant. The more of these items that are used, the more likely

> it is that an association with the 2012 Games will be created.
> – An Olympic-style torch/flame
> – Use of the five colours of the Olympic symbol
> – Use of designs which reproduce or closely resemble the official designs of the 2012 Games
> – Images of venues to be used for, and closely associated with, the 2012 Games such as the Olympic Stadium or Aquatics Centre in Olympic Park
> – The depiction of Olympic and/or Paralympic sports…
> – Words which capture the essence of the 2012 Games and/or qualities associated with Olympism, (eg: "Spirit"; "Endeavour"; "Friendship"; "Winning"; "Determination")
> – "XXX" or "30th" (the 2012 Games will be the Games of the XXX Olympiad).[9]

The looseness of the terms used here is worrying; how is anyone to know in advance what may be interpreted as a word which captures "the essence of the 2012 Games and/or qualities associated with Olympism?" Would you be able to get away with "trying hard", "doing your best", "giving it your best shot", or even "friend", "winner", "try"?

In Basingstoke the business community set up a steering group "initially to explore the issue of training camps"; this steering group was called Basingstoke 2011+1, allegedly to avoid infringing the 2006 Act. Other apocryphal stories suggested scenarios such as street parties being closed down because children had been asked to contribute 10p to the cost of a cake, or fee-paying events in the capital having to choose between date and place in their promotional literature.

At some stage LOCOG clearly realised that public opinion had picked up on the issue of control of words and was reacting adversely to it. Could it be that LOCOG had failed to explain its message that it was actually protecting these words from unauthorised use, and by doing so serving Britain's financial interests? An explanatory document was needed, and duly appeared:

> Several misleading ideas have appeared in recent media reports about the Government's proposals to restrict ambush marketing around the 2012 Olympics. This factsheet counters some of these myths and explains what the London Olympics Bill will actually do.
> Myth: Only official sponsors can use words like "games" and "gold"

> Fact: The Bill stops businesses unfairly cashing in on the London Olympics by wrongly implying that they have some form of association with the Games. But the Bill does not prevent the mere use of words like "games" and "gold". Instead it creates the London Olympics association right, which means LOCOG can authorise certain persons – most likely official sponsors and commercial partners - to associate themselves with the Games. The Bill sets out a list of words, including "games" and "gold", which when used in certain combinations by unauthorised persons may be used by the LOCOG as evidence of infringement of the association right. This measure is based on the model which Sydney developed before the 2000 Games. Our legislation fulfils the requirements of the International Olympic Committee to prevent ambush marketing and thereby protect their sponsors, who are vital to the economic well-being of the Games. London committed itself to fulfilling the IOC's requirements during the bidding process...
>
> Myth: Using words like "games" and "gold" will attract fines of £20,000
>
> Fact: People will not be fined simply because they have used words like "games" or "gold". However, if individuals or organisations use words like "games" and "gold" in combination to seek to create an unauthorised association with the Games, the LOCOG would be able to take civil action against them. It will have to be decided on a case by case basis whether infringement has occurred. As this would be a civil law suit, where infringement had occurred fines would not be levied. Instead it would be for the judge to determine the level of damages to be paid, if appropriate.[10]

Other "myths" to be "busted" include:

> Myth: Legislation like this is unprecedented
> Fact: The IOC require that we take all necessary steps to prevent ambush marketing. Sydney put very similar legislation in place before it hosted the 2000 Games. The words in the Bill which, when used in combination, are seen as likely to have created an association with the Games, are based on the Sydney legislation.[11]

It is rather worrying that the 2006 Act creating LOCOG should engender both a document in which LOCOG indicates how it "interprets" the Act, and then this myth-busting document, which uses the phrase "words like 'games' and 'gold'". What does "words like" mean, and is it meaningful legal English? The legislation is claimed to be in line with previous legislation, but the Government's own website states that the legislation is "novel".[12] As conflicting messages continue to appear the only safe courses of action are either to have a very good lawyer or to go nowhere near using any of the words, images or ideas in question.

One myth which failed to be busted concerned those people who had been using the "listed expressions" before the Act came into force on 30 March 2006 (Schedule 4, by the way, is effective until the end of the year when these physical contests of speed and strength and so on take place). On 14 June 2011 the BBC news website reported the following:

> An art event called the Great Exhibition 2012 says it has had legal action threatened by Olympics organisers over its use of "2012". The exhibition is due to take place between the Olympic and the Paralympic Games, next August… London 2012 team said it was "legally obliged" to ensure firms did not "create unauthorised association". Julie Benson, founder of The Great Exhibition Company, based on the Isle of Wight, said she has spent the last 12 years planning the art event, including going through the trademarking process… Ms Benson said: "This apparent 'bullying' from Locog to bring down an event aimed at championing Great Britain and supporting British tourism and industry gives a shocking insight in to the 'true spirit' of the Olympics.
> "It's preposterous."[13]

It might be claimed that Ms Benson acted with some disingenuity in laying plans to name her event "the Great Exhibition 2012" in 2005 (the Great Exhibition's website states that she 'founded The Great Exhibition Co UK Ltd and launched the Great Exhibition 2012 when Britain was announced as the winner in the bid to be host nation to the world for the Olympics').[14] Should she or her advisers have done more research into what sort of "brand protection" was likely to happen? Perhaps, but this situation indicates what appears to be retrospective legislation. Common sense, good faith, the spirit of the law and so on notwithstanding, her event was initiated, and presumably its name registered, even if only in the publishing of a website in the public domain, before the legislation was passed.

The prospect of firms being prosecuted as the date approaches opens up the possibility of organisations and individuals testing the legislation. On 2 September 2011, *Private Eye* showed photographs of rioters smashing windows and throwing bricks, captioned "judo", "shotput" and so on, each with the Olympic logo and the words "Welcome to London" in inverted commas. The internet is beginning to disseminate satirical versions of the Olympic logo adapted to form recognisable symbols or words. Will LOCOG attempt to prosecute them?

The feeling that special measures are being applied for the purpose of scaring people off is further strengthened when we see how the Government has extended penalties and limits specifically for this legislation. New words are added to the list – in August 2010, the word describing a spear thrown at a sporting event, and the term traditionally used between "Up to your marks" and "Go", became protected (restricted use) words.[15]

From the 2006 Act's explanatory notes Section 21: Offence, Paragraph 56[16] we learn that the upper limit for the infringement penalties has been specially raised: "In the Magistrates' Courts the maximum fine will be £20,000, which is higher than the maximum fine which Magistrates can normally impose." This is justified on the grounds that the offences are expected to be committed by corporate bodies, and "the offence is considered to be highly lucrative". The phrase "higher than the maximum fine which Magistrates can normally impose" may for clarity be interpreted as "four times the amount that a Magistrates' Court can normally impose for a summary criminal offence".

The nature of English law being what it is – roughly speaking the Government makes a law, it is tested in court, and precedents are established – all this is providing a flurry of discussion among lawyers and journalists on questions such as the burden of proof; there is also a lack of clarity as to whether infringement is a criminal or civil offence. But one thread runs through most reporting on the Act: its powers mark a previously unseen extent of control. In 2007 Davenport Lyons, a leading business law firm, published on its website a brief survey of the 2006 Act, with the opinion that the laws relating to the events in question "are probably the most restrictive ever in their scope".[17] Section 22 of the 2006 Act also allows the police or an enforcement officer to remove articles offending against the 2006 Act, granting powers of entry onto private property with a warrant from a justice of the peace.

Further use of words as a power-tool includes the terms and conditions document (assent required for ticket purchase) published by LOCOG, which is 7,350 words long. According to the *Telegraph*, those attending will not be allowed entry onto the site if they are carrying any of the following items:

> Food, alcoholic and non-alcoholic beverages, liquids in containers of greater than 100ml in size, umbrellas, horns, whistles, drums, rattles, musical instruments, or any other devices that in the opinion of LOCOG may disturb a session (including mobile telephones), flasks, Thermoses and in general any material that LOCOG may deem dangerous or that may cause damage or disruption to a session.[18]

Ultimately the Act and following documents seem confused, variable, and threatening. Hugh Robertson, Minister for Sport and the Olympics, was quoted in another article in the *Telegraph* as saying "'a light touch proportionate to the offence" would be adopted by officers from the ODA responsible for enforcing the regulations.[19] In the spirit of *timeo Danaos et dona ferentes* ("I fear the Greeks most when they come bearing gifts"), how should we take this assertion? Is the government able and prepared to police the Act? Is LOCOG likely to prosecute a few test cases to intimidate possible offenders? Will any such cases stand up in a court of law? Do the 2006 Act or LOCOG's publications support big business at the cost of small entrepreneurs? Is quadrupling the maximum Magistrates' Court fine "a light touch"? Was not the idea of throwing controls round basic words an enormous false start? With accusations of governmental bullying, selling the language, fears of police entering private property, the "spirit of the Olympics" seems to be less "*Citius, altius, forties*" (faster, higher, stronger) than "more government-authorised marketing, more control, more money".

Reportage and artwork ("incidental inclusion in a literary work, dramatic work, artistic work, sound recording, film or broadcast", according to the 2006 Act) are excluded from the list of potential infringers, but intellectual discussion of the four-yearly event or the LOAR is not excluded; since this entire business is about the use of words and images, is there a risk of infringement merely by discussing the subject in an essay format? It is clearly not possible to write about the revels without using either the "listed expressions" or words "so similar to a protected word as to be likely to create in the public mind an association with the Olympic Games or the Olympic movement". There may be a defence under the "'honestly made statements' exception". If not, the foregoing "announcements or notices of any kind of a non-commercial nature" about certain physical competitive events happening somewhere at some time may be read within 200 metres of Stratford station; and being to the potential advantage (financial or otherwise) of this writer's career this could be construed as an infringement. See you in court.

Cathy Ward and Eric
Wright, Before the
Gold Rush, 2009

London 2012 Brand Protection – What You Need To Know

ALISTAIR SIDDONS

The Visual Identity of the Olympic Games

The visual identity of the 2012 Olympic Games ("the Games") – the five interlocking Olympic rings – is well known to individuals and to small and large businesses because of the strategies put in place by the Agency for the Protection of the Games (APG) to ensure just this outcome. It is no accident that this visual identity ("the identity"), is so readily associated with London 2012. Companies of all sizes, as well as individuals, are invited to look at it and to admire its simplicity and the power of its message. The rings have come to symbolise something that is protected, reinforced and strengthened by various powers including statutory powers. Accordingly, this image gives rise to feelings of security and trust directed towards those officially retained for the purpose of safeguarding the general population. Just as we protect the symbol, so it protects us all.

We, the APG, are entrusted with safeguarding the visual identity of the Olympic Games, and all associated intellectual property. We are invested with the authority and power(s) to prevent material or symbolic harm to any real or symbolic likenesses of the visual identity of the London 2012 Olympic Games. By these powers, we are entitled to and indeed obligated to move swiftly and decisively to close down any action, howsoever identified, that may occasion harm to the visual identity of the Olympic Games, or to deny or reduce the operational capability of any agent identified as having the intention, means or capacity to take in vain the whole or any part of the visual identity of the London 2012 Olympic Games.

By "agent" we mean any person, being, organisation, entity, device or thing, whether living or otherwise capable of making images, whether mechanically or electronically or by any other means. This list includes camera operatives, whether professional or amateur, as well as cameras, including still and video cameras, scanners, photocopiers, flash memory cards, hard drives and mobile phones.

London 2012 – numbers and The Games

Because of the significance of the number 2012 to the words "London 2012 Olympic Games", this number has been accorded special protection by legislation enacted in parliament on behalf of the APG. We call this "deep protection", because it goes to the very heart of the number. The prime factorisation of 2012 is 2 squared x 503. Hence, both 2 and 503, which constitute the foundation of 2012, are also protected. 2012 may also be expressed as 1500 + 8 cubed = 1500 + 512 = 2012. Accordingly, the integers 8, 500, 1000 and 1500 are all protected.

Likewise, 2000 is protected, and so are 10 (along with 2, a constituent of 12) and 12 itself. Since we say "twenty – twelve", 20 is granted protection. Also since 12 = 6 x 2, 6 is protected, and since 6 = 3 x 2, 3 gains protection. Additionally, 1 is protected, since it stands for the number of 10s in 2012. Similarly, since there are five rings, the number 5 is also protected.

In summary, all of the following numbers are protected: 1, 2, 3, 5, 6, 8, 10, 12, 20, 500, 503, 512, 1000, 1500 and 2000, as well as 2012.

Making of false images – definition under the Olympics (Protection of Intellectual Property Act) 2007, amended 2011

Under the Olympics (Protection of Intellectual Property Act) 2007, amended 2011 ("the Act"), any spectator at the 2012 Olympic Games may not record any image during any events taking place as part of the Games. Spectators include those who have paid to watch events, those who are present in order to watch events, even if they have not paid, and those who are in a position to see events, even if they are not or do not claim to be present primarily in order to watch events. Such persons include coaches, managers and friends and relatives of athletes; athletes, whether about to compete, competing or eliminated from competition; those transporting or escorting athletes from the Olympic village to stadia, arenas, pools and other competition facilities; ticket collectors, refreshments and merchandising sales personnel, maintenance workers, electricians, plumbers, fitters and all other trades people, delivery drivers, security guards, police operatives, members of the armed forces and paramedics; and any personnel employed under any capacity for the duration of the Games or for any fraction of the duration of the Games, including the period of the Games, or for any period longer than the Games. Under the Act, an image is any piece of data larger than one pixel wide by one pixel high, or, if the image is recorded on traditional film emulsion, an image whose dimensions would exceed one pixel high by one pixel wide after digitisation of the film.

Under the Act, any image so made is defined as a false image. Any false image, along with the device that was caused to make it, may be seized without advance notice. Also any image suspected of being a false image may similarly be seized. All manner of devices are proscribed from being caused to make a false image. A list of these devices includes, but is not restricted to: cameras integral to mobile phones and smart phones; webcams; helmet cams; security cameras; 35 mm film cameras; 35 mm digital cameras; medium format cameras using film or digital backs; large format cameras using film or digital backs; vintage cameras of any description including roll film cameras, whether twin or single reflex; 35 mm vintage film cameras including reflex cameras; plate cameras; binoculars with digital imaging capabilities; telescopes with digital imaging capabilities; camera obscuras, whether manufactured or home-made; pinhole cameras, whether manufactured or home-made; film cameras of any age or format, including digital film cameras; and moving film cameras and movie cameras using negative film of any gauge.

Sound recordings

No sound recording may be made, distributed or kept, whether as part of a film or on its own, that has as its point of origin any of the events of the Games. No recording device may be taken into, held or carried in any stadium, ground, arena, pool or field having to do with the Games. All types of microphone are banned, whether held or worn, and whether designed for professional or amateur use. All types of recording equipment are banned, including dictaphones, devices with digital memory of all kinds, whether integral or external, and whether or not part of a personal computer. Devices using magnetic tapes are similarly outlawed, whatever the dimensions of the tapes. Micro-cassettes are not permitted, and nor are earlier generations of tape, including those used in combination with reel-to-reel recording devices, whether using integrated circuits, transistors or thermionic valve (or electron tube) technology, whether operated by mains voltage or battery.

Press entitlement to use images of the Games

Bona fide members of the press who have registered with the authorities and passed the necessary approvals may make images using any method, provided they submit to the authorities any images that are surplus to the completion of their current assignment.

Whether they are salaried members of staff working in a news-gathering capacity, or freelancers working in a similar capacity, they are bound to hand over any material that is not immediately used for broadcast, or to destroy it. Library tapes may not be kept by news-gathering organisations, but may be submitted to the relevant authorities, who, in exchange for a fee, will safeguard such tapes and make them available for use at a later date.

Thus, a news-gathering organisation may acquire a temporary licence to obtain and broadcast material that it does not initially select for broadcast, and which has been returned to the APG. The authorities assigned with the protection of all intellectual property associated with the Games are entitled, under the Act, to search the premises of any organisation that is listed as having been granted the approvals necessary to make images of the Games. Individuals are required to co-operate fully with any search. If they do not, the APG is entitled, under the Act, to require payment of a fine. Individuals and companies may be fined. Individuals and companies commit a criminal act by failing to pay a fine levied as a result of non-cooperation with a search.

Details of how to register with the authorities are held at the offices of the APG, and may be supplied in email, as a PDF document, or, in exchange for a fee, as a printed brochure supplied by post.

Picture libraries

Picture libraries are not authorised to buy, acquire or otherwise gain hold of any images of the Games. Any images that are so acquired, bought or gained are held unlawfully and deemed to be false images. The APG is the only organisation authorised to operate a picture library for the Games.

Personal enjoyment of the Games

We want people to enjoy the Games within the spaces accorded for enjoyment of the Games – the stadia, arenas, pools, grounds and all other spaces allocated for competition during the Games.

However, the Act redesignates as being under the jurisdiction of the APG some spaces previously assumed by custom to be private spaces. All spaces within the 10 square metres surrounding a broadcast receiver, radio or television set, or any device for replaying broadcasts ("on-demand"), whether the land on which it stands is owned by an individual or by a company (or corporation), are deemed to be "satellite spaces" of the Games.

These spaces are governed by the same regulations as govern the Olympic Park and all London 2012 sites; therefore, the regulations defining the making of false images in any London 2012 site apply equally here, as do those applicable to the making of sound recordings. Such spaces may be in a home or office. They may be in a dental or doctor's surgery, hospital or hospice, school, college or university, whether in halls of residence or private accommodation. They may be in a tent, car, camper-van, hostel, hotel, motel, guest house, inn, bed-and-breakfast, prison, vicarage, rectory, parsonage, army or air-force barracks, on board a merchant or Royal Naval vessel, or in any other form of residence, whether temporary or permanent.

Satellite spaces may not be occupied by more than one person at a time without a licence. Such licences, which are performance licences only, and do not entitle you to own any of the material being broadcast, may be obtained on application in advance to the APG in exchange for a fee, whose costs are on a sliding scale. Therefore it is not ten times as costly for ten people to view or listen to a broadcast as it is for one person – economies of scale apply. In order to help you pay the appropriate per-use fee, the APG has set up a streamlined online payment service for satellite licences.

Conclusion

We want people to enjoy the 2012 Olympic Games. We also want people to feel sure that all intellectual property apparently originating from the Games is genuine, and for that reason the spaces in which the Games are to take place will be policed by the APG in order to prevent the making of false images. We feel that by preventing the making of false images, it will be easier to delimit the subsequent distribution and dissemination of false images. We also want people to appreciate the audiovisual material they are able to access from satellite spaces. Since we consider these spaces to be *de facto* extensions of the London 2012 Games venues, we need to preserve the innate value of this material by charging for its use. Not to do so would be to cheapen the Games and so cheapen your experience of them.

We want people to be able to look at the visual identity of the Olympic Games in the certain knowledge that this, too, is not a false image. Likewise, we want people to hear recordings that are genuinely the intellectual property of the Olympic Games, and not recordings that are passed off as real. Although ideally we would want people to be able to engage in discussion of the Olympic Games without any restriction in private, we also want you to respect that all semiotic matter describing the processes of the Games in a permanent form, whether in writing or by broadcast, deserves special protection if it is to be recognised as authentic and regarded as fresh, relevant and in finite supply. That is why we have delimited the meaning of private for the duration of the Games and for a reasonable period afterwards. That is the reason why we are protecting the usage of all possible media having to do with all aspects of the London 2012 Olympic Games. And that is the reason why we have caused to be enacted the Olympics (Protection of Intellectual Property Act) 2007.

AdiZones: Rewriting the 2012 Olympic Legacy as Permanent Branding

ALBERTO DUMAN

Right from the outset, the notion of "legacy" has been predominant in articulating the value of hosting the 2012 Olympic and Paralympics Games in East London, the argument being that the long-term regeneration benefits would ultimately prevail over the aggressive land restructuring, everyday disruption and unbalanced socio-economic shifts characteristic of the years leading up to the 2012 Games. Subsequent to the awarding of the 2012 Games, the emphasis placed on such explicit non-sporting benefits as added long-term values has been confirmed as one of the most decisive assets of the London bid, contributing a great deal to the final awarding decision by the IOC.[1] This legacy, we are told, is why the London 2012 Games will be "unique" and "different", a pledge clearly spelled out through "five promises to set the scale of our ambition":

1. To make the UK a world-leading sporting nation
2. To transform the heart of East London
3. To inspire a generation of young people
4. To make the Olympic Park a blueprint for sustainable living
5. To demonstrate the UK is a creative, inclusive and welcoming place to live in, visit and for business.[2]

Although the national dimension of these ambitions is clearly emphasised, a more specific focus is placed on "transforming the heart of East London", to "create a well-planned and well-managed environment in and around the Olympic Park which will attract business investment and promote recreational and cultural use for years to come".[3]

But while these Olympic-driven strategies of urban regeneration and business market development have been produced in a contingent climate of lofty financial euphoria, the reality in which they are and will be developed is rather less jubilant. A phase of economic restraint and market uncertainties has now replaced it, with tougher control on banking and finance mechanisms, curtailed public spending and cuts in culture and education budgets as some of the most evident consequences. As the sudden moment of rupture in late 2008 has developed into a more prolonged condition with unclear long-term prognosis, doubts are cast over the resources and financial climate necessary for the legacy

All pictures in this essay: Alberto Duman, AdiZones, 2011

plans to be implemented.[4]

And although arguably the much publicised ArcelorMittal Orbit tower designed by Anish Kapoor will be a tangible legacy as much as a liability to contend with after the Games, another much less sizeable but equally controversial and remarkable inheritance of London 2012 has already been implemented in several sites within the five Olympic host boroughs of London:

> Constructed in the shape of the London 2012 logo, adiZones provide a highly visible and tangible legacy from the Games. These innovative multi-sport areas, designed and developed by Adidas, the Official Sportswear Partner of London 2012, aim to inspire the local community to get involved in sport. In this way they can help councils to achieve their physical activity targets.[5]

Quoting both the notion of zoning derived from the vocabulary of urban planning and the out-of-time state of mind reached through high-performance physical activities,[6] the adiZones are Adidas' and LOCOG's idea of a "free" sporting legacy for the London 2012 Games.

These dense, hypnotic and highly branded insertions on public parklands are standardised 25 m × 25 m areas, where cluttered symbolic opportunities to participate in sport, play, movement and fitness outdoors 24/7, 365 days a year, are rolled together with unique branding opportunities; over 15 Adidas logos are contained within the oversized 2012 logo of any adiZone.

When in September 2008 Adidas committed £1 million to "the development of a new sporting venue in each of the five London boroughs hosting London 2012",[7] expectations might have been different, but given the strict IOC rules restricting forms of advertising in the Olympic stadia or other competition areas during the Games, Adidas heeded the call to maximise its marketing opportunities with a relatively small financial commitment.

Nobody sings "My Adidas"[8] any more, but surely the marketing visionaries responsible for these "zones" know very well the mechanism and advantages of endorsement and the currency of their brands; in every adiZone there is a "wall of fame" comprising only Adidas-endorsed athletes and singers, contemporary followers in the pioneering footsteps of Run-DMC back in the early 1980s.

Capitalising on the rich symbolic exchanges between the brand Adidas and its most-prolific youth market established in the early 1980s with the emergence of the "BBoys" phenomena in New York's Bronx, and further strengthened by its evolution into the Hip-Hop scene in the 1990s, the cultural currency traded

Jade
Johnson

between the Olympic Delivery Authority (ODA) and Adidas through its first-tier sponsorship association with the London 2012 Olympic and Paralympics Games is rather self-evident. The ODA provides Adidas with privileged access to its urban strategies and processes on the territory under its "transformative" legacy agenda, and Adidas provides through its branding association an immediate sheen of "cool" and "bling" to what is essentially an Olympic driven top-down urban restructuring and social re-engineering project in the heart of areas where the legibility and value of such branding is maximised – read Beckton for Bronx.

But more importantly, it is the unique presence of the 2012 legacy agenda and its redemptive, quasi-humanitarian drive for a sweeping and radical change that legitimises the explicit and outlandish branding operation of the "adiZones" and their characterisation as "multi-sport" areas. When encountered in the flesh, the adiZones appear incongruent with such expectations, resembling a montage of sampled suggestions for a variety of physical activities rather than proper sporting or fitness venues; such quotations of full-scale facilities only highlight the doubts over their future provision within the 2012 legacy, a matter of concern and contestation in years to come.

Initially conceived only for the five host boroughs, the adiZones were then rolled out all over the UK. Costing £150,000 each and delivered in UK by the Great Outdoor Gym Company, the adiZones – as stated by the marketing material distributed by Adidas – are "a perfect solution to the Government's target of the 5 hour offer",[9] since "with rising obesity levels it is obviously in the Local Authority's interest to invest in activities that can get people more active".[10]

Given that in many cases the fitting of an adiZone constitutes a renovation of existing public playgrounds they don't even need to get through the planning process. In 2011 there were adiZones in Thurrock, Yarmouth, Swansea, Sandwell, Southampton, Littleport, Derby, Colchester, Preston, Scunthorpe and St Albans – with more to come.

But despite the unique penetration in otherwise brand-free public spaces that each adiZone represents for Adidas, their costs are only partly borne by the company, with the remaining 50% matching funds distributed between government agencies and local authorities, which are also in charge of the £5,000 yearly administration and maintenance costs included in the package. The adiZones equipment life expectancy is 20 years, and any possible removal from its current sites must be negotiated beforehand with Adidas.

Pushing further the hybrid proximity between public authorities' target obligations and private companies' demands for deeper branding integration

in everyday life, the adiZones appear as a symptomatic confirmation of the established trend towards the corporatisation of contemporary cultural life in the UK and beyond. Branding as marketing stretches freely between the macro and micro scale collapsing the illusory private-public divide; if the adiZones are small and localised interventions of private interests in public spaces rewritten as "public service", public authorities are constantly branding themselves and the opportunities their territory offers to global investors.

At the Singapore 2010 World Fair, the London Borough of Newham presented its investment prospectus and produced a short film to promote its land portfolio to the world of property and business. Its opening statement reads: "A Regeneration Supernova is currently exploding across Newham London."[11] For once, the bombastic and hypocritical promotional language of regeneration has caught up with its reality; whoever conceived such memorable semantic embodiment of creative destruction on a mass scale has set its aspiration on a cosmic level, a Grand Plan to pale even the most radical urban development agenda. In this document, vast areas of the borough are outlined in shocking pink on oversimplified maps, promoting the "abundance of land for development" of which the Olympic Village is the most high-profile good on sale.

The emergence of the adiZones as a typology of urban landscape of sport, fitness and leisure appears both as a departure and a point of arrival, an innovation and a regression. Their permanency ushers more durable sponsorship opportunities usually limited to the specificity of "world-class" events and their timeline, a marketing legacy extending momentary instrumental alliances into strategic partnerships, with the result of imprinting at a capillary level the passage of such events into the urban built environment.

But at the same time, the character of such intervention revisits a whole history of branding legacies that belong to the pavilions of world fairs and world expositions of the 1930s and 1950s, a model that has clearly influenced the overall sponsorship strategy of the London 2012 Olympics Games, eager to offer to its sponsors available avenues to circumvent the IOC restrictions on branding during the Games.

The London 2012 legacy has been insistently promoted as a progressive, socially beneficial approach to the value of hosting the Olympic Games, a kind of bona fide pre-emptive statement of intent sold as an antidote to the reoccurring evidences of monumentally redundant structures in previous Olympic host cities. However, by consciously deflecting the attention from the Games itself towards the added long-term benefits of the legacy, the Games' organisers have raised the expectations for the effective delivery of such a long-term

benefit. Whether or not the Stratford Westfield Shopping Centre can be considered a "long-term" benefit, the much vaunted "transformation of the heart of East London" holds its own secret promises within the use of such generic and unspecific turn of phrase, but – like any heart operation – the responses will continue to be emotionally charged.

As a prologue to future acts of tangible urban transformations, the adiZones appear as frightening forecasts of the effective value of the legacy and its branded inheritance. Like an Olympic "Groundhog Day" in 3D, their protracted presence, eternally returning within previously unbranded public spaces, might in time become one of the most effective ways of measuring the history of branding legacies that belong to the pavilions of world fairs and world expositions of the 1930s and 1950s, a model that has clearly influenced the overall sponsorship strategy of the London 2012 Olympics Games, eager to offer to its sponsors available avenues to circumvent the IOC restrictions on branding during the Games.

The London 2012 legacy has been insistently promoted as a progressive, socially beneficial approach to the value of hosting the Olympic Games, a kind of bona fide pre-emptive statement of intent sold as an antidote to the reoccurring evidences of monumentally redundant structures in previous Olympic host cities. However, by consciously deflecting the attention from the Games itself towards the added long-term benefits of the legacy, the Games' organisers have raised the expectations for the effective delivery of such a long-term benefit. Whether or not the Stratford Westfield Shopping Centre can be considered a "long-term" benefit, the much vaunted "transformation of the heart of East London" holds its own secret promises within the use of such generic and unspecific turn of phrase, but – like any heart operation – the responses will continue to be emotionally charged.

As a prologue to future acts of tangible urban transformations, the adiZones appear as frightening forecasts of the effective value of the legacy and its branded inheritance. Like an Olympic "Groundhog Day" in 3D, their protracted presence, eternally returning within previously unbranded public spaces, might in time become one of the most effective ways of measuring the actual impact of the London 2012 Olympic and Paralympics Games in its most immediate surroundings and beyond.

Bower Birds

JUDE ROSEN

Through the glass and haze of the eucalyptus tree
you could see the pile growing: blue fluff, two
powder blue feathers, royal blue plastic peg
that caught my eye, so huge for a small bird to push
into place. Did he do it with his nose?
Why did he want to hoard blues? It seemed such
a particular obsession. So coming back
to the Lea Valley to find it wrapped up tight
in blue corsetry, holding in its contours
its heart pulseless, its complexion grey ashphalt
the air, brown dust, I was struck by the attraction
for bower birds of the Olympic authorities.
The best of everything has gone into this…
the best materials. There are stores of it –
Dulux Trade Water Resistant Gloss - on site -
blue scurf curling off the swollen plywood.
Key parts of the fence will be branded…
Everyone's 2012. Demolish,
Dig, Design! Regeneration, in 3D,
patrolled at night by private security men.
Imagine the bower birds coming, stripping off
the valley's body armour to adorn
the bowers they'd build with the blue detritus.

A Fragment from the Long Poem
Reclamations: Voices and Narratives from the Olympic Zone

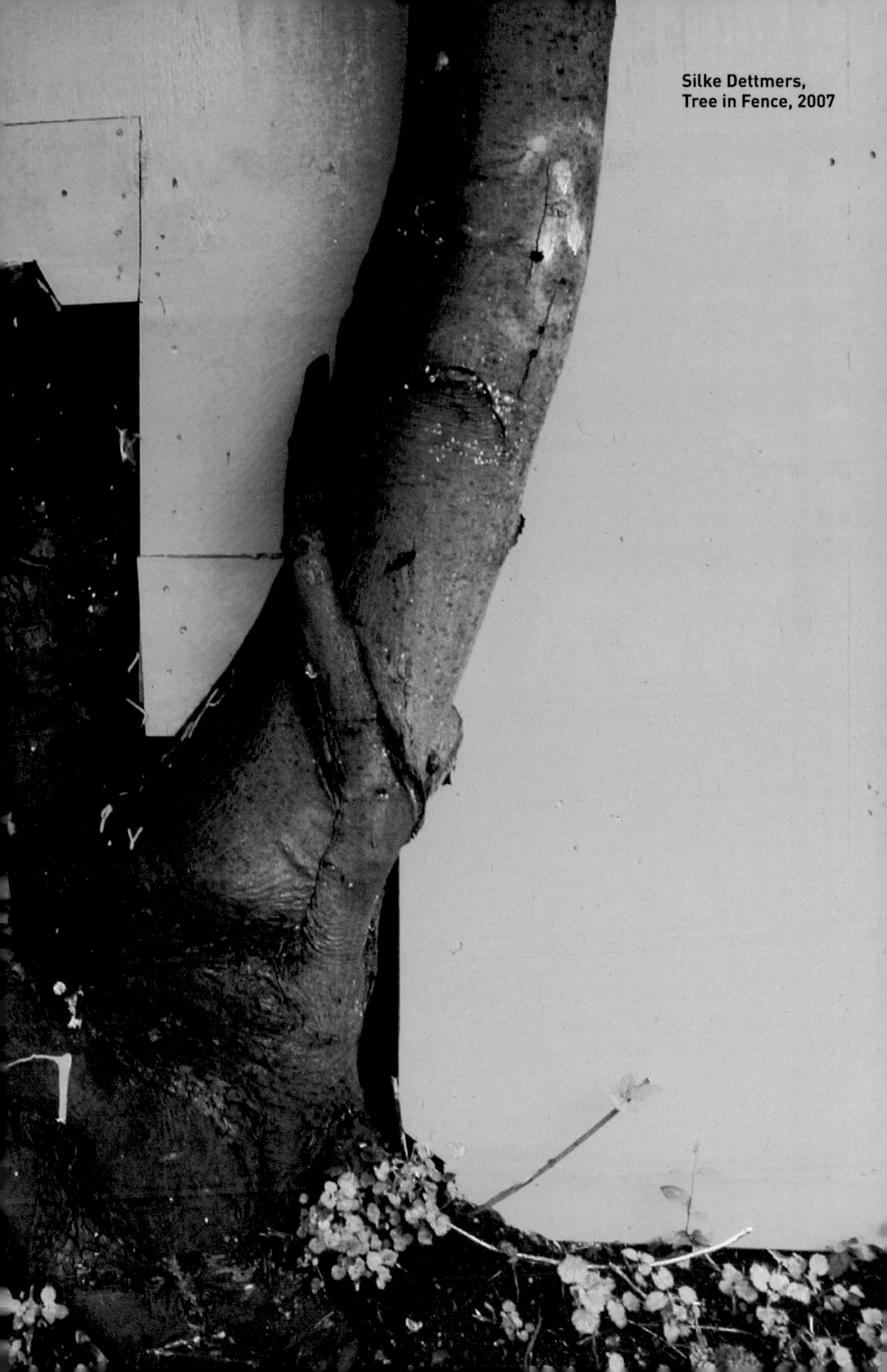
Silke Dettmers,
Tree in Fence, 2007

Point of View:
The London Olympics' First Public Viewing Platform

VICKY RICHARDSON

I've never been a critic of the Olympic development. I'm a supporter of London hosting the Games, and I think that the project of creating a new urban quarter in east London is one of the few truly brave public projects of our time. Perhaps that's why I felt so annoyed in the summer of 2008 when I innocently visited the Olympic site, hoping for a view of the construction works, only to be met by security guards, a three-metre high blue fence, and not a clue as to what was going on beyond it.

The blue fence came to symbolise the defensiveness and paranoia of the Olympic Delivery Authority (ODA). Dealing with the ODA's press office was no easier: it drip fed announcements, but refused to provide information on request, and we discovered that the architects working on the site had been intimidated into silence. I was editor of *Blueprint* at the time, and the job of producing informed articles about architecture of the Games was virtually impossible.

The Blueprint team was driven by a sense of injustice that summer. Our deputy editor Tim Abrahams flew to Beijing to visit the new Olympic facilities, and against the odds managed to gain access to the Birds Nest Stadium before its official opening. If we could break through the Chinese Government's information blockade, surely we could make an impact on the ODA in London. Faced with cuts at the magazine, we felt we had nothing to lose, and angered by the ring of silence around the Olympic park, we decided to take direct action. We contacted the Office for Subversive Architecture (OSA), a small firm run by Bernd Truempler and Karsten Huneck, and commissioned them to design a viewing platform to be located alongside the blue fence. They were not deterred by the two-week deadline, the non-existent budget, or the possibility of being arrested. They designed a simple but effective structure, and fortunately we had a student working in the Blueprint office, Amy Tipper, whose dad was a joiner with a workshop in Leytonstone and willingly agreed to build it for us.

On 12 June we installed the first public viewing platform at London's Olympic site. At 6am Huneck, Truempler and Blueprint staff lifted it into position in deep vegetation alongside the blue fence on the Greenway at the southwest corner of the Park. The architects applied the finishing touch, spraying 'Point of View' onto the side with a stencil. We then formed an orderly

Office for Subversive Architecture, Point of View, 2008

queue, and took it in turns to climb the six steps to the top of the platform, gloriously taking in the view towards the foundations of the Olympic stadium.

All this was recorded for the August issue of *Blueprint*, in which I wrote (I admit somewhat disingenuously): 'We placed Point of View alongside the fence not as a provocation but as a gesture of friendliness, openness and enthusiasm for the Games – a spirit seemingly unknown to the official bodies organising them.' Point of View stayed in position for 60 hours before being removed by ODA officials. Several members of the public were witnessed using the platform in that time.

The year after, in 2009, the ODA and its partners installed a public visitor centre of their own. The View Tube was a slightly more elaborate structure than ours, made from recycled shipping containers. Run as a "social enterprise", with a café, educational programme and arts spaces, the View Tube has been highly successful. But this makeshift solution evidently came about as an afterthought, and followed several years' debate about how to handle public interest in the site. I would like to think that our intervention may have played a role in high-lighting the need.

The failure to provide a proper visitor centre from which the public could witness the development of the Olympic facilities was not just an innocuous omission. It says much about the peculiar relationship between the authorities and the public. On the one hand the community is urged to be part of the process through elaborate and expensive consultation; and on the other the public is kept at arm's length, viewed as a security threat.

Indeed the longer history of the visitor centre is revealing. Something that was seen as an add-on in the early days of planning for the Games has slowly been understood to be fundamental. The original budget for the Games did not include a plan for a visitor centre. For several years VIP visitors were taken to the top of a residential tower block in Stratford (Holden Point), where a portakabin, which accommodated 15 people, had been placed on the roof to act as a viewing gallery. The Queen was even taken there in 2005, shortly after London won its bid to host the Games.

Stratford-based architecture group Fundamental, which engaged school children with the Olympic development, resorted to using the roof of a multi-storey car park as a viewing gallery for the site. Later on this became the location for Dining East, a pop-up restaurant designed by architect Carmody Groarke.

During 2007 the Department for Culture Media and Sport undertook numerous costly feasibility studies that looked into providing a visitor centre, including one study by the organisation Open House, which concluded in March 2007 that there should be a "virtual architecture centre". For some months OSpace was run by the Commission for Architecture and the Built Environment, before it quietly disappeared, presumably when they realised how a website could be no substitute for actually being there.

In 2011, in my new role at the British Council, I was invited into the Olympic site by the Olympic Park Legacy Company (the public body which took over from the ODA). Dressed in fluorescent padded jacket, protective glasses, gloves and boots, I walked along the banks of the River Lea, where wild mushrooms were sprouting from the Hargreaves-designed landscape. I was there to visit the site of the North Park hub and playground, one of the facilities that will welcome visitors to the new Queen Elizabeth Olympic Park in May 2013. I'd been invited to chair the jury for an architectural competition for the "hub", with the emphasis on creating a "special place where local residents and community groups, as well as regional and international visitors will feel at home". The issue of community was uppermost in our minds as we prepared to interview the design teams. Who would use the hub; how would they find their way to the park; and who would actually make up the "community", given that most new housing surrounding the park would not be complete until 2016?

Several times that day I remembered the summer of 2008: Blueprint's homemade viewing platform and our demand for access to the site. The irony was inescapable: for so long the public was kept away from the park; the challenge now was to get them back.

All Aboard:
Creating Extensions to the Olympic Blue Wall by Painting Objects Found in the Vicinity

JEAN-FRANÇOIS PROST

The colour, opaqueness and sheer size of the Olympic blue wall attracted a lot of attention and criticism. Graffiti and stickers appeared regularly on its surface. In order to remove these frequent and various forms of visual expression, several employed workers regularly inspected and repetitively stripped and repainted the 10-foot-high wooden barrier.

One day, while observing the site and on a routine walk around the perimeter, I found a discarded bucket of the Olympic blue paint (called All Aboard) lying on the ground. Taking into consideration that possibly nothing but blue could or would survive on the wall, the "All Aboard" "adaptive action" was developed to test whether unplanned additions and extensions to and around the wall would survive if they were blue and, if so, for how long?

In the vicinity of the bold and well-maintained blue wall laid an incredible quantity of rubbish and abandoned objects. As the fence was routinely repainted blue, I started extending it by painting surrounding chairs, toys, tools, stools, tables and so on. While others looked for graffiti and stickers I searched for interesting objects to fix, reuse and relocate, to reveal their existence or question their prolonged abandonment. Through this repetitive activity, I progressively discovered the life around the site, its concealed aspects.

Jean-François Prost, All Aboard, 2008

The Blue Fence Project

STUDIO SUPERNICHE*

> "It is important to know the mechanism of transformation and above all to establish how we can act in this situation – not, I believe, through the total control of the process of change."
> Aldo Rossi, *The Architecture of the City*

Eleven miles of blue plywood landed in east London in 2006, inscribing a vast ring around 200 hectares of the Lower Lea Valley: the site for the 2012 Olympic Games, incarcerated with an endless fence. As a continuous billboard, the blue wall trumpeted the arrival of wholesale regeneration, projecting the promise of an imaginary post-Olympic legacy-scape: 12,000 new homes and 10,000 new jobs emerging from pristine grasslands, across six themed quarters – our very own Magic Kingdom of the East End. The irony wasn't lost on local residents, disenfranchised on the wrong side of the fence.

In 2009, the blue wall came down, making way for a Guantanamo-style electrified version, and some of the ubiquitous plywood fell into the hands of Studio Superniche – a group of four architects and product designers, brought together to champion the cause of the niche against the tide of the generic. Attempting to demonstrate an alternative future for the site, we began to develop an Olympic Legacy Toolkit, a catalogue of provisional urban furniture designed to encourage local re-appropriation of this vast terrain in the aftermath of the fleeting sporting funfair.

Once the travelling Olympic circus has upped sticks, the site will be left bare, a tabula rasa to be somehow transformed into a vibrant, mixed-use city quarter – by 2050. But, because of the sheer scale of the site, and the waning confidence of the market, it has become clear that much of the 200 hectares will remain vacant for years to come, earmarked as "transition zones" in a 40-year plan of "field evolution". And herein lies the opportunity.

Through encouraging temporary use on the site, our Toolkit proposes a bottom-up alternative, a counter to the conventional top-down masterplan issued from on high. Using the very material designed to keep people out, we have developed a series of low-tech, ephemeral pavilions to suggest possible ways of inhabiting the site, taking inspiration from community groups that were forcibly displaced by the Olympic project, to inspire the reclamation of the empty landscape as their own.

From bird hides to allotment sheds, portable galleries to boat houses, this series of functional follies aims to provoke debate about potential uses for the site's vacant plots in the wake of the Games and demonstrate the power of propositional critique in challenging the received wisdom of the planning authorities.

In recession-struck London, temporary intervention can provide a snapshot of the possible, a physical means of demonstrating alternatives. Public consultation – the souped-up roadshows of interactive maps, board games and Post-it notes so beloved of developers – can be transcended in favour of building a version of the real thing, at no risk and little cost. By showing what is possible, temporary uses have the power to rewrite the rules of the plan, forestalling final judgement on what plots of land might be worth, and what kind of activities are appropriate there. Interim users have the potential to open up fundamental debates on land use classification, temporary permissions suggesting the slackening of more permanent restrictions. Ultimately democratic, they must prove their self-sustaining viability through their own vitality: if spaces thrive and become established before the developers arrive, they can redirect the development agenda as facts on the ground and turn the whole masterplan upside down.

The recession has marked a watershed in conventional systems of masterplanning, from which we can only move towards a process-driven model of incremental, evolutionary development. Newly politicised, there is an opportunity for design to be oppositional once again, to battle the tide of win–win consensus planning. Like never before, the future of the city is in the hands of its users – and the holes in the legacy plan provide an opportunity to offer up a radical alternative.

* Studio Superniche is Kieren Jones, Will Shannon, Ottilie Ventiroso and Oliver Wainwright.

Birdhide

The area around the Olympic Park is a popular site for bird-watchers, with over 200 different species of bird known to frequent the Lower Lea Valley. Many of these will have been displaced by the noise and dust of the development, but there are plans to encourage their return with the inclusion of wetlands and reedbeds in the legacy park. This birdhide provides a place for bird-watchers to shelter, with a second storey to allow an elevated view over the landscape.

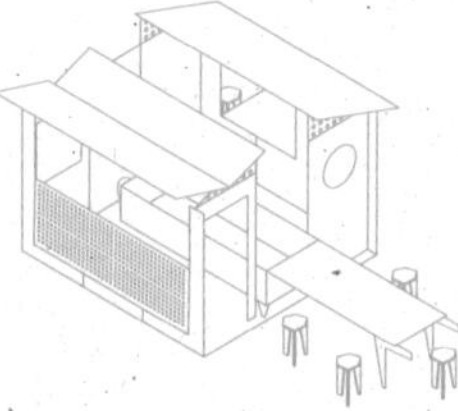

Allotment Shed

Before development began, the area was home to several heavily-used allotment sites, which are planned to return to the park after the Games. This openable shed responds to the way the allotments had become a centre for social interaction. With a sliding table and portable growing bed, it allows the conventional storage space to transform into an area for sitting, eating and exchanging produce.

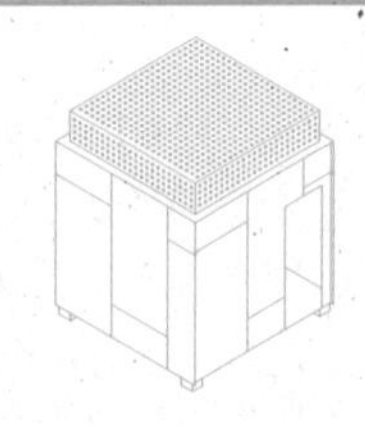

Gallery Cube

London's 'Cultural Olympiad' has attracted funding of over £50m, several million of which will be spent on high profile public art for the park. At the same time, East London is home to Europe's largest concentration of artists, most of whom are being excluded from these large commissions. This modest gallery cube provides a flexible, itinerant, backdrop, an open platform for smaller artistic endeavours. It could equally be erected around an existing feature to elevate it from the everday.

The Olympic Legacy Toolkit

StudioSuperniche©

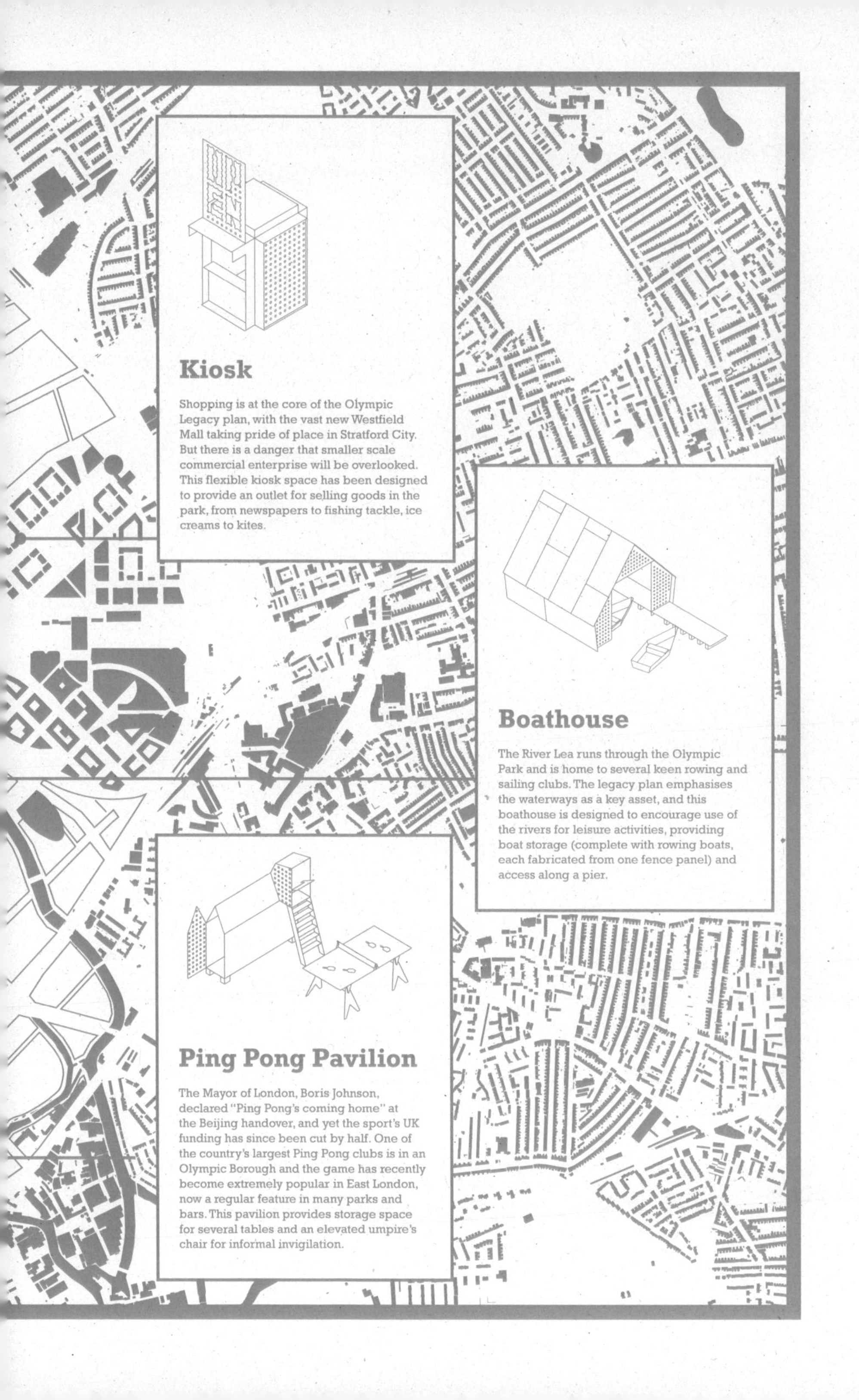

Kiosk

Shopping is at the core of the Olympic Legacy plan, with the vast new Westfield Mall taking pride of place in Stratford City. But there is a danger that smaller scale commercial enterprise will be overlooked. This flexible kiosk space has been designed to provide an outlet for selling goods in the park, from newspapers to fishing tackle, ice creams to kites.

Boathouse

The River Lea runs through the Olympic Park and is home to several keen rowing and sailing clubs. The legacy plan emphasises the waterways as a key asset, and this boathouse is designed to encourage use of the rivers for leisure activities, providing boat storage (complete with rowing boats, each fabricated from one fence panel) and access along a pier.

Ping Pong Pavilion

The Mayor of London, Boris Johnson, declared "Ping Pong's coming home" at the Beijing handover, and yet the sport's UK funding has since been cut by half. One of the country's largest Ping Pong clubs is in an Olympic Borough and the game has recently become extremely popular in East London, now a regular feature in many parks and bars. This pavilion provides storage space for several tables and an elevated umpire's chair for informal invigilation.

An East London Border

MARK WAYMAN

16 November 2007. The Olympic Park Viewing Gallery, 22nd floor, Holden Point, Stratford. We are in the vie

edge of it. The first photograph was taken at the corner of Angel Lane, just the other side of this (points thro

it. And that is the perimeter fence [...] This sign here... there's a lot of boat racing on the Lee Navigation and

strangely, a bird table inside a glass box. "Is that a work of art?" (woman in audience) Who knows? [...] One

in audience) Dentures? Ah, Right. There's the Grim Reaper! [...] This is the new Forman and Sons building. T

llery for a great East London construction project. The presentation which I'm going to give today shows the

window) cigarette-shaped tower block, of the redbrick council estate that you can see just down there below

nk this sign refers to the finish of a boat race. Excellent catering facilities. And more catering facilities with,

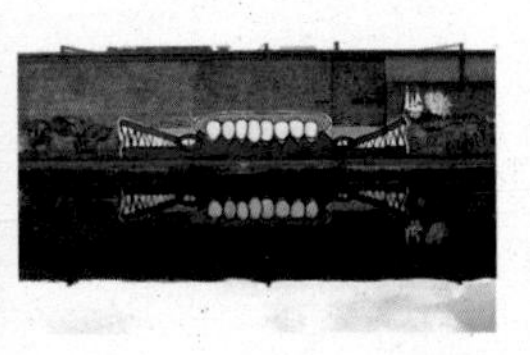

he artists who's done a lot of this work seems to have a particular theme of making teeth. "Dentures" (man

had to move from what is now the zone of nothingness, and this is their new site and they are fish smokers.

This is another quite spectacular artwork which is actually a swan, a very long, thin swan, that goes right th

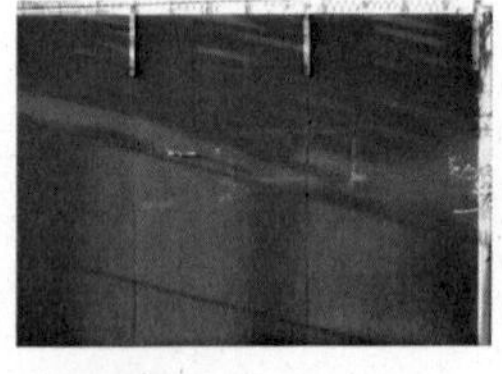   

And there's a guy maintaining the winch [...] This is the beginning of the Greenway, which you can see. It is

(woman in audience). The Greenway? "Yes. You can't actually smell it there, but if you go down the other en

for that. [...] This is at the bottom of the Greenway, where it's hemmed in by the zone of nothingness, and be

Pudding Mill Lane, and this is an industrial estate that is off to the side of it. Different kinds of wall surface.

ay along this building. And here's the back of it, with the Lee Mean Clean Machine. And this is Old Ford Lock.

ne of trees. It is on the route of a disused railway viaduct. "I thought it covered the Northern Outfall Sewer"

n in audience). That's interesting. I did smell it the other day, and I didn't realise what it was. Ok, thank-you

nd that other thing, straight ahead. You can see the sign that says "Greenway", up there. This is the start of

nother waste management company. It does seem to be a popular means of making money around here.

Sound Proof:
In a State of Becoming Olympic

MONICA BIAGIOLI

Sound Proof is a series of yearly exhibitions that take the Stratford site of the London 2012 Olympics as a point of departure for commissioned artworks with a focus on sound. Since 2008 it has provided artists with an independent platform from which to respond to and explore the London Games. The project was inspired by a tour of the site led by a member of the Ramblers Association in 2007. During the visit, he led us along the waterway paths, pointing out sites soon to be transformed. It was a space suspended in time, in a state of becoming. Not quite what it appeared to be, not yet the place envisioned.

Sound Proof 1 was co-curated by Colm Lally and me at E:vent Gallery (London) in 2008. We focused on artist walks of the Olympic site, with the aim to capture and preserve sonic readings of its essence at that time – to retain a record of something that would disappear and re-shape into new forms when construction commenced. "Sound as cartography" became the theme for the first exhibition, in which six artists participated: Brown Sierra, Angus Carlyle, Jem Finer, Sara Heitlinger and Frank Purg, Miller and McAfee Press, and Vessna Perunovich with Boja Vasic. The tone of contributions varied according to the artists' perspective of the site and Sound Proof as a whole reflected a complex response to the space. For the exhibition, we wanted the focus to be on sound, so we decided to carve out space for each piece through the measurement of time. A thin blue line of text on the wall surrounded two loudspeakers set in the centre of the space, and each artist was allocated a one-hour time slot.

Sound Proof 2 responded to the changes in the area already apparent in 2009 – the blue wall had been replaced by see-through wire fencing, renderings of future buildings, and messages and images encouraging public participation. New temporary structures were on the site and the main stadium was taking shape. The thematic focus became archaeological, with an emphasis on "sound as artefact". What could constitute a material artefact within this site in development? Four artists, Isha Bøhling, Daniel Jackson, Sheena Macrae and John Wynne, were invited to explore the issue. The works were then exhibited in a warehouse space in Canterbury Court in London, and a vinyl multiple edition of 300 was published.

For John Wynne and Daniel Jackson the artefact was extracted not from the physical site, but from public consciousness. Wynne uncovered the Olympic

Jem Finer, The Rise and fall of the Olympic State, 2008

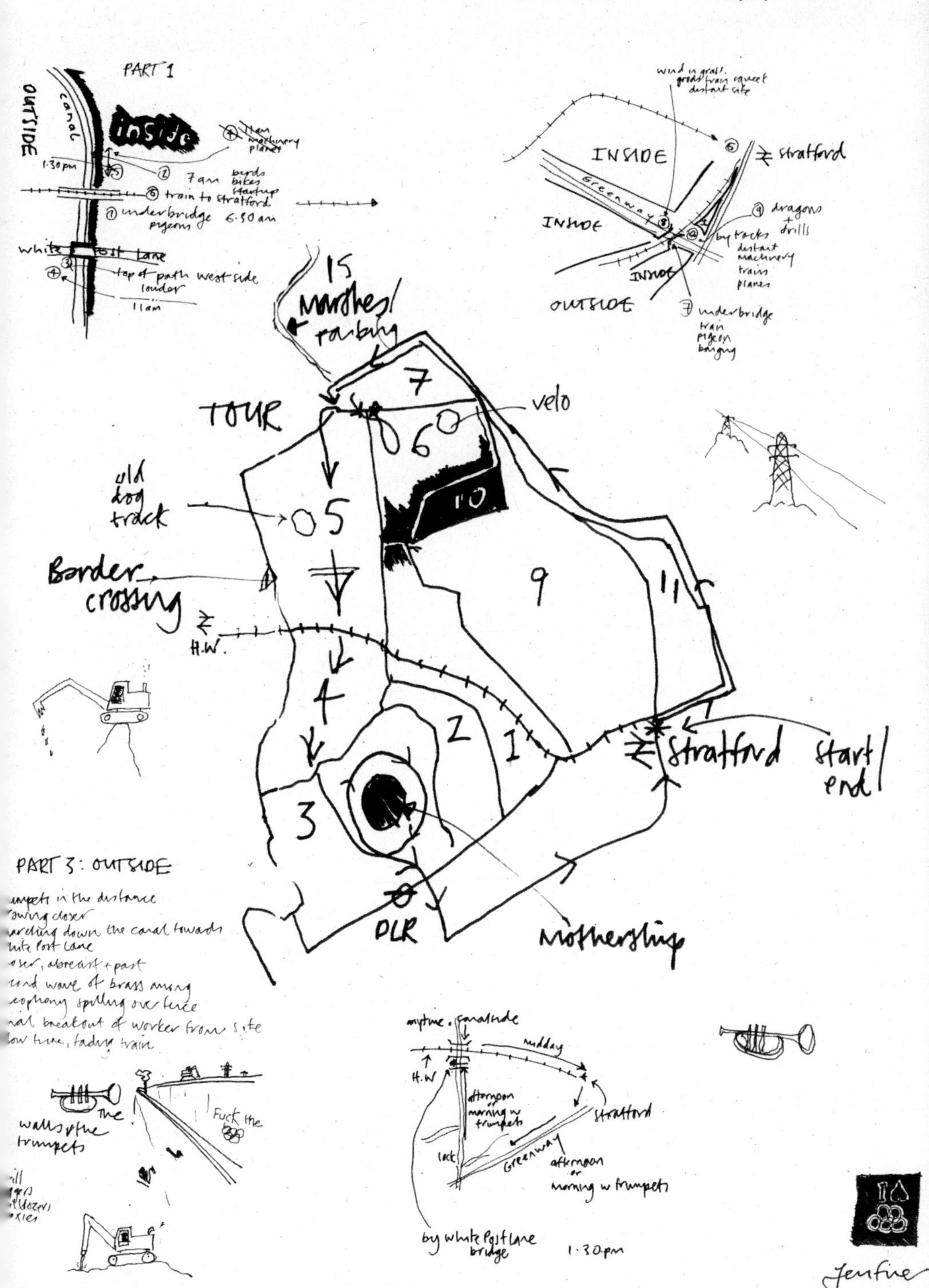

logo as a site of conflict manifested in graffiti, stickers, banners and blogs. In Jackson's conceptual soundwork, the physical site existed as numerical reference points. The visual manifestation was a play on the word "Olympics", represented through the five rings, where the word was taken apart and put through a filter that imposed a rhythmic structure determined by statistical data from the construction site.

For Isha Bøhling and Sheena Macrae the archaeology was personal. In "Prize", Bøhling excavated a family history: her grandmother Ruth Bøhling was the Danish Open Water Kayak Champion for the eight years leading up to the 1936 Olympics, but relinquished her chance to compete in Berlin under the Nazi regime and joined the boycott. Working with composer Paul Robinson, Macrae examined her personal sonic signposts as someone who had lived in the Pudding Mill Lane area before the site became designated Olympic. Her piece "Beginnings, Middles, and Ends" layered ten of Robinson's film compositions simultaneously, stratifying the cinematic coding into a phonic range of poignant moments, a quintessential film score to punctuate a personal history.

By this point my perception of Sound Proof was that it operated as an open platform inviting differing responses and views through the works shown in the exhibition, rather than presenting a position of its own. I invited Julie Penfold of PVA MediaLab to co-curate Sound Proof 3 with me. As she was based in Dorset, where the sailing competitions would take place, Penfold could provide the perspective and focus from that area. Sound Proof 3 became a dialogue between two sites of the 2012 Olympics, connected through a conversation between artists. Sheena Calvert and Denna Jones in London and Claire Burke and Joe Stevens in Dorset responded to the theme "sound as text" through a live tweet conversation during the B-side Festival in 2010 – later represented as a wall text piece on the foyer wall at Homerton Library, near the Olympics site in Stratford.

The dialogue between Olympic sites continued in Sound Proof 4, where I explored the link between London and Barcelona, host of the Olympics 20 years earlier. The theme was "sound as legacy" and four installations with sound – two from Barcelona (Roc Jiménez de Cisneros, and Barbara Held, Yapci Ramos and Matt Davis) and two from London (Leigh Clark and Jon Fawcett) – were curated. The co existing installations formed a type of environmental sculpture, allowing the works to speak to each other through the context of the exhibition.

In its yearly iterations Sound Proof has acted as a memory track of how London was built up towards 2012, reflecting a complex layering of moods and views through the filter of artistic responses.

Sara Heitlinger and Franc Purg, What is it that moves us?, 2008

Symbolic Resistance: Turning the Rings

JOHN WYNNE AND HELEN LENSKYJ IN CONVERSATION

HL: I was an active member of Toronto's Bread Not Circuses Coalition from 1998. At the time, Toronto was bidding for the 2008 Olympics, using the slogan "Expect the World". Our subverted version, "Expect the Worst", showed various images suggesting homelessness, police surveillance, public debt and so on. We put these images on banners, leaflets and stickers, and throughout our anti-Olympic bid book, as a counter to the official bid images that saturated the city. The rings are a popular image for Olympic resisters to subvert and distort. As they're universally recognised as "Olympic", it's easy to present them in a way that raises public awareness. Images from Vancouver and Whistler artists portrayed the rings as handcuffs, barbed wire and dripping blood. Other Vancouver and Whistler activists wrote and performed satirical songs, with subverted images, which they put on YouTube.

JW: It was the graphic subversion of the Olympic rings that first inspired me to make this piece. It's unusual for me to begin from a visual perspective rather than an aural one, but when I was in Vancouver I noticed the imaginative ways that people were subverting the Olympics symbol – through graffiti, stickers, banners and blogs – and I knew I wanted to work with some of them. Strangely enough, despite the five rings being, as Angus Carlyle put it in an email to me, "ripe for *détournement*", when I returned to London I was unable to find many similar graphic subversions in public view. The perimeter wall that surrounded the London Olympic site for years had so many coats of blue paint that perhaps the graffitists just gave up.

HL: We saw the effectiveness of convergence in the 1999 anti-globalisation protests in Seattle, again in Australia in 2000 during the Olympics, and then in 2010 in Vancouver. The rallying point for the NO 2010 protest in Canada was "No Olympics on Stolen Land" – the province of British Columbia is not covered by a treaty with the Indigenous peoples – and this approach brought together Native people, environmentalists and a wide range of community activists across Canada. Some of the visual images that NO 2010 created focused on these concerns, and you have some of them in your installation.

JW: The Vancouver Olympics were very divisive among Native com-

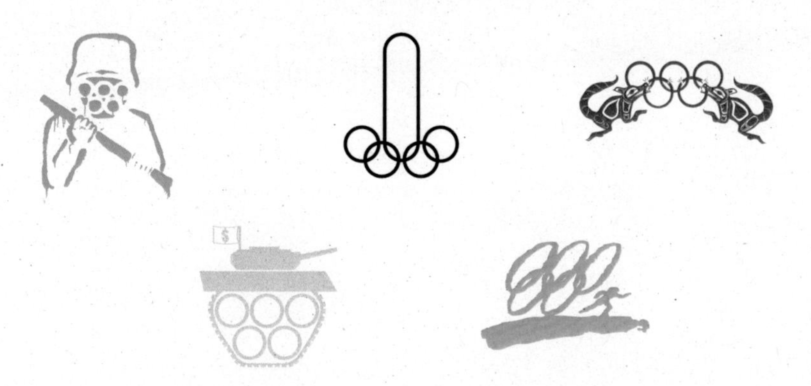

John Wynne, Faster Higher Stronger, 2009 (includes Wolves not Sheep, by Ange Sterritt)

munities in British Columbia – some people were satisfied with the arguable benefits of employment, money and exposure they got from the presence of the games, but others saw exploitative tokenism and pointed to the hypocrisy of the "Green Games" being used as a smokescreen for environmentally irresponsible and culturally insensitive acts, like the destruction of Eagle Ridge in order to widen the Sea to Sky Highway between Vancouver and Whistler. I was happy to discover that one of the appropriations of the rings that attracted my attention online was by an artist from the Native community in which I recently did a project focusing on their language, one of several endangered indigenous languages in Canada. Ange Sterritt is a Gitxsan artist whose graphics have been widely used by the No 2010 campaign, and she kindly gave me permission to include her Wolves not Sheep image in my installation. I spotted the phallic image (which some apparently prefer to see as a finger) as a sticker on a lamppost in the downtown east side of Vancouver, which is where I also saw the police figure with a five-ring mask spray painted on lots of walls and utility boxes. The tank was a response to the games in China, which I found on the internet, and you sent me the image of a figure running from the rings which was used by Bread Not Circuses in Toronto. But all except Ange's work remain anonymous, despite my efforts to trace their origins in order to acknowledge the artists.

HL: The Olympic industry has a mega-budget for global publicity, and more than a century of history as the world's biggest sporting spectacle. This makes it difficult, almost impossible in some cases, for Olympic resisters to get our message out to the public. The mainstream media are mostly uncritical supporters of all things Olympic, and "feel-good" human interest stories are the norm. "Bringing politics into sport" (as if sport was somehow exempt) is presented as "a bad thing", and attacking (or appearing to attack) athletes is even worse. In my books, I've critiqued "the myth of the pure Olympic athlete and pure Olympic sport" because their celebrity status often blinds people to the fact that they are not by definition good "role models" simply because they are faster and stronger than most of us.[1]

JW: It's hard to argue against something that people think stands for brotherly love without sounding like a curmudgeon. Running continuously in my piece is an electronic tone that seems to rise continuously in pitch – forever. This is an illusion, of course – a sound that truly got higher and higher in pitch would soon go above the range of human hearing and would therefore become inaudible quite quickly. I'm using the tension created by this rising tone to suggest both the relentless and inescapable hype that follows the Games around the world and the often unchallenged assumption of the benefits of endless progress in technology, culture and physical performance. The arguably illusory public image of the games relies heavily on the ideals of goodwill, social development, international peace and brotherhood to mask the underlying commercialism and profiteering of what Chris Shaw refers to as "the Olympic machine".[2]

Faster Higher Stronger also marks the first time I've used sounds I have not recorded myself. I use booing sounds from sound effects libraries to simultaneously give voice to the protests and to reflect some of the aggression that seems to be an integral part of high-level sport and, at times, of its spectators. Sometimes, as George Orwell wrote in "The Sporting Spirit", "Serious sport... is war minus the shooting".[3] It's a five-channel sound piece and the graphic images are actually flat speakers so that each image has its own "voice".

HL: Olympic industry officials and their lawyers put a lot of energy and money into protecting Olympic symbols. There were examples in Sydney where they went after an Audi car dealer who used that company's four rings in a way that suggested the five rings of the Olympics. Most copyright concerns are purely financial, to prevent "ambush marketing" and protect the multinationals who have paid enormous sums for the title "Olympic sponsor".

JW: I don't live close to the Olympic site, but it seems that the suppression of protest – at least in the form of publicly visible graphics – has been particularly successful in London. The police may not use their powers under Section 22 of the London Olympic and Paralympic Games Act 2006 to use "reasonable force" to enter "land or premises" to remove and destroy protest materials, but the fact that such legislation exists is worrying evidence of the power of the International Olympic Committee (IOC) to "shape a country's domestic policy, at least in the short term", as you have written.

HL: During the Olympics, spectators are screened to ensure they don't have clothing or banners that promote a competing product or convey a political message. One of the most imaginative protests in recent Olympics happened during Sydney 2000's closing ceremony. While the group Midnight Oil was singing "Beds are Burning", they wore clothes with SORRY written on them – a powerful political statement referring to the Government's longstanding refusal to apologise to the Stolen Generation of Aboriginal peoples. As children, they had been forcibly removed from their families to live in boarding schools, where they were frequently abused.

Exploitation of Indigenous peoples, their cultures and symbols is a regular feature of the Olympics. Sydney 2000 officials wanted "Aboriginality" in their logos, with the dots in the final version representing central Australian Aboriginal dot paintings. In the case of London, the bid committee took children from East End immigrant families to parade in front of the IOC during its selection meeting.

JW: I thought it was interesting and appropriate in relation to both the "No Olympics on stolen Native land" campaign and Vancouver's appropriation of an arguably unsuitable Inuit symbol for its logo. that the CEO of the Vancouver Organizing Committee is reported to have said, "The five Olympic rings could be used to sell snow to the Eskimos". George Monbiot wrote in the *Guardian* that the reality of the Games is that for some people they are simply "a licence for land grabs".[4] And the value for sponsors of having their logos associated with the Olympic brand and of the restrictions on competition within Olympic sites is massive, regardless of how little their products might relate to notions of good health and social responsibility, as in the case of McDonald's. One of my influences for the visual presentation of this piece was the sort of logo-covered walls that people stand in front of for press conferences, interviews and product launches. Like Orwell, I want to question what he referred to as "the modern cult of sport", which is even stronger now than in his day, and to draw attention to what goes on behind its façade.

susan pui san lok, Faster Higher, a photo-essay comprising stills from the artists' eponymous five-screen installation, interweaving rarely-seen archive material, Chinese documentary newsreels, and footage filmed around the London 2012 site.

The installation (2008) was commissioned by Film and Video Umbrella and BFI, and supported by Arts Council England. The photo-essay (2012) includes material which is © the artist, © Olympic Television Archive Bureau, and © ITN Source.

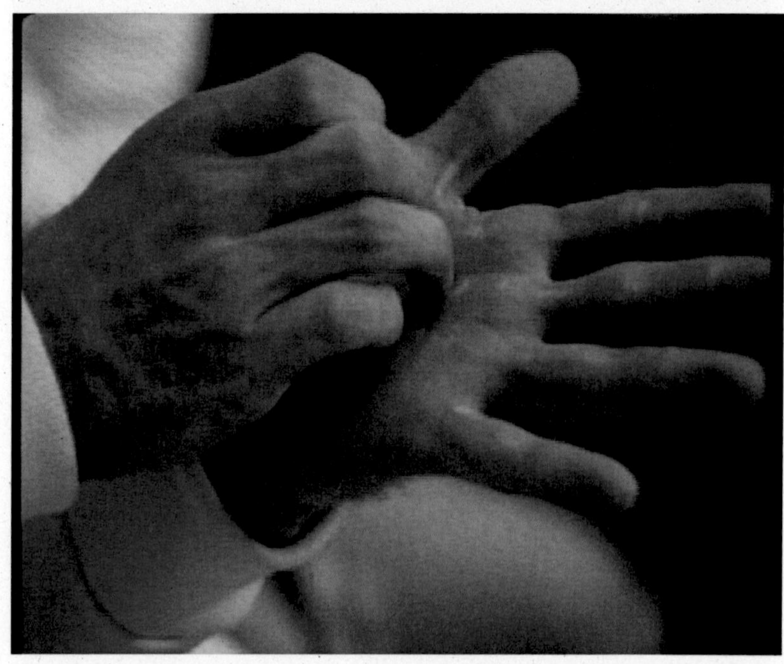

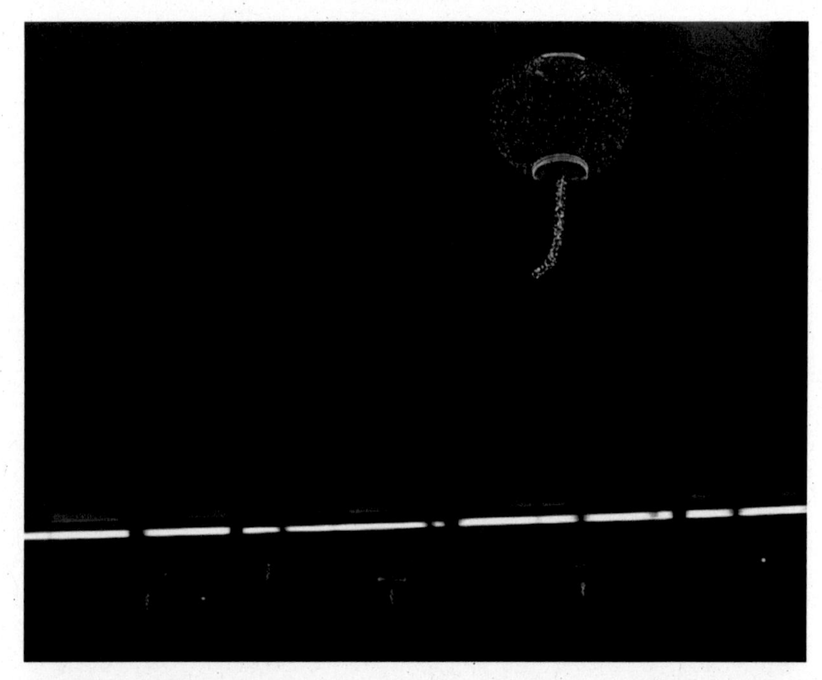

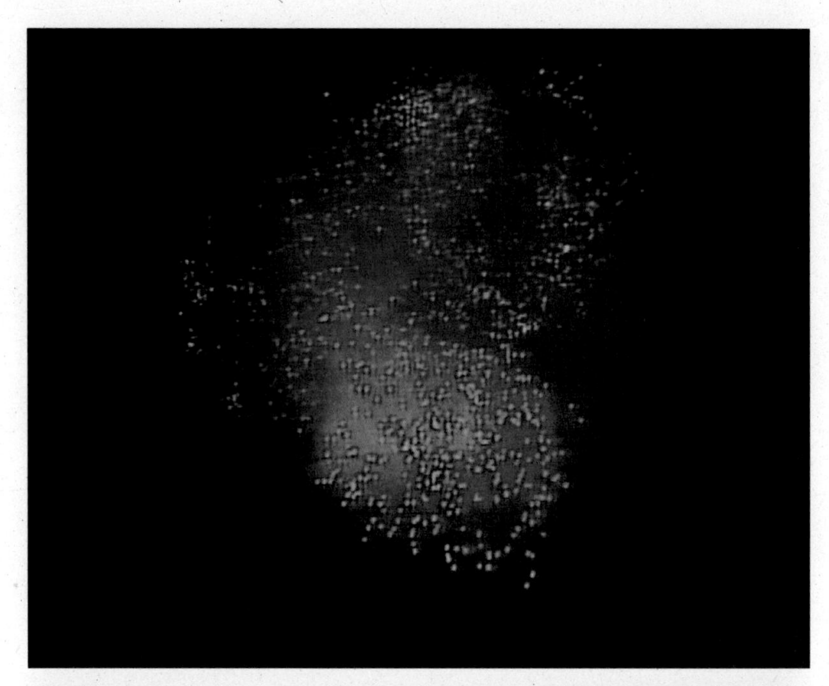

The Games:
Playing for Time in East London

INTERVIEW WITH HILARY POWELL BY ALI MACGILP*

Hilary Powell's short film *The Games* stages a surreal Olympics amid the sites set to become the 2012 Olympic Park. It documents a condensed competition of absurd sporting activities performed under guerrilla conditions: discus-throwing with old car hub caps, trampolining on abandoned mattresses, weightlifting with tyres. Leaping over rubble and debris, the athletes overrun the decayed urban landscape of this forgotten part of London, which stands poised on the brink of total transformation.

Powell obliquely passes comment on the real impact the 2012 Olympics, heavily marketed to Londoners as a Good Thing, has on our environment and communities. When this area is appropriated and transformed into a glossy Olympic Village, what will become of its histories and memories? Powell's film takes a humorously subversive look at the psycho-geography of this area by projecting the future into the past.

AM: For me your film is the antithesis of the heroics of Leni Riefenstahl's *Olympia*. With its school sports day aesthetic, it is joyful and nostalgic with a certain English eccentricity. Where did you find you the initial inspiration for *The Games*?

HP: It's very much inspired by London's earlier Olympic Games of 1908 and 1948 – most particularly the 1948 Games and its post war DIY attitude. London was war scarred and still subject to rationing and yet, in the spirit of making do and getting by, amateur athletes practised in parks and literally amid the rubble, stayed in RAF camps and the women of the teams were sent the patterns to make their own kits! I loved these stories and the fact that it was the first televised games, and used this as a source of inspiration for our DIY outing into the Olympic zone. For me, it's not about nostalgia or recreating the past but gleaning elements, inspiration and methodologies that perhaps could teach us more about the future. It was about taking the iconography, ritual and symbols of the Games – from Olympic torch to podium ceremony and subverting or making them ridiculous and comical.

Iain Sinclair also refers to the film as a "parodic restaging of Leni Riefensthal's overblown epic"[1] and this reference to and emphasis on an element of parody was important within the film's development. I was playing more on the spirit

Federico Figa Talamanca, Hilary Powell's The Games (production still), 2007

and requirements of amateurism associated with the early modern Olympiad than the elite athleticism and body of today's international competition. A similar notion of ideal form was being applied to the local landscape Sinclair described as the "panorama of blight" and this was the key thing I wanted to counter – the idealised Photoshop visions of the future that were being rapidly overlain on the reality of this area – I wanted to make a tragi-comic epic of the real place, to shun the ideal and idealised and play with the pomp and ceremony adding in a good dose of the absurd.

The BBC was on site early filming for their long-term series *Building the Olympics*, and activist film makers were busy documenting the individual community plights within this story. I wanted to find my own way of marking these changes in a creative, provocative way. My training in scenography underpins all my work with a belief in a total scenography or form of "event art" in which place is no longer a backdrop but the core component of any action. The Lower Lea Valley was the main character in this film, with the clumsy movements of the athlete's ventures articulating and highlighting the diversity of communities and sites poised on the brink of destruction. Derek Jarman's *The Last of England* was a core source as a critical and creative occupation and comment of a site (the London Docklands) on the brink of massive change. For him and many others the Docklands development represented a deliberate act of erasure and forgetting. Peter Ackroyd states in his biography of London, "It was as if time, and London's history, had for all practical purposes ceased to exist. In pursuit of profit and instant gratification, the past had become a foreign country."[2] The same can be applied to the Olympic site, particularly in the context of its materialisation during boom and bust – the film has been referenced as an Olympics "after the crash".

AM: As a local, what's your relationship or personal connection with this area of London? What changes have you noticed or been affected by?

HP: Living in a factory warehouse in Hackney Wick, dog walking on the marshes and cycling the streets with a camera meant that little glimpses of the changes to come could be seen early on. As the capital geared up for the bid the area underwent both subtle and drastic changes. The massive Hackney Wick Sunday market was closed down early on, "fridge city" and the Acme studio factory next door disappeared. At the same time, as news reporters struck the area – jumping out of vans to present a piece to camera in front of glamorously, tantalisingly derelict sites – the graffiti started to appear:

NO BIDS NO GAMES and FUCK SEB COE. Graffiti removal vans moved in to keep up with the pace of change and more and more prowling documentarians patrolled the site as its transformation seemed ever imminent.

Local photographer Stephen Gill has taken photographs of glimpses of "future archaeology" – the painted crosses on doomed trees and the surveyors lining the canal paths. For me, Wim Wenders' belief in film as an "archival activity" resonated; he witnessed his Berlin film *Wings of Desire* become both an architectural document and work of mourning for a city that no longer exists. He stated that "the fact that something is due to go is always a good reason to include it in a scene",[3] and this impetus to document and highlight the impending disappearance of multiple sites drove the production of *The Games*.

Most of the sites in which we filmed are now completely gone or on the brink of further transformation; my handmade location map of *The Games* is now a map of vanishings. A new landscape has been moulded and hardly any points of reference to this past remain within the total cleansing of tabula rasa urbanism.

AM: Could you tell me about the making of your film? How long did it take? Who are your actors?

HP: The film required a lot of logistics and people. It began with creating montage collages of athletes transplanted into the area, followed by more detailed storyboards. There were many funding refusals, no real exhibition strategy and the site was changing so rapidly I knew our window of opportunity wouldn't be open for long. We were lucky to gain the support of Urbis in Manchester just before Christmas 2006, with the help of the Office for Subversive Architecture, which supported the film and worked on set construction. This gave us the deadline of March 2007 for its fortuitous inclusion in Urbis' exhibition "Play: Experience the Adventures of Our Cities".

It was certainly an adventure – all filming was done guerrilla style with no site permission, and by its nature had to be organised at the last minute, with constant visits to check sites were actually still accessible as construction work really began in earnest in the area. While getting together costumes I cycled around every day, meeting people in Clays Lane Housing estate, Manor Garden Allotments and so on, asking for permission to use their locations. A lot was achieved under cover of darkness, which helped, and any kind of road closing activities worked out fine as there weren't any cars! Even our fireworks and bonfire went undisturbed.

The people involved were a great mixed bunch of friends and contacts, actors and locals. It was filmed over two weekends in freezing cold conditions, with everyone wearing thin white shorts and vests, and running around in soggy mud. I had arranged to use the Griddlers Café on Carpenters Road as base camp and Rosie the owner was brilliant. Sharing the café with construction workers we set up a screen in the corner for kit change and the massive portions of sausage and chips really helped combat the cold. We did encounter a few problems with the early breed of marauding security guards, complete with army fatigues and Alsatians, but generally our hit and run method went unhindered. It was just good timing – any later and the security was pumped up and what was once a "wild west" zone became more and more policed and surveyed.

AM: Where has working on *The Games* project led for you? Have you become something of an expert on the 2012 Olympics and the regeneration and gentrification of the area?

HP: It's become an inadvertent and ongoing project. We drove the roads of the "zone" the night before its final closure, saying goodbye to what had become in a way our "adventure playground", but it was really just the beginning. The rise of the blue fence in 2007 instantly cordoned off this landscape for good – it prompted anger and resentment in the area but was also a provocation – a call to keep patrolling the area and find ways of intervening in the over-arching narratives of regeneration, progress and exclusion. I continued to work consistently, some may say obsessively, on various projects, including "Pudding Mill River" (also in this volume), guerrilla screening events, "Salon de refuse Olympique" debates, and even a monthly newsletter listing creative projects engaging with the politics and poetics of the rapidly changing area.

It has been at times an emotional and wearing endurance exercise and a real test of the key question what happens when you stay and maintain an ongoing commitment to and working practice within a specific place and landscape, maintaining a creative, critical and independent voice amid the flurry of sponsored cultural initiatives and regeneration agency branding exercises?[4] This book and my three-year Arts and Humanities Research Council Fellowship in the Creative and Performing Arts (Bartlett, UCL) appropriating the traditions of etching and pop-up books to create an archive of demolition and dissent is what happens in this case.

* A first version of this interview was published as "Interview with Hilary Powell", *Art Vehicle* 33 (2007).

Double Games:
Red In Tooth And Claw

FANTICH & YOUNG

"To compete is the highest form of humanity" - anonymous

In the mid-1800s, gymnastic apparatus was adapted from its historical military training application and re-employed in private educational institutions. At the turn of the 1900s, the apparatus was introduced into the physical education (PE) curriculum of state schools. This implementation reflected the evolutionary idea that improving the physical condition of students would enhance intelligence, class and race regeneration. PE's theoretical base married the scientific theory of evolution with the pseudo science of eugenics. Physical exercise was equated with adaptation, strength, survival, intelligence and class – all of which could be hereditarily transferred to the next generation. This was in keeping with the eugenic doctrine: the improvement of human stock and the war against the weak. Gymnasium apparatus was introduced into PE for its form, and function was fully compatible with this ideology: challenging the participant's inner competitive impulse as well as encouraging a competitive instinct within the collective. Baron Pierre de Coubertin, founder of the International Olympic Committee, was deeply interested in education, particularly in PE and the role of sport in schooling. In 1883, he visited England for the first time and studied the PE programme instituted by Thomas Arnold at the Rugby School. Coubertin credited these methods with leading to the expansion of British power during the 1800s and advocated for their use in French institutions. The inclusion of PE in the curriculum of French schools would become one of his ongoing pursuits and passions.

Double Games: Red In Tooth And Claw employs 300,000 Sheffield steel stanley blades, which have been integrated into vintage school gymnasium apparatus: a climbing rope, fixed wall bars, a gym bench, a vaulting horse, a vaulting board and a medicine ball. The sculptures enhance the competitive attributes embedded in the design of the apparatus, elevating them into a wider reflection about the struggle between winners and losers. *Double Games* was conceived, produced and exhibited in Hackney Wick, in the context of the arrival of the Olympics to London and in appreciation of the parallels with some of the city's traits: ruthless competitiveness, hierarchal objectives and statistics-driven targets.

Fantich & Young,
Double Games: Red in
Tooth and Claw, 2010

Victoria Lenzoi
Lee, Olympic
Terra, 2009

EXCAVATIONS

AGAINST THE SYSTEMATIC ERASURE AND EFFACEMENT OF THE HISTORY OF THE LOWER LEA VALLEY CARRIED OUT BY THE OLYMPIC-LED TRANSFORMATION, THE WORKS IN THIS SECTION GLEAN AND CARESS THE MINOR STORIES AND HISTORIES OF THE VALLEY - AN ARCHAEOLOGY OF THE RECENT PAST IN ANTICIPATION OF THE NEAR FUTURE. THIS COLLECTIVE WORK OF ACTIVE MEMORY REVEALS A RICH HUMAN AND NATURAL LANDSPACE, HIDDEN AND UNREGULATED. OBSESSIVELY DOCUMENTING AND WANDERING IN A WORLD THAT WAS SOON TO DISAPPEAR, MANY OF THESE ARTISTS SEEMED TO BE SUFFERING FROM A FORM OF "TOPOPHILIA" - THAT IS, A LOVE OF PLACE AND A NEED TO CAPTURE ITS RAPID TRANSFORMATION.

Stephen Gill, from the series Buried, 2006

Stephen Gill, from the series Buried, 2006

Buried by Stephen Gill and Hackney Wick: an excavation

BEN CAMPKIN

> "Stephen Gill has learnt this: to haunt the places that haunt him."[1]

> "[T]here is something to be gained in focusing explicitly on an archaeology of the present, on an archaeology that engages with the here and now."[2]

In the mid-2000s, London-based photographer Stephen Gill published a number of special edition photographic books through his own imprint, Nobody.[3] Eight of these contain photoworks documenting Hackney Wick and the London 2012 Olympic Park area before its reconfiguration as such.[4] Here, I consider one example, *Buried* (2006), featuring photographs Gill took of Hackney Wick and subsequently buried and exhumed. Which sites did Gill choose to document like this, and why? What does the act and metaphor of burial mean in relation to this contested site, and the manner in which its redevelopment proceeds? In what contexts can we situate Gill's methods and *Buried*'s motifs?

In this project, Gill combines low-tech equipment and simple photographic formats with the labour intensive process of burying and retrieving his photographic prints. The resulting images engage the photographer and viewer in more dynamic exchanges with the sites they depict than the utilitarian photographs typically produced by professionals involved in urban change – those of construction contractors, architects and archaeologists. Gill's archive makes visible structures and spaces that have since been demolished, removed or assigned new uses in the area's restructuring. In *Buried* Gill produces an image from – materialises – the properties and movement of the ground, the "bioremediation" of which has been central in justifying the need for "regeneration", an ambiguous and contested term.[5]

The photographs in *Buried* pointedly contrast the seamlessness and lack of context of the idealistic "photo-real" simulations and architectural photographs circulating according to the official communications agendas of the Olympic development process. Such images are highly controlled at the macro scale of master-planning, and the micro scale of specific architectural schemes. The writer Iain Sinclair, one of the most vocal critics of the Olympics, evokes the projective renders associated with the redevelopment as "CGI smears on the blue fence", drawing attention to their abstracting tendency, and suggesting their potential to blur reality in disorientating and deceptive ways.[6] The fence he refers to is itself an image as well as a physical boundary. It encircled the perimeter of the construction zone when demolition began in the summer of 2007. It quickly became an especially contentious boundary for many artists and photographers. They had previously wandered freely in this area, recording it as they wished, but were now prevented from doing so as this large "piece of the city" was "locked down".[7] Early on in the construction phase the Olympic Delivery Authority (ODA) anticipated criticism of a lack of visual accessibility to the site, installing twenty webcams streaming live footage of the construction zone to their website. The ODA's top public relations priority was to communicate the progress of the site towards its idealised future, the Olympic dream. Aware of the power of images, the ODA prioritised spending on visual communications, and the production of a photographic and film archive to record the site as work proceeded.[8] The webcam images and time-lapse photographs, and the "CGI smears" Sinclair refers to, were precisely intended to "bury" certain things, closing down the area's pre-existing identity and history, neutralising any sense of controversy about the form of redevelopment, suggesting "transparency" while keeping spectators and unauthorised image-makers at a safe distance.

Of course, numerous other professional groups have produced their own archives of the site as part of their day-to-day work. These kinds of photographic documentation normally serve to fix and stabilise an urban area in the throws of physical and social transformation, making sense of it as works progress, rationalising it. Photographs "clean up" an architectural or archaeological site, "freezing" time in order that it can be understood. Within the proliferation of publicly available images produced by built environment professionals associated with the Olympic redevelopment we hardly encounter any that depict a sense of process, or the messy realities of construction. As the works reach completion, polished architectural photographs become the norm, those that typically "present a newly completed and unsullied ideal".[9] This is what makes Gill's photographs so unusual.

Taken and disseminated during the pre-construction phase, Gill's work emphasises process, chance and a subjective and intimate understanding of the area's qualities before its possession by the ODA. Traces resulting from the burial of the original prints expressively record the photographer's material interaction with the site, as well as the physical influence of the site on the photographs. Marks, smears, scratches and dirt take the "witness" aspect of documentary photography to a new dimension, communicating the photographer's presence directly, while also quoting from the site through the voice of its own materiality. In this, Gill's photoworks poetically and forensically open up urban transformation in all its emotional, material, spatial and temporal complexity.

Surface

Buried is a small A5 book, packaged in a stone coloured cardboard slipcase: self-consciously nondescript and earthy. As well as the book itself, inside there is a plain envelope containing a photograph, as if a treasure hunt clue. In edition number 007 this is a snapshot of an overgrown and mossy concrete verge: a definitively urban manmade feature reclaimed by wild plants and flowers. The format and proportions of the image and frame recall an over-sized Polaroid. The slipcase also contains the book itself, smeared with earth, actual abject dirt: evidence of its recent burial. The first time I handled one of the 750 editions was in the sanctuary of the British Library's Rare Books and Manuscripts Reading Room, an orderly and carefully controlled environment, which heightened the surprising out-of-place textures of its dirtiness, as well as bringing to mind the usual function of archives to protect against damage and material decay.

The book's title, "Buried", is in a version of a rounded serif font, Cooper Black, eroded underneath, as is the name of the author, Stephen Gill. The positive and negative images of the letters suggest simultaneously a pile of dirt and an excavated trench. The colour of the text hovers between grey, brown and black. The author's name is obscured by actual dirt, so that you would have to pick at it to reveal it. A sense of abjection, prompted by the dirt's unknown origin, and its connotation of a rotting object, might put you off.

Inside are 27 images that echo the format of the enveloped one. In contrast to that pristine print, here the images and their white borders are damaged and distorted. Three explanatory paragraphs include the information that "the photographs in this book were taken in Hackney Wick and later buried there". They were deposited at various depths and positions, for variable lengths of time.[10] The suggestion is that the reader should take the single unblemished photograph and bury it themselves, joining a collaboration with the authors, identified as "Stephen Gill and Hackney Wick".

Buried is a c-type – chromogenic colour – print book, designed by Melanie Mues, and is one of a series of photobooks published with the intention of "making the book the finished expression of the photographs, rather than just a shell in which to house them".[11] This method gives Gill maximum possible control over the presentation of his photographs, and has meant that the many he has taken of Hackney Wick have been disseminated in publications printed and bound in the area. Close identification with place, and with Hackney and Hackney Wick, in particular, have been consistently important for Gill. He has become well known for his methodical documentation of everyday urban sites and lives, through understated, self-consciously low-tech snapshots, revealing patterns and complexity in ostensibly simple and familiar scenes, objects and city features.

Gill took the photographs in *Buried* with a secondhand plastic Coronet camera, purchased for 50 pence in a market local to the sites they depict. How are we to read the frugal use of such low-tech equipment, and the sparse understated quality of the work? The camera lacked focus and exposure controls, and knowledge of this communicates the virtue of unpretentious yet skillful craftsmanship, and an association with everyday amateur photography. The recycling of a discarded piece of equipment made redundant by more recent technology suggests creativity and pragmatism in Gill's approach to photographing an area rich with history as a "landscape of production" and industrial innovation. This same area was portrayed as derelict in the regeneration discourses, and contaminated beyond remediation except in the most dramatic – *tabula rasa* – form, intended to transform it into a "landscape of consumption".[12] In the context of the Olympics and elsewhere many artists have taken against such dramatic modes of restructuring the industrial zones that were the lifeblood of modern London; and have themselves revelled, sometimes romantically, in the informality, and socio-economic and material diversity, on offer.

Gill's attitude to the Olympics is equivocal but much of his work appears to lament what has been or will be lost. On his website he comments:

> The games… will bring many good things to the area: new transport links and much-needed infrastructure. But there will be losses, too. There is another side to Hackney Wick. Away from the noise and chaos nature has somehow managed to find and keep a place for itself. The canals and rivers and secret allotments (known only to their dedicated gardeners) are home to many birds and animals. These hidden paradises have a vibrancy of their own which will soon be muted by the dust that will cover them.[13]

This statement indicates Gill's appreciation of a poetics of dust and burial, as well as his interest in the spontaneous forms of urban nature that existed in this industry-saturated environment before the Olympic redevelopment. The photographs in *Buried* depict a range of views that highlight the area's complex metropolitan nature. Two pylons, iconic landmarks conveying manmade power and energy, are shot from below, set pictorially against a grey sky in an overgrown park. They are harmonious outcrops rather than incongruous eyesores. As we move through the book we view industry and infrastructure, street scenes, workers, workspaces, snapshots of local residents, discarded objects, scrap yards and the anonymous interstitial background architecture of industrial parks, alongside blurry close-ups of plants and flowers, allotments and their guardians.

Each visual fragment coheres within the series through a common presentation format, and the consistent interruptions of scratches, specks of dirt, stains, watermarks, fingerprints and other traces, indexing the burial of the original prints. The degree to which these disrupt the image varies. Some photographs are just lightly speckled, but towards the book's centre the original subject matter becomes virtually unrecognisable, erupting into kalaedoscopic explosions of psychedelic colour, alien forms that bleed, bubble and blur into one another. These result from the emulsion on the original photographs' surfaces breaking down in contact with the water and chemicals in the soil.

If the link between reality and the photograph was inscribed when Gill originally pressed the shutter, the blemishes record a second interaction with the site, analogous to the exposure of light on film, more direct and literally grounded in the site's materiality, yet less controlled and predictable to the photographer. In one image the process has produced a new multi-coloured coral reef-like landscape. Another shows a jumping dog, seemingly bursting through intensely orange layers of flame that spontaneously combust the picture plane. In the shot of the two pylons, the clouds of the overcast sky float into the white border. An image of a man inspecting a marrow on his allotment has a dirty frame: added realism, involving us in the scene, surrounded as he is by piles of earth. At the same time, these supplements to the photographs – as with the collages of plants in his later photobook *Hackney Flowers* – disrupt the conventional photographic illusion of reality, making us aware of the photograph as material artifact.

Although the sites featured often seem low key, definitively ordinary, as a group they represent a number of important locations in the controversies encircling the area's Olympic-led redevelopment. The pylons were among the first features removed from Hackney Marshes, replaced by power-lines buried neatly underground at high cost. Another shot shows water bursting through a lock in the Lea Navigation system. The management of these waterways since the ODA took over has been challenged by those who argue that the area's already rich ecology, and its natural bioremediation following the closure of heavy industry, is being destroyed in favour of a sanitised biodiversity that better fits a managerial, neoliberal image of the good city.[14] The photograph of a man inspecting a marrow is presumably taken at Manor Gardens Allotments, from which the owners were evicted in 2007.

Sometimes Gill's strategies are pictorial, as when a shot of a bridge over the Lea in another of his photobooks, *Archaeologies in Reverse*, echoes Claude Monet's *Bridge Over a Pond of Waterlilies* (1899). At other times, less so: urban nature has an edge, rather than being pretty; it can be disorderly and unfinished rather than formally laid out. In *Buried*, a cormorant sits in front of a graffitied concrete wall. A grassy bank has been sectioned off with plastic construction safety fencing: surgery imminent. Water streams through mossy canal gate timbers and wildflowers bloom through chainlink fences. These images of urban nature well illustrate architectural historian Antoine Picon's notion of contemporary cities as the primary form of landscape experienced in the contemporary world. We have moved away, Picon argues, from a traditional experience of landscape as relaxing and contemplative, towards "anxious landscapes", where nature is experienced in the process of reclaiming environments saturated by man's technological endeavours.[15]

Gill's photoassemblages of artifacts, organisms and settings suggest a subtle understanding of the city as an environment with its own nature, the meaning of which is constructed dialectically between manmade and natural images and objects. Here is a pre-existing biodiversity at odds with the ODA's vision of formal parklands, which might not be economically productive, but which Gill (and others) celebrate as a positive and meaningful feature of the city, and a space for creativity and imagination.

Contexts

Gill belongs to a lineage of artists and writers who have highlighted the urban everyday, running from the surrealists and situationists, to the psychogeographers of present-day London, including Sinclair, and, in photography, Richard Wentworth and Mark Atkins. Gill, like Atkins, has collaborated with Sinclair. Both have engaged with Hackney in a sustained way through multiple projects with overlapping motifs. Gill's work, rather than taking a formalistic approach to the built environment, is rather a kind of intuitive documentary, "suggestive of how buildings and cities are occupied and acquire a personal, emotional resonance".[16] He displays a psychogeographer's interest in the flows of life, energy and entropy that collectively shape the experience and imaginaries of the area: what he calls the "spirit" of place.[17] He gives emphasis to the process of photography as one of "reaction to place" rather than straightforward documentation.[18] As in Wentworth's *Making Do and Getting By* (1974–), Gill often identifies and highlights formulaic patterns in urban and material culture – as in his series of the back of advertising hoardings, ATM machines and lost people in *A Book of Field Studies* (2005). The rigid structure and repetition involved in such work contrast, on the surface at least, with the writings of Sinclair, who also highlights value in interstitial spaces and familiar things, but through ambulatory connections.

Roger Luckhurst's critique of the contemporary London literary psychogeographic tradition is helpful in thinking about Gill's work, given his direct association with the authors Luckhurst discusses. One of them, Sinclair, has commented that Gill has learned "to haunt the places that haunt him", and in this statement he suggests how the photographer's investigations of east London connect with what Luckhurst describes as a "master trope" of the uncanny, and a "contemporary London Gothic".[19] Pursuing a strategy of spectrality, which itself contains the ghost of Jacques Derrida's *Spectres of Marx*, the literary exponents of this mode share a number of characteristics with Gill, and with *Buried* specifically. They use motifs of haunting as a mechanism to "excavate" repressed traumatic memories, and lost or threatened histories. They focus on banal or degraded spaces and structures – conduits through which overlooked histories and mythologies erupt into, and disrupt, the present.

Contemporary "regeneration", and especially the form of the "Demolish Dig Design" *tabula rasa* approach typified by the Olympic redevelopment, either denies, fictionalises or neutralises the past. Driven by what Derrida calls "heritage fever", it may construct specific reductive historical imaginaries that legitimise – or at least do not conflict with – the forms and directions it pursues. The implicit political strategy underlying the Gothic imaginaries of ruination, burial and exhumation at work in London's contemporary psychogeographic practices instead reveal the city as a complex "polytemporal assemblage" – Bruno Latour's term, invoked by Luckhurst – in which different times collide. For Derrida, according to Luckhurst, hauntology was a way of thinking through the "ghosts" of Marxism – its association with totalitarian regimes – in relation to his philosophy of deconstruction. In the London context, he observes, "the buried Gothic fragment… operates as the emblem of resistance to the tyranny of planned space".

This approach has the potential to reveal forgotten times and repressed histories in order to intervene critically, stimulating alternative urban imaginaries, countering a collapse of imagination in urban development.[20] Yet Luckhurst raises a number of important limitations. First, "the generalized structure of haunting is symptomatically blind to its generative loci"; second, the "deadpan mythology" of its authors makes their political intent ambiguous; third, the celebration of London's ineffability tends towards a aestheticising "supernaturalisation", distancing us from the city's shifting political structures; and finally the mode itself, even if it is subversive, is "necessarily occluded and interstitial, passed on only between initiates".[21] Gill's intent is implicit rather than explicit. The language and mode he uses are more readily available to a cultural elite familiar with the wider body of recent London psychogeographic work than they would be to anyone else. However, his "collaboration" with the site certainly addresses the first of Luckhurst's critiques. The soil powerfully brings to mind the physical, political and economic restructuring taking place in a specific place.

We can also connect Gill's interest in "degraded" working-class urban environments and the people who live in them with what the art historian Julian Stallabrass identifies as the emergence of an "urban pastoral" in late twentieth century British art. Stallabrass comments that such work "is about seeing something valuable in something trivial associated with the less advantaged sections of society, and bringing that to the attention of art lovers".[22] The mode, he suggests, can be described as touristic or "quasi-anthropological", operating through repeated, formulaic, patterns. It focuses attention on particular "raw", degraded or seamy urban environments, encouraging a fascination with and desire to venture into such places. These qualities could apply to Gill's work. In his case the quasi-anthropological moves into the quasi-archaeological, connecting both with Robert Smithson's notion of "ruins in reverse", and a body of recent London-based artists, overlapping with the psychogeographers, such as Wentworth and Mark Dion, who have adopted archaeological methods and metaphors in their work.

Sifting the soil

The acts of literally burying these photographs and photobooks, and metaphorically burying the people and places that are their subjects, moves photography beyond the passivity and neutrality of official site documentation, instigating a necessarily more involved encounter with the land "in motion". Instead of flat images or records of places that have since been lost, or of the processes of demolition or construction themselves, the energy – both creative and destructive – and physical substance of urban change are made more directly and materially manifest. The architectural photographer's conventional play between distant overviews, involved but partial fragments, and constructed boundaries, are supplemented by visual and tactile information added through contact with the site, and extending beyond the picture plane.

These are what the archaeological photographic theorist Michael Shanks terms "photoworks" rather than straightforward photographs, in the sense that that they are explicitly interpretative, and they highlight the photographic image as material artefact, comprised of paper and emulsion. The materiality of photography is reasserted at a time when, through digital technologies, photographs are being detached from the material and chemical processes that once defined their limits. The chance actions of soil, air, water and other elements in the ground shape each image as a unique artifact. Like archaeological photographs, the "truth" of these images can only be understood in relation to multiple temporal and spatial scales. In *Buried*, photographic time pertains to the presencing of the pasts of each site recorded, the present of each original photographic act, and each burial and retrieval, and the viewer's present, the moment of reading, with or without knowledge of the site's transformed condition. Right now, there are ongoing debates about the nature of the changes happening, although the place is already radically different from the moment the photographs were taken.

That the images have been influenced by the chemical properties of the soil, and thus draw our attention to it, is fitting given the expense and complexity of its bioremediation in preparation for construction work and the Games. This was a key feature of the Olympic "regeneration" narrative, invoking the biological connotations of a term that originally referred to spiritual improvement. The justification for washing the soil was to remove hydrocarbons and heavy metals: indicators of the site's industrial use, mainly as landfill. Between 2007 and 2008 over 500,000 tonnes of earth were processed through a soil treatment centre.[23] The ODA has very successfully communicated this in the media as a key benefit of the redevelopment process. However, critics have observed that much of the landfill buried in the area had been safely secured under 2–3 metres of topsoil in the 1970s, and that ironically the recent treatment of the soil had a hazardous effect on local people during the construction process, in which they were subject to dangerous dusts and high levels of radioactivity.[24] Furthermore, contaminated waste is still buried beneath the velodrome, and some of the remaining waste is now only buried to a depth of 60 centimetres.

The act of burying the photographs and books raises important questions beyond the artist's own statement, which appears on the surface to be quite politically neutral, that his intention was simply to collaborate with the site, and introduce a chance element to his practice. Challenging the notion of "dirt as matter out of place", the definition popularised by the anthropologist Mary Douglas, this is dirt drawn into the circulation of capital, and here used by Gill to narrate place, referring us to the soil's embodiment of the area's history. Rather than being "unnatural", this earth has its own historically and geographically specific nature formed through a unique mixture of properties: minerals, decomposing organic material, chemicals and industrial pollutants.

In Gill's work dirt is introduced as a material for more than just its potential for "distress" aesthetics.[25] He makes high art from base matter, and the "damage" to the photographs indexes the effects of time and wear. Through burying the photographs Gill highlights the materials, site, means of production and labour in his own practice, as well as those of the Olympic development process. This counters what Marx would term the process of fetishisation at work in the spectacular results of contemporary *tabula rasa* redevelopment: abstract environments and iconic built objects. In the process of his work Gill changes the value of the dirt in which he buries his photobooks. This brings to mind the most fundamental "regeneration" taking place: not only the mechanised bioremediation of the soil, but its revaluation as an asset, and the transfer of its ownership, from local residents and businesses and the state to elite private investors.[26]

Digging up the contemporary past

As a project in conceptual archaeology *Buried* emphasises that the discipline of archaeology itself – as with the "heritage industry" more generally – is inextricably bound to neoliberal redevelopment, and limited in its critical possibilities. In contrast to the archaeological work taking place within the contractual frameworks of the Olympic development, Gill's archaeological metaphor is more akin to experimental "archaeologies of the contemporary past".[27] In the 1990s, such projects sought to destabilise the archaeological production of knowledge, and the scientific distancing of archaeology's object of enquiry – the past – through performative archaeological acts intended to scrutinise present-day ("contemporary past") material culture, and emotionally charged situations. Similarly, in the context of Gill's work, burial and excavation refer us to the processes through which information and criticism have circulated, or have been prevented from circulating – buried, suppressed, repressed – within the regeneration discourses.

In discussing repression and the operations of image and archaeological metaphors within psychoanalytic thought, art historian Griselda Pollock observes:

> Repression at once erases and encrypts traumatic memories. They are buried and thus preserved like relics in the unconscious which is, as Derrida has helped us to recognise, the Freudian archive. Analysis is not only excavation; it is at the same time something more shocking: exhumation. In this double form, analysis does not, however, aim at merely re-archiving relics in the psychic museum.[28]

Taking her lead from Freud's archaeological metaphors, Pollock thus sees psychoanalysis as an archaeological method of exhuming and "working through" traumatic memories. This therapeutic analogy could equally apply to the potential of contemplating the "traumas" enacted on the various sites and communities in the Olympic Park development through the medium of Gill's photoworks. In the context of a *tabula rasa* redevelopment, buildings and other structures are razed to the ground, returned to dust. The soil becomes an archive, with archaeology being the only means to extrapolate the knowledge it contains. In burying images of the area's everyday architecture and inhabitants, Gill appears to want to preserve a set of memory-images. Once retrieved, their interactions with the land have leant them primal, elemental qualities. They have changed dramatically, quickly, and now seem like evidence of a long lost culture, its customs and rituals quite alien. As with memories, when the images are recovered they have partly been distorted or erased, some seem banal, while others are intense, vivid or traumatic. They form a dream-like sequence of flashbacks rather than a coherent narrative.

Conclusion

Gill's work prompts us to think about the different and conflicting "place images" of the area – the active imaginaries, rather than passive representations – through which individuals and groups have identified with it as a materially, empirically and perceptually knowable entity. The fact that the photographs and books have been buried and ornamented with dirt from the area makes a binary understanding of reality versus representation more complex. The strategy adopted is the antithesis of the developers' own highly codified "photo-real" CGI imaging of the site. Gill has created an archive featuring aspects of the area that have been overlooked or actively denied – buried – within the official discourses of the regeneration. He has then put that archive at risk, subject to chance chemical reactions, damage and decomposition. The photobook containing the archive is a "fetish object" in a psychoanalytic sense – an object that stands in totemically for displaced traumatic memories. Like a trauma from the past that re-emerges to the surface when prompted by new events in the present, *Buried* takes on new meanings, beyond Gill's original intentions, as the redevelopment proceeds, and as the soil becomes increasingly significant as the restructuring takes place.

In Gill's photoworks, there is an excess of image, overflowing from the frame. The method highlight's conventional photography's limits – its lack of power to represent properly the ways that architecture and cities are made, the difficulty of documenting the complexity of social, spatial and material restructurings of urban space, and the necessarily reductivist, abstracting tendency of all kinds of photography.[29] These contextual, literally bottom (ground) up images are presented to us in a situation where images are playing a powerful role in promoting and implementing a particular form of top-down *tabula rasa* redevelopment. Gill's intuitive approach contrasts with the form of business-led managerial planning that has characterised the Olympic redevelopment process. Critical fine art photography still has the power to reveal aspects of urban change that officials might not necessarily want us to see, and to prompt us to question its processes, and the authorities' own use of images.

We are an established East End company harvesting and producing deliciously wild edible provisions and beverages. Our company ethos and history grows out of the very earth of our surroundings and we have gathered, gleaned, scrumped and processed the fruits of the Lower Lea valley for generations, We are inextricably and passionately bound to the changing landscape that yields our produce and are constantly surprised by its blithe spirit of urban evolution. Recent developments mean that our potent ingredients are currently gathered solely from the fringe-lands of London's 2012 Olympic Park. In this time of great change, the very instability of our potent harvests makes them all the more precious – a fugitive, threatened but resilient and valuable bounty that we are committed to sharing.

Under our generous boughs an eccentric, some may say visionary fusion of sporting, community, festive and Olympic spirit survives as, in our potent recipes we capture something of the spirit of the age lost amid the under and over growth of the Olympic fringe lands. In spite of soil cleansing and the removal of archaeological evidence the past is alive and looking to the future with a curious mix of hope and foreboding in both the landscape and culinary delights of Pudding Mill River.

Choose from a delicious range of wild products from juicy Bow Back Blackberry jam to the ultimate Olympic Spirit in the form of our intoxicating Sloe Lea Gin. All our products are seasonal. Vintages from 2007 available.

www.puddingmillriver.com

LSO AVAILABLE: *East Marsh Elderflower Fizz and the Rose range (including Waterden Gypsy Rose hip jelly donuts).*

Guide to the Wastelands of the Lea Valley

LARA ALMARCEGUI*

The Lower Lea Valley will be the main location for the 2012 Olympic Park, and is going through a period of rapid urban transformation in preparation for the Games and for the years beyond 2012. The places that appear in this guide are unprotected and will disappear over the next few years, absorbed by the growing, regenerating city.

These places are some of the few in London that are not subject to any design or used for any particular purpose. Because they have been left alone, natural processes of decay, transition and entropy - processes which affect all places but which are hidden in the rest of the city - can be observed. They are in-between places where almost anything is possible, where time seems to have stopped. Independent of the rhythm of the city, they offer a paradise for vegetation and for visitors, though perhaps not for much longer.

Old Ford Locks. Towing Path, Greenway Path. Stratford

This terrain is bordered by the Lea Navigation and a Lea tributary. Its relative inaccessibility means that it has never borne heavy or light industry, although on the opposite bank of the river there were once printing and chemical works.

This site was undeveloped in the 1860s and was cut off from the adjacent territory by a compensation reservoir channel. It was also the site of an access ramp carrying people and vehicles onto the ridge of the sewer. For some time, it has been used by the Metropolitan Water Board, who maintain the adjacent sewage line as well as the former water storage reservoirs, which were replaced by larger reservoirs at Walthamstow and further up the Lea Valley.

The site was the home, for 42 years, to an ex-fireman and Royal Navy veteran who became the first person to be evicted as a result of the 2012 Olympics plans, in 2007. He lived in a detached house in the centre of the terrain owned by the water board. At the time of his eviction, his home was practically invisible owing to the thick vegetation surrounding it.

The site is now owned by the London Development Agency. It plans to keep it as dense woodland, part of the extensive green spaces of the Legacy project. Immediately to the south, a building for checking athletes' accreditation is planned. The area is also shown as green space in the Lower Lea Valley Planning Framework, the strategy for the area approved by London's mayor and in the London Borough of Newham's Unitary Development Plan.

The Greenway. Wick Lane, Pudding Mill Lane, High Street, Canning Road. Hackney Wick, Stratford, West Ham

This five-mile long site follows the Northern Outfall Sewer line, which was designed by civil engineer Joseph Bazalgette in the 1850s. This comprehensive new sewage system was a response to three related things: outbreaks of cholera; the increasing use of flush toilets, which vastly increased the flow into London's open sewers; and the 'Big Stink' of summer 1858, when the smell of sewage overwhelmed the city. The new system was made up of extensive sewers both north and south of the river, which were connected up along the edge of the Thames at Victoria Embankment and carried to this single main outfall. The system still carries the majority of north London's sewage out to water treatment works at Beckton, and remains under the control of Thames Water.

The sewer forms a ridge at Hackney Wick and runs almost uninterrupted until Beckton. This grass-covered ridge was originally intended to function as a public road through the marshes but instead it was used as an informal leisure area by local residents for nearly a century.

In 1964 the terrain was included in the 1964 proposal for the Lea Valley Regional Park, a plan which led to the formalisation of the whole valley as parkland. In subsequent decades the ridge was branded The Greenway; new signage, gates and access points were provided by local councils, particularly Newham.

The Greenway runs through the centre of the 2012 Olympic site and early plans suggest its use as a pedestrian route to the games. New signage, materials and street furniture are proposed, and a strategy has been prepared by architects Adams & Sutherland. Subsequent proposals extend plans for The Greenway beyond West Ham to Beckton and eventually to the river Thames.

* This guide was commissioned on the occasion of the exhibition *Radical Nature – Art and Architecture for a Changing Planet 1969–2009* at the Barbican Art Gallery, London in 2009. Research: David Knight. Copy editing: Anna Wood.

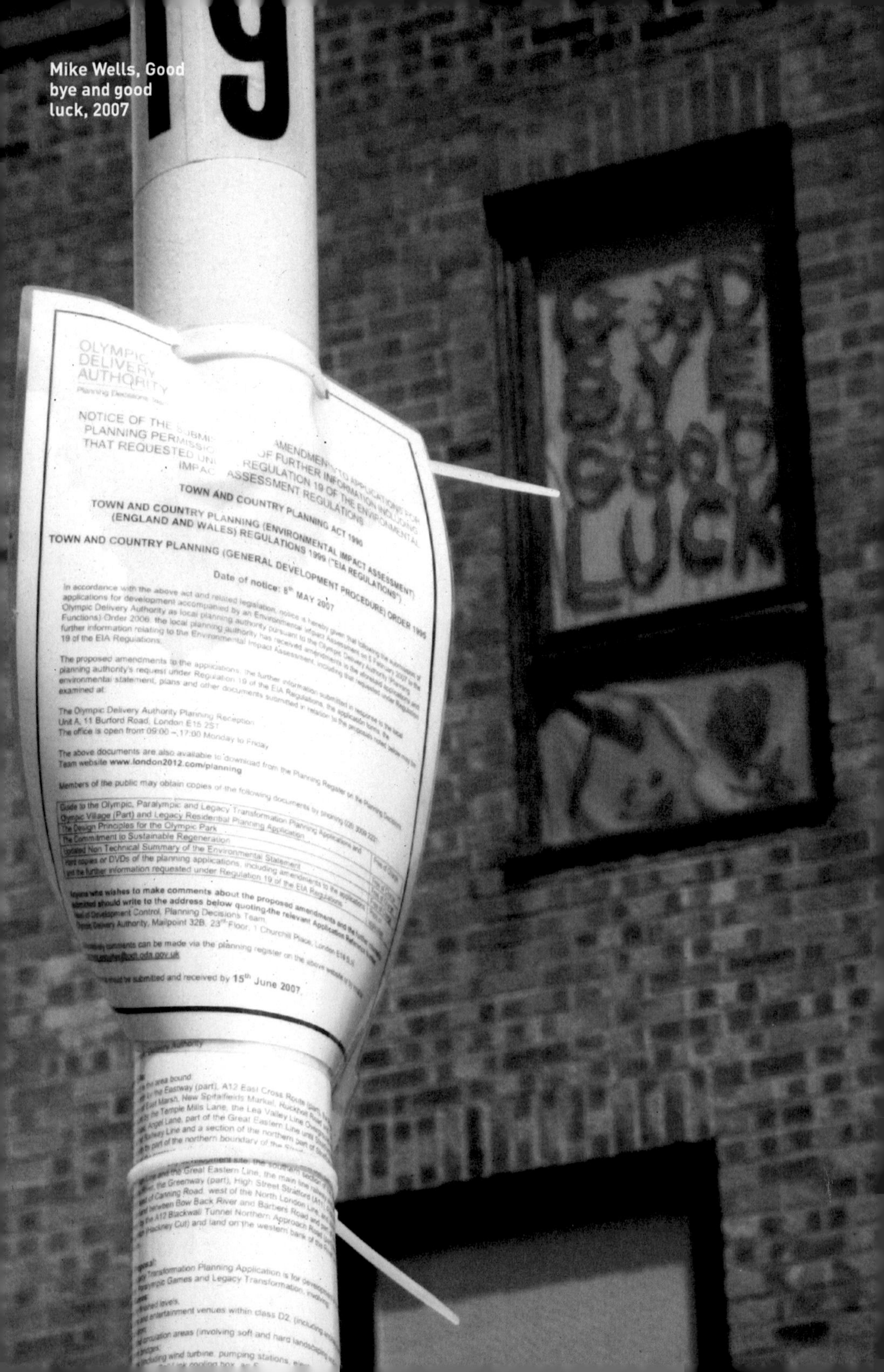

Mike Wells, Good bye and good luck, 2007

Ghost Milk

IAIN SINCLAIR

"Milk is the subtlest of insults." Don DeLillo

I remember R.D. Laing, in July 1967, sitting at the back of the Roundhouse, talking about the artist and illustrator Tomi Ungerer. How he relished the state of siege, living close to 42nd Street in the heart of Manhattan. "He's dressed in military uniform. He is conscious of the smog biting into his eyes, destroying his skin, eroding his lungs. He's aware all the time of the enormous pollution, the noise. It's impossible to smell anything anymore because all the interior environments are air-conditioned and pumped with the most sickly scent. You can't smell each other's sweat. You don't know who to trust."

Now, forty years on, I understood Ungerer's attitude: homeopathic doses of horror to prepare ourselves for the dark day. Circumambulations of the Olympic Park were becoming an addiction. Richard Mabey, author of *The Unofficial Countryside*, a book I twinned with Ballard's *Crash* as the great edge-land testimonials of the 1970s, accompanied me on another forlorn excursion. He travelled with binoculars, not a camera. He pointed out the feathery clumps of fennel growing at the cropped margin of the canal, near the Mare Street bridge. He told me that coots and ducks would be unaffected by radioactive spillage into the water table. They breed quite happily, and often, in the teeth of eco disaster. He was impressed by the duckweed lawns clotting the Lea, near Old Ford Lock.

The telling moment on this walk came with our arrival at the stack of yellow containers that operate, in playfully ironic mode, as café, viewing platform and learning centre, on the Greenway overlooking the Olympic Stadium. We explored a thicket that ran along the side of the railway, where wild nature, profligate and without imposed narrative, thrived in blossom and berry. Hacking our way out of the tunnel, we emerged on a strip of bare, baked earth beside the yellow tin box. Mabey examined, in grim fascination, a cluster of dying saplings. At which point, a young woman emerged from the education centre to tick him off for having the temerity to intrude on the few yards of precious ground reserved for the education of the disadvantaged children of the Olympic boroughs. Richard pointed out that the pathetic plantings were choked of sustenance, uncared for, coughing their last. And if she really wanted to let the children see something grow, all she had to do was take down the rickety exclusion fence and a fruiting, thrusting wilderness would sweep across from the embankment.

Among the cargoes regularly transported down the railway line, through the heart of London's major development, the site where countless thousands will soon be arriving from across the globe for the great B&Q self-assembly Olympics, are flasks containing highly radioactive nuclear fuel-rods, shipped from Sizewell in Suffolk, and Dungeness in Kent, to Sellafield on the Cumbrian coast. When the Nuclear Trains Action Group (NTAG) contacted the Olympic Development Authority to ask if these convoys would continue to run through the period of the Games, they received no reply. Mayor Johnson knows nothing, remains silent. He has other, more pressing problems.

A protest rally, marching from Victoria Park to Stratford Station, staged a "die-in" in front of the CGI Westfield promotional panels, well aware of the official Olympic clock clicking down the seconds like the nuclear triggers in Stanley Kubrick's *Dr Strangelove.* Such oddities are part of a conflicted topography: protest into art, political rhetoric into psychotic babble. The Angel Lane bridge over the railway, the route we walked from Chobham Farm to Joan Littlewood's Theatre Royal and the High Street, has been demolished. Mounds of scoured earth appear overnight, mountain ranges of a rigid formality thrown up by some new collision of the earth's tectonic plates.

At the junction of the Hertford Union Canal and the Lea Navigation, I came across an Olympic art manifestation which stopped me in my tracks. Here at last was a conceptual piece that took the breath away. Between Whitepost Lane and Old Ford, water gushed, cascaded, out of the enclosed site, through the fence, into the turbid and duckweed-infested canal. New barriers had been erected to deny access to potential paddlers heading for the main stadium. It was shapely, the way the water folded, curved and shimmered: a dwarf Niagara coming out of nowhere.

A jogger paused alongside me, hands on knees, taking in this unexpected water feature. "Twenty-eight years," he said. "And now this." He had come from Hong Kong and settled on an estate in Hackney Wick. Every morning he ran the same circuit, now his path was blocked. He never knew when he set out which way he would be allowed to return home, or if his home would still be standing. "There has never been such division between rich people and poor." He gestured towards the cliff of green-glazed windows on the spit of ground opposite us: a man-made island, the triangle between the Hertford Union Canal, the Lea Navigation, and the A102 Blackwall Tunnel Approach.

This was no art work, in the sense of being funded, approved: punctured

Victorian pipes on the Olympic site. No water in the taps for much of Hackney. The security guards brought in to protect the rapidly assembled plywood barriers were old-fashioned bouncer types, amiable and suspicious, nervous of saying the wrong thing in an unfamiliar language. The inner ring, close to the stadium complex and the construction convoys, was now guarded by regiments of Joanna Lumley's diminutive and unreadable Gurkhas.

It was only when I studied privately commissioned reports of investigations into the extensive radioactive contamination of the 2012 site that I appreciated the implication of the gushing pipes. The dispersal cell holding many tonnes of treated and untreated soil, in layers under a permeable skin, was positioned right here. As Ian Griffiths revealed in an article in the *Guardian*: "Documents obtained under Freedom of Information (FOI) rules reveal that, contrary to government guidelines, waste from thorium and radium has been mixed with very low-level waste and buried in a so-called dispersal cell". A cell which was placed about 500m to the north of the Olympic stadium. The setting for the involuntary water feature.

Bill Parry-Davies convened a meeting at which Mike Wells, who had been sifting thousands of documents and invigilating the progress of construction activity with numerous photographs, gave a lucid and alarming account of his findings. You could not nominate, in all of London, more challenging ground for a landscape blitz, a ticking-clock assault on the devastated residue of industrial history: insecticide and fertiliser works, paint factories, distillers of gin, gas mantel manufacturers, bone grinders, importers of fish-mush, seething dunes of radiant maggots.

Waste: dumped, buried. Disturbed. Distributed.

Decay.

Putrefaction.

Tyre mounds.

The crunched metal-and-glass of innumerable breakers' yards hidden behind convolvulus-draped fences, under the flag of St George. Snarling dogs. Shirtless men smashing white goods with hammers.

And the dust.

The particulates. Hot cinders.

Blind warehouses with bundles of rags and damp paper waiting for insurance fires. Petrol reek. Black ash.

Oily smoke saturates cloth, fouls underwear.

In the dirt, they prospect: the pinstripe outsiders, compliant bureaucrats. Sanctioned buck passers.

This was where London University carried out experiments with a now-decommissioned nuclear reactor. An area so far off the official map, so hidden within a nexus of dark waterways, that it functioned as the dumping ground of choice for what Parry-Davies refers to as "uncontrolled deposits of radioactive thorium". In an OPEN-Dalston blog, Bill presents a photograph by Mike Wells showing "clouds of dust, and a skip with unsealed bags of asbestos material, during demolition of the Clays Lane estate."

In the Leabank Square estate, from which the Chinese jogger had emerged for his restorative morning circuit, mediating rather than remediating the territory, residents were concerned about dust from the Olympic site. "A recognised pathway to contamination," Parry-Davies said, "is by a person inhaling radioactive dust particles. Thorium is particularly hazardous." On the estate, as the summer barbeque season opened, families found themselves "literally eating" a relish of airborne dust, a mega-chilli bite on their steaks and sausages. When their worries were published on a website, the ODA threatened the Leabank whistle-blower with legal proceedings. And sent in a dust-sweeping vehicle to patrol the yellow-brick avenues.

Rumours were rife. I was told that the only consequence of the remediating exercise was to spread low-level radioactivity across the entire landscape of the Olympic enclosure, the divided fiefdoms of competing contractors. Toxic soil, removed from the stadium was stored alongside bundles of Japanese knotweed, suggesting delirious *Quatermass* mutations, vegetal Triffid creatures slouching towards Westfield to be born. Richard Mabey pointed out that all Japanese knotweed, along the Lea, is female; the bounteous harem of a single potent male plant.

The Olympic Park was a newsreel of the fall of Berlin run backwards, from present boasts about urban renewal to the bombed and blasted killing fields, as the Russian advance decimated a pitiful remnant of boy soldiers, cripples and SS fanatics, in the Götterdämmerung endgame of Hitler's insane vision of a capital made from neo-classical facsimiles. In the Reichssportfeld, beside Berlin's 1936 Olympic Stadium, tanks, emerging from the woods, demolished trenches dug for military rehearsals. A sergeant, in command of a ragtag group of frightened children, had the only bazooka. When he stood up to fire it, his head was blown from his shoulders. What remains in these ravished topographies is a category of war-zone architecture: concrete bunkers, electrified fences, unexplained posts, burnt-out warehouses, stripped woodland, fouled water. Grand Project development is accidental archaeology. A séance with future ruins.

On Dalston Lane I met the globe-trotting Sicilian photographer, Mimi

Mollica, a native of Hackney Wick. He swerved through the traffic to embrace me: a friendly face in a bleak environment. Many of his Wick neighbours had been expelled, the free-floating anarcho-communal days were over. There was a general drift in the direction of Berlin: more space, a vibrant culture. With the capture of Hackney, there was now a clear direction of travel: Berlin or Dagenham. Go east, young man. With his rent pitched at an impossible level, Mimi relocated to one of the generic blocks on Dalston Lane. A pristine apartment in all probability conceived by a Russian developer. If I wanted to follow the story, I would have to mug up my Fritz Lang DVDs and book a flight to Berlin.

"You have a name for your book?" Mimi said.

"*Ghost Milk*."

"What does this mean?"

"CGI smears on the blue fence. Real juice from a virtual host. Embalming fluid. A poisonous soup of photographic negatives. Soul food for the dead. The universal element in which we sink and swim."

"Crazy, Mr Sinclair," Mimi said. "Crazy again."

Gesche Würfel, BMX Track 1, 2006, from the series Go for Gold!

Gesche Würfel, Media and Press Centre 2, 2006, from the series Go for Gold!

Gesche Würfel, Olympic Stadium 3, 2007, from the series Go for Gold!

Gesche Würfel, Olympic Village 2, 2007, from the series Go for Gold!

Re-shoots – Photographs 1986-2011

CHRIS DORLEY-BROWN

Re-shoots is an ongoing archive project that uses my own photographic archive as well as images from historical public collections as reference photographs for subsequent re-staging and re-making. A kind of concurrent journal emerged unexpectedly alongside the pictures – it helps to explain the daily grind and the experience of making pictures in an urban landscape that appears to have gone temporarily insane.

1st November 2010, 11am Pudding Mill Lane E3

Camera on a tripod pointing at the Olympic Stadium, an illegally parked Porsche is being winched onto a flatbed truck. A Police BMW slows beside me, the two officers clock me, drive forward and then U-turn back towards me. My hand is inside my coat with the shutter release cable. I squeeze off a couple of frames as the WPC in the passenger seat gets out the jam sandwich and approaches me: "Remove your hand from your pocket sir."

She doesn't wait for a response. In a swift movement she has my wrist and shoves me in the back seat; she keeps a flat hand on my chest. I feel totally immobile. Also, strangely, I am slightly aroused; she is quite handsome. Before I can spell out the second of my double barrels, my date of birth and other unreadable information speed types itself onto a screen on the dashboard: "So you have been stopped by Police quite a few times recently sir?"

"Yeah but I didn't know you were keeping score," I say.

The routine conversation ensues, I establish my non-membership of Al -Qa'ida; they let me know they are only doing their job. "Probably the same people who pay both our wages." Good point. The driver gives me a business card:

Metropolitan Police
Specialist Operations
Olympic Unit
Working together for a safer London

There is a mobile number below. "Next time," he says, "ring this and say the following phrase to the person who answers and you will be ok."

"Er... right, what's the phrase?"

"Hello boys I am on the ground."

Have I just been the victim of a stag-do prank?

16th November 2010, 9.30am, Wick Lane, Hackney

I am in a cul-de-sac, but it has a name and post code. There are two car repair yards at the end; the road is caked with sump oil. Attempting to photograph the Olympic stadium through a gap formed by two newly finished but unlet blocks of flats that wouldn't look out of place in Benidorm, I don't get the viewfinder to eye-level before I hear "Oi" beside me, a Dublin accent: "You are on private land mate, what are you doing?"

"I just want to photograph the stadium, and err... this is not private land."

"It is my land, and bollox to your stadium. Go suck on the dole you bastard."

There followed a brief but rather one-sided discussion about civil rights, employment opportunities, my sexuality and a sincere promise of physical congress at our next meeting. The encounter was carefully observed throughout by his colleague, who was holding a spanner large enough to loosen a nut the size of a birthday cake.

I haven't been on the dole since 1983.

17th January 2011, 11am, Wallis Road, Hackney Wick

I am removing my tripod from its neoprene quiver, my mood is workmanlike; it must be the New Year resolution. The Police (again), they seem to appear from nowhere, except this time they don't look like Police: they are wearing green chinos, blousons, kind of casual for a copper, more like security at Lidl, more like American Police. For some reason I find this unnerving. The routine conversation: my membership of al-Qa'ida has lapsed, forgot to send the forms off. I am an artist I tell them. I usually avoid the word – I prefer "photographer" – and I regret it immediately. I obviously don't believe it myself, my voice is querulous, they've tumbled me – I am a fraud.

"Do you know, sir, that this area has the highest concentration of visual artists in Europe, more than a hundred just in Hackney Wick alone?" I remain silent but can vaguely feel my wrists merging together behind my back, ready to receive the cuffs. "What kind of artist are you?" asks the fat one, the passenger, the aggressive one. Before I can answer he offers me a prompt to help get me started: "Conceptual?"

I am not in the mood to discuss relational aesthetics with a rozzer; he'll wipe the floor with me; he's probably got a PhD from Goldsmiths. I change tack: "In all honesty would a potential terrorist really be out in broad daylight with a big camera on a tripod standing in the middle of the road?"

"Well sir, they like to test the security systems by making themselves more conspicuous." Genius.

24th November 2010, 3.30pm, Hackney Wick

The towpath outside the Coffley energy centre (under construction); a tabarded worker is repairing the steel gates for the third time in a week. Overnight the freshly painted walls have acquired thick, black, confident lines, caricatures of demonic paranoia; the defiance is overwhelming and moving.

"They shit everywhere," he says, gesturing at the empty print works across the canal.

31st January 2011, 11.30am, canal towpath, corner of Hertford Union and Lee Navigation

A film crew on the western side of the towpath, a crane-mounted movie camera is rising and swooping down to synchronise with a passing double scull rowing boat. Take after take, the rowers and camera crew return to their marks under the orders of a drill sergeant assistant director, the megaphone amplifying his frustration as the light fades. They are shooting a Visa commercial.

The rowers are dressed in a Great Britain strip. The backdrop to this scene is the main stadium, which now "looks" finished. The foregrounded canal contains about eight "traditional" narrow boats moored at regular intervals along the eastern towpath. A set dresser is moving from barge to barge, arranging flowers in enamel jugs and sitting them on the roofs. This is the version of canal life that is acceptable to the corporate big sell, a cliched rewind of bygone imagery. The muddy bikes, unsightly piles of stuff, are disguised and obscured. Floaties and boaties are being gently goaded out of shot or below decks of their own craft: "It's okay we should be done in half an hour tops and you can have your life back."

31st January 2011, 2.10pm Counter Café, Fish Island

An overheard exchange between a young couple sitting at a corner table:

Him: "Shall I bore you with it?"

Her: "Yes."

25th March 2011, White Post Bridge, Hackney Wick

The canal towpath was finally fenced off on its western side at 9 o'clock this morning. Cyclists and pedestrians who rely on this subterranean byway to go about their daily business are feeling the Olympic noose tighten; the eastern flank was closed two months ago.

A friendly landscape engineer from Barnsley representing the contractor May Gurney has drawn the short straw and been given the job of relaying the bad news, via a mantra repeated every 30 seconds or so as if on a tape loop: "Sorry mate/luv, the towpath is shut until July 11th, you have to go the long way round." This meets with an array of responses, like, "Why don't you just shut the whole fucking city down?" or "Olympricks more like" or "Land thieving ***ts" (popular one that). He gets no empathy for "just doing my job". This is the reality: the monster has now seized control.

I am more interested in talking than photographing today. Maybe this is evidence that the assignment is nearing completion, or maybe I am bored by my feeble attempts to really nail this complexity. I like the Yorkshireman's pragmatic take on progress; he makes it all sound like common sense: "Then we going to rip that fence down and put a nice gentle slope in down to the canal, it will look lovely." I believe him; he is proud of his work; he wants to do a good job. He will tell his grandchildren about it one day.

*During 2010 and 2011 Chris Dorley-Brown was commissioned by SPACE to make new photographs for an exhibition and publication. "The Cut" was published in newspaper form in July 2011 and included newly commissioned work from Jessie Brennan and Daniel Lehan as well as rare archival material from British Waterways.

Chris Dorley-Brown, Fish Island, south-west from Dace Road Bow, 1986 - 2011

IRONWOR

Chris Dorley-Brown, Duckett's Canal and River Lee Navigation, Hackney Wick, 1999 - 2011

London Borough of Hackney Archives (L) and Chris Dorley-Brown (R), Wallis Road, Hackney Wick, 1948 - 2011

BOSS

The Lower Lea Valley:
From Fun Palace to Creative Prison

ANTHONY ILES

The Lower Lea Valley, formed by strips of common land, canals and marshes separating the Metropolitan Borough of Hackney from the Victorian suburbs of Newham, Walthamstow and Leyton, was an agricultural then industrial area characterised by railways, greenhouses, warehouses and light manufacturing until the end of the Second World War. This zone, shaped by the successive waves of redevelopment that have assailed its wild, industrial and playful nature, has over the last five years become the largest building site in London.

Regeneration, a buzz word of the Blair era, is contemporary parlance for the violent forms of destruction and displacement which have accompanied capitalist development throughout industrialisation, but now appear loosed from the production of competitive advantage for the growth of capital. Instead, these "industries" now grow on their own, producing competing world cities entirely at the behest of the tourism, entertainment, financial, insurance and real estate economies. The London 2012 Olympics promises to transform not only the specific zone of the Lower Lea Valley, but also the whole of east London to suit the interests of these so-called industries.

In 1964 the architect Cedric Price and theatre director Joan Littlewood made plans for a "Fun Palace" to be sited in the Lower Lea Valley in the zone between Stratford and West Ham, close to the site of the 2012 London Olympics. The Fun Palace was to be the culmination of the socialist theatre director's dream for a flexible theatrical space open to all and shaped by its users' interests, a space where "the latest discoveries of engineering and science can provide an environment for pleasure and discovery, a place to look at the stars, to eat, stroll, meet and play".[1]

In the London of the early 1960s Littlewood's popular agit-prop theatre met Cedric Price's novel ideas of architecture as "social means". The Fun Palace was to be the very model of Price's radical principles in architecture, embodying flexibility, indeterminacy, mobility and openness, and employing cheap lightweight industrial materials. "Since Littlewood's 'idea' prescribed no particular programme or fixed activities, Price decided that it should have no specific plan and no fixed floor plan."[2] The Fun Palace was to include a retractable corrugated roof, two gantry cranes on rails spanning the full 73.2 metres of the two central bays, service towers producing a grid of interlocking squares, stair towers, pivoting escalators and moving walkways, a rally area, temporary modules and kiosks, no entrance, open access on the ground floor, and a complex system of "environmental controls generating charged static-vapour zones, optical barriers, warm-air curtains and fog dispersal".[3]

Price was obsessed with containerisation. As an integral part of the Fun Palace design, gantry cranes would move building modules around the site. Reyner Banham had celebrated the aesthetics of containerisation in his article "Flatscape with Containers", suggesting that the modular aesthetic of the container challenged architecture to develop an anti-monumentality in line with the new conditions that the age of mobility and indeterminacy brought with it.[4] Price's architecture was thought of at the time as pragmatic and anti-symbolic, yet even the "cultural" use of industrial materials can be seen to have its own symbolism, as well as a practical application, particular to his de-industrialising times.

A promotional pamphlet for the Fun Palace promised activities such as: "Kunst Dabbling, Genius Chat, Clownery, Fireworks, Rallies, Battles of flowers, Concerts, Science Gadgetry, Juke Box Information, Learning Machines". There were to be big screens with live feeds from a number of sites around the city, such as hospitals, police stations and football matches.

Keith Khan, shortly after his appointment as head of the Cultural Olympiad in 2007, indicating an interest in user-generated content with a distant relation to Price and Littlewood's enthusiasm, said he was "keen to embrace the 'iPod generation' with the use of digital technology and concepts used by websites such as MySpace and YouTube".[5] We may well understand the internalisation of the "open" status of art and creativity by culture administrators as appropriate to a political situation in which everything is contingency, vague statements and buzzwords set in motion by open-ended projects sustained by hot air:

> But this is all process, structure and construct. The philosophy of culture and creativity taking its place at the heart of London 2012 was there for all to see in the bid. The intellectual architecture was won in the values and vision for the Cultural Olympiad that emerged last summer. Now we have systems, criteria and brand mark to offer the hope of practical reality.[6]

New leisure or New Labour?

From the start of the Fun Palace project, Cedric Price and Joan Littlewood had explicitly framed their project as mending the false division between work and leisure: "[It was] essential to eliminate [the] unreal division between leisure and work time."[7]

Like many radicals (such as Alexander Trocchi, Constant Nieuwenhuys and others), Price and Littlewood were influenced by the expectation of the "new windfall of leisure time" provided to the working classes by mechanisation and automation:

> Those who at present work in factories, mines and offices will quite soon be able to live as only a few people now can: choosing their own congenial work, doing as little of it as they like, and filling their leisure with whatever delights them. Those people who like fiddling with machinery and pressing buttons can service and press buttons in the robot-manned factories.[8]

Or, as Trocchi put it: "Thus freed from all economic responsibility, man will have at his disposal a new plus-value, incalculable in monetary terms, a plus-value not computable according to the accountancy of salaried work... play value."[9]

It is interesting to read these utopian predictions of the end of work in the light of our now apparently wholly de-industrialised society, where work continues by other means. What is activity after work? Perhaps more importantly, how is capitalism to extract value from workers, after they are "free" from work?

Price was concerned that this new leisure time be spent productively, in training for the new forms of work. He applied himself to the problem of the "brain drain" Britain was perceived to suffer from. So, while government planners were concerning themselves with reproducing workers with more free time as "workers", Price was devising new forms of training and education disguised as "leisure". Leisure was to be, after all, much like work, co-ordinated activity. The word "fun" was essentially a trope for new "productive and constructive uses" of free time.[10]

Flatscape with containers

Although many of the pioneers of radical thought of the 1960s were celebrating the new struggles for free time and a qualitatively improved life, there were important labour struggles taking place. Some of those struggles may not have fitted the notion of what Price and his peers might have considered "progressive". One area of conflict in particular directly related to the contested role of new technology that so fascinated Price and Banham is related geographically to the liminal zone which the Fun Palace was to occupy: "the dockers' fight against the containerisation of goods which cost jobs. The dockers had been fighting this throughout the 1960s but it exploded as an issue in 1972."[11] These efforts by dockers were not an attempt to express themselves freely in a world after work, but rather defensive campaigns to keep hold of what work they still had. By pure coincidence, the testing ground for the introduction of containerisation into the Port of London took place on Chobham Farm, a goods yard behind Stratford station, on what is now part of Stratford City and Westfield East: "Three London dockers were threatened with prison for picketing the Chobham Farm container base in June. Some 35,000 dockers struck unofficially throughout Britain in support of the pickets, and hundreds joined the picket of Chobham Farm the day the arrests were expected."[12] These protests spiralled from a defensive campaign to protect jobs into one the largest actions by organised labour since the General Strike: around 250,000 workers struck unofficially, picketing Fleet Street and closing down several national newspapers until the arrested dockers were released.[13]

In 1951 the Port of London was the second largest dock in the world. So, while it is claimed that the docks and the extensive canal traffic that served them were wound down because of the impossibility of getting larger ships up the Thames, containerisation has also played a pivotal role in the transformation in the Port of London's fortunes. It was no accident that London's docks had historically contained some of the most militant unions and labour organisations. "With the use of larger ships and containerisation, the importance of the upstream port declined rapidly from the mid-1960s. The enclosed docks further up river declined and closed progressively between the end of the 1960s and the early 1980s."[14]

The building around the London 2012 Olympics completes a triangulation of East London by the City, the London Docklands and a retail and transport hub in Stratford. This is not by any means yet a smooth space, one tuned to and reflective of the abstract flows of money managed at these other sites, but it is a space very much in the process of being smoothed out. While on the one hand Docklands Light Railway and London Underground links converge on Stratford, bringing people to and from the Games and Westfield retail centre, below, rail links bring containers to and from Tilbury, New Spitalfields Market and beyond.

The London Development Plan

In the 1951 London Development Plan there is no mention of the advent of larger ships or the technical necessity of containerisation as an argument for the transformation of the docks. Rather, the displacement of industry from the river and canal side is argued for to confront the twin evils of blight and pollution, and cure them through the virtues of parks, open space and picturesque views. In 1951, 85.1% of the riverside below Blackfriars Bridge was used for industrial and commercial uses. In 2012 at least the same percentage is occupied by luxury apartments. As early as 1951, there is a glimpse of the potential for the docks as a former site of messy work to be transformed into a scene of leisure and conspicuous consumption. But this development would not only affect the river, canals and former docklands. It is symptomatic of a broader shift across the UK to a services-based economy and a built environment that would both reflect and arguably engineer that shift.

The County of London Plan, 1943, and the 1951 London Development Plan "opened the post-war attack on London's four main defects – traffic congestion, depressed housing, intermingled housing and industry, and insufficiency of open space".[15]

The key strategies to achieve this "attack" were:

- decentralisation of industry;
- decentralisation of population from the "congested centre";
- "a substantial increase in riverside open space";
- slum clearance;
- a substantial programme of building housing undertaken by local councils with support from the London County Council (nonetheless resulting in a net displacement of the existing population);
- planning for organised leisure space;
- clearance of "use-rights";
- clearance of "non-conforming industry"; and
- "population management".

Rather than looking for the discontinuities between the (supposedly utopian) plans of the post-war Labour Government and the current plans for the Olympic Games and legacy, it might be a more interesting and contentious project to look at the continuity between them.

A good example is the way in which Michael Heseltine's proposals for a Thames Gateway development to extend from that of the Docklands, balancing the west London intensification around Heathrow, was picked up by Gordon Brown's Labour Government. Similarly, we could go back to Patrick Abercrombie's redevelopment plans for post-war London – The Greater

London Plan, 1944, the 1951 London Development Plan and the Civic Trust's plan for a Lea Valley regional park, 1964. We can trace in those early examples of the management of space explicit arguments for de-industrialisation and the formulation of "healthy leisure", management of urban nature all pre-figuring the tenets of the approach by the London Development Authority (LDA) and the Olympic Development Authority (ODA) to planned domestication of the wilder aspects of city life in the present day.

Price and Littlewood's plans, despite being unrealised, represent a significant response to the conditions and arguments steering the post-war reconstruction of London. Moreover, we can see the "visionary" principles explored in the plans for the Fun Palace: the collapse of distinction between leisure and work, the mechanisation of play, administered participation and user-generated content as the very virtues and values celebrated in the post-Fordist paradigm.

Output of modified people

In order to facilitate an environment that was to be "continuously adaptable, acknowledging change and indeterminacy in a continuously evolving process",[16] Littlewood and Price put together an interdisciplinary group of collaborators and consultants from engineering, design, theatre, cybernetics and technology. Although Price and Littlewood are interpreted as utopian visionaries working with the advanced technologies and ideas of their times, some of the ideas of the Cybernetics Group for the Fun Palace seem in retrospect profoundly sinister. A good example is Gordon Pask's sketch "Organisational Plan as Programme", indicating in a circuit-like diagram describing a feedback loop between the "Input of Unmodified people" arriving in the building and the "Output of Modified People" interacting as they leave.

Unfortunately, neither Littlewood nor Price can be saved from the implications of their patrician positions, playful as they may have been. As Joan Littlewood put it in a letter to Gordon Pask, head of the Cybernetics Group:

> We can to some extent control these transformations, though, in this case, we and our machinery act as catalysts and most of the computation is done as a result of the interaction taking place between members of the population, either by verbal discourse, or by cooperation to achieve a common objective. The paradigm for the control of such a population is the maturation of a child, the subtle interplay of action and the existing language to produce thought, and the development of meaning to control action in society.[17]

In an attitude typical of colonialism, the proletarian test subject is imagined as less than adult, suitable to experiment on and not necessarily in full possession of their own volition. There is at least a sense in which this experiment conducted by bohemian researchers would genuinely provide for surprising feedback, unexpected stimulus or response. Its staged freedom is a world away from the secured environments visitors will be funnelled in and out of around the 2012 Games. What is crucial about the approach though is that Price, Littlewood and Pask sought not only to change and control an environment, but to employ an environment to induce a change in the subjects that moved through it. In this sense, Price's architecture anticipated post-Fordism itself.[18] Open architecture would act as project, soft policing and springboard for social transformation. As Price said of a later project, "Like the Fun Palace, the Potteries Thinkbelt was not an expressive or symbolic building, but an interactive device in which the subject could undergo a transformation."[19]

So what was this new or ideal subject being produced and to what purpose? It fits the description Brian Holmes excavated from management literature and social commentary of the late 1990s:

> I call this ideal type the flexible personality. The word "flexible" alludes directly to the current economic system, with its casual labor contracts, its just-in-time production, its informational products and its absolute dependence on virtual currency circulating in the financial sphere. But it also refers to an entire set of very positive images, spontaneity, creativity, cooperativity, mobility, peer relations, appreciation of difference, openness to present experience... you can say that these are our creations, but caught in the distorting mirror of a new hegemony.[20]

This in turn corresponds to the new forms of subjectivity training and behaviour modification at work in the futuristic projections of the 2012 Olympic site and the arguments by which it is framed by planners and politicians:

> The new Olympic Park under construction in the Lower Lea Valley will revive one of the most deprived areas in the country. Thousands of jobs will be created. Transport links will be transformed. Thousands of homes for key workers will be built. Parts of the landscape that have been wasteland will spring to life.[21]

Alessandra Chilá, Output of Modified People, 2008

Other less tangible benefits the London 2012 Olympics is expected to bring to the area are improved health, education, social inclusion, ecology, housing and employment.

Creative prison

Of course to anyone who grew up near the area, the Lea Valley is familiar as a place where people make their own entertainment, from allotment holders, footballers, anglers, kite flyers, ramblers, cyclists and nature lovers to ravers and free party-makers, under-age drinkers, graffiti artists and scooter thieves. It is no accident that all these activities require a minimum of services and equipment and yet produce the altered states, collective bonds, social communication and physical exertion that are the very stuff of life. Organised without licence (usually) nor permission... without planning or costly amenity.

This is the very opposite of what we see in the projections for the new Olympic site of the Games and in legacy mode. Instead, we have a harmonious managed nature, organised and safe exercise, communication technologies – mobile phones, water, the Docklands and city – centres of international financial flows. These images are also characterised by a multiculturalism peculiar to neoliberal development – the dream image of difference without conflict and most importantly without work or workers – no one who has actually built or contributes to the running or servicing of this place appears in these visions. Whereas Price's model disposes of labour through automation, the LDA's vision hides labour in dream like reflections, glass, water, smoke and mirrors.

A recent example by one of Price's most successful disciples, Will Alsop's Creative Prison project, gives us a flavour of the direction in which Price's ideas have travelled since their inception:

> The layout of the prison mimics that of a college campus with separate living modules, or "blocks", as Alsop calls them (though I prefer module since block is still such a carceral-centric term). While being typically brightly coloured like most of Alsop's work, the inmates would "live in clusters of between 12 and 15" and would "be able to control how long they spent in their cells at the end of a day of work or training".[22]

Alsop has been extremely successful in so-called Creative Britain, building among other things Peckham library, flagship of regeneration, and a stem-cell research centre in Whitechapel. His architecture frequently deploys key ideas popularised by Cedric Price and contemporaries such as Archigram. The Creative Prison was the culmination of a consultancy project to address the poor conditions and chronic overcrowding of Britain's prisons. This kind of blue sky thinking should not surprise; as well as promoting creativity, New Labour had also innovated in criminalisation. Over 3,000 new criminal offences were created during the last decade under the Labour Government.

There are increasingly vocal critics of the "creative economy" celebrated in Britain and exported by its boosters elsewhere. It seems that under its shiny surface there are problems, namely that its booming appearance is simply the knock-on effect of a financial sector which only drains wealth from the rest of the world: "Britain's financial sector is parasitic on healthy growth elsewhere, mostly in East Asia".[23] GLA's Alan Freeman, one of the creative industries' biggest boosters, has described the City's advantages as "artificial conditions sustained in the metropolis by the superexploitation of the rest of the world".[24]

It seems no coincidence several of the promotional images for the London Olympics Park are framed by the two key financial districts, Canary Wharf to the south and the City to the west.

Playland

> Playland is a country whose inhabitants are busy celebrating rituals, and manipulating objects and sacred words, whose sense and purpose they have, however, forgotten.[25]

The kind of architectural space of pre-emptive unfreedom shored up against conflict common to Price and Littlewood's Fun Palace, the London 2012 Olympic Park and the Creative Prison can be related to the dense layers of financialised risk, described by Randy Martin, on which the production of such spaces economically depends:

> If bringing the future into the present is the temporality of financialized risk, pre-emption is its preferred mode of activation. Acting before action has coalesced, intervening before the enemy has emerged, punishing before the crime is committed, measuring before the outcome is achieved, selling before the product is produced – all these join the hyperactive attention-deficit inducing disorder we have come to treat so kindly and readily.[26]

The collapse of distinction between leisure and work means that play mimics work and all is work. The Olympic playland is a dystopia predicated on the dream of omni-surveillance and super-exploitation. A creative prison we find being constructed all around us today.

If the Fun Palace can be considered a pre-vision of the emerging post-industrial society, we can wager the London Olympics won't be that society's crowning success. Rather, these designs represent the return, as farce, of Price's visionary dream – a plasticated world populated by unreal avatars repeating gestures rehearsed on TV. The very creation of this landscape will be underpinned by debt, exploitation and public bankruptcy. What if we think like Price and take a visionary stance towards the future? We could reject the poverty of choosing between the shiny service work jobs and the policed leisure offered and instead imagine what might be built out of the ruins of the financialised city after the new economy.

Polly Braden and David Campany, Centre of the Planned Olympic Site, from Adventures in the Valley, 2007

Polly Braden and David Campany, Biking on the Greenway, Sunday Afternoon, from Adventures in the Valley, 2007

Polly Braden and David Campany, Grafitti, Lower Lea Valley, from Adventures in the Valley, 2007

Polly Braden and David Campany, Saturday Morning, November, Stamford Hill, from Adventures in the Valley, 2007

Duck! You Regeneration Sucker:
Anja Kirschner and David Panos' Trail of the Spider

NEIL GRAY*

> "Only that historian will have the gift of fanning the spark of hope in the past who is firmly convinced that even the dead will not be safe from the enemy if he wins. And this enemy has not ceased to be victorious." Walter Benjamin

> "Watch them now. All bold, like they discovered the place... maybe we can't stop them, but we can't give them an easy ride. Let them feel some loss!" Doctor Dynamite

Stepping confidently out of the specialised ghetto of "artists cinema", Anja Kirschner and David Panos' film *Trail of the Spider* (2008) dramatically explores the material and psychological conditions brought on by gentrification through the refractory prism of the Western genre. The film, a self-described "Western made in London and Essex", deploys the vanishing frontier motif and subversive Western genre tropes in complex yet unambiguous terms to examine contemporary "regeneration" strategies in east London. By doing so, it skilfully mobilises multiple historical narratives into a fraught but productive relationship with the present. The universal theme of gentrification, reimagined through the tropes of the Western, conjures a rich inter-textual feast for all those interested in the burdened intersection between cinema and politics.

The plot is replete with all the key motifs of the Spaghetti Western genre: an existential anti-hero; "the Man with No Name"; a wronged woman; the inexorable forces of modernity in the form of surveyors, land barons and the steam train; and pusillanimous townsmen, lawmen and small businessmen seeking personal profit over collective gain. The Man with No Name wanders this unruly "genre setting", seeking only rest and solace, while surveyors haunt the frontier lands, mapping and carving the land into new enclosures of time and space.[1] Frontier and genre conventions are deployed here not as retro gestures or deconstructive discourses on signifying practices. Rather, they are marshalled as part of a layered discourse dealing critically with a range of historical experiences and registers. Much of the viewing pleasure in *Trail of the Spider* is derived from this engaged reworking of historical and aesthetic references: an implicit challenge to an art world culture of repetitive reference and citation, which almost uniformly fails to redeploy and transform culture for radical social ends.

Stewart Home has argued that the difference between *detournement* and appropriation is precisely the difference between a transformational praxis and a slavish citation that refuses to theorise, never mind renovate, its historical moorings.[2] The currents which inform *Trail of the Spider*, by contrast, are rooted in the objective conditions of postwar Europe and filtered through the lens of historically situated subjectivity. The idea for the film, according to Panos, was derived in part from Munich-born Kirschner's "very German interest in cowboys". The devastation of Germany's production and distribution facilities during the Second World War granted the US film industry an industrial stranglehold on West German cinema, rendering Germany prone to a "re-education" programme in the form of rereleased US films – a vast new market for the products of American culture. The cowboy was then the archetypal American hero; in his celluloid form, devoid of competition, he was ready to conquer German cinema. The terms of this occupation were disinterred by a character in Wim Wenders' *Kings of the Road* (1976) who ruefully observed, "The Yanks have colonised our unconscious."

The cowboy narrative, however, developed along divergent lines in the GDR, where production facilities were rebuilt relatively soon after the Nazi era. The film industry quickly developed its own ideological contours under Communist rule. Relative autonomy from US influence spawned, by the 1960s, the bastard Indianer Filme: an estranged, inverted breed of Western where cowboys were capitalists and Indians were proto-communists challenging North American capitalism. This non-compliant appropriation of the Western, shorn of regressive Stalinist ideology, irradiates the narrative and provides a rebellious genre background for *Trail of the Spider*. The Man with No Name character (immaculately played by Hackney activist Floyd) finds echoes in the subversion of racial ideology in R. W. Fassbinder's *Whity* (1970), the heroic "half-breed" avengers of Sergio Corbucci's *Navajo Joe* (1966) and Enzo G. Castellari's *Keoma* (1976). "Marnie's place" (the tavern in Turnwood) deliberately evokes Joan Crawford's gender-busting saloon in Nicholas Ray's *Johnny Guitar* (1954) and Marlene Dietrich's "Chuck-a-Luck" rebel hideaway in Fritz Lang's "feminist" *Rancho Notorious* (1952). Meanwhile, references to *Django* (1966) and *The Great Silence* (1968) impregnate the film with Corbucci's "communist" take on the Spaghetti Western genre more commonly associated with cruel, existential pathos.

These references (and many others) work to inscribe dissenting discourses into the prosaic conventions of genre narrative and, more importantly, the discursive terrain of contemporary land-grab scenarios. Yet the process by which Kirschner and Panos redeploy history and genre myth recalls most forcefully the philosophical method by which Walter Benjamin set out to rescue history from "historicism's bordello". Benjamin's conception of montage ("the ability to capture the infinite, sudden or subterranean connections of dissimilars as the major constitutive principle of the artistic imagination")[3] fought a constant battle on behalf of history's victims, in order to detonate the slumbering time of the present with the fractious constellations of the past. Interviewed about one of her previous films, *Polly II: Plan for a Revolution in Docklands* (2006), Kirschner said:

> To some extent the plot of *Polly II* was based on actual events from the 18th century… But I'm not depicting or referencing these moments so they can be measured against so many subsequent defeats or presented as easily digestible celebrations of "heritage" or downright nostalgia… Rather, I use them because they penetrate the present like so many callings and loopholes whose explosive potential still speaks to us.[4]

These "callings and loopholes" are dramatically precipitated when the Man with No Name observes Surveyor's masked henchmen lynching a local man. A close-up of a wound in the Man with No Name's stomach dissolves into a rapidly edited montage that violently implodes a dense personal and collective history of repression and injustice (signified here by a lurid red filter). Later, when the Man with No Name is beaten to near unconsciousness by Turnwood for his bounty, the red filter is redeployed as a deep signifier of emotional as well as physical turmoil.[5] This defeat is given historical and cinematic resonance by the incessant, rhythmic pounding of a steam train and the beating of fists, on a soundtrack pulsing with the pressure of brutal and seemingly irresistible forces.

Kirschner and Panos understand, just as Benjamin did, the need to fight and refight the battles of the past. The film re-enacts and reorders the repressed racial history of the West through scenes and inter-titles that reference a frontier history more commonly epitomised by erasure and disavowal. The moribund landscapes of contemporary east London – through which the Man with No Name restlessly wanders – are given a mythic register and reanimated to mirror "The Unassigned Lands" where the US government of the 1860s forced Indian tribes to "cede back" inalienable territory so that settlers could pursue a ferocious land-grab. "The Trail of Tears", through which the Man with No Name makes his sorrowful way to his old flame Marnie, condenses his journey with the forcible displacement and relocation of Indian tribes from the American South to Arkansas and Oklahoma after the passage of the Indian removal Act in 1830. "The Great Dismal Swamp" (evoked in the film through judicious close-ups of snakes, lizards and spiders) is both the location for "Turnwood Town" and a reference to an actual location in North Carolina where runaway settlements ("maroons") of African and Native Americans escaped from slaveholders to form their own rebel agricultural and trading communities.

The interaction of these mythic landscapes with present tense actuality "brushes history against the grain", placing elements of past and present into new dialectical images that attempt to address a critical understanding of history.[6] Patterns of montage within and between images allow the landscape to be read as a palimpsest, containing multiple discursive layers. The epic Western landscape, for instance, is imaginatively conjured from landfills, "wastelands" and gravel pits with direct links to the construction of the 2012 Olympic Park, conflating both historical and contemporary land-grabs.

Pioneers and pariahs – the new urban frontiers

> If Hollywood wanted to capture the emotional centre of western history, its movies would be about real estate. John Wayne would have been neither a gunfighter nor a sheriff, but a surveyor, speculator, or claims lawyer. The showdowns would appear in the land office or the courtroom: weapons would be deeds and lawsuits, not six guns.[7]

The notion of the frontier and its inverse relation to wilderness and "the other" are particularly pertinent here. Neil Smith charted this territory when he established the ongoing currency of Frederick Jackson Turner's 1893 essay "The Significance of the Frontier in American History".[8] Turner envisioned the expansion of the Western frontier as "the outer edge of the wave… the meeting point between savagery and civilization… interpenetrated by lines of civilization growing ever more numerous."[9]

In this interpretation, the frontier is represented as an evocative combination of economic, geographical and historical advances by robust pioneers. Yet Turner's frontier line was extended less by individual pioneers and rugged homesteaders and more by "banks, railways, the state, and other collective sources of capital".[10] By the mid- to late 20th century, the potent imagery of wilderness and frontier was being reapplied to inner city areas in major cities back East. Inner city slums were increasingly demarcated as "urban wilderness" or, worse, "urban jungles" in a "discourse of decline", which came to dominate representations of the inner city.[11] By the 1970s and 1980s, market-led discourses of urban renaissance retooled frontier imagery (with the African American as its stigmatised "other") to legitimise "a political geographical strategy of economic reconquest".[12] The property market unleashed a wave of "urban scouts", "urban pioneers" and "urban homesteaders" on the margins of the inner city. And just as the original "pioneers" reductively envisioned native Indian populations as no more than a constituent part of the wilderness, so the "new folk heroes of the urban frontier" saw the residents of the contemporary frontier as "not yet socially inhabited" or "less than social".

Trail of the Spider exhumes this discursive current of conquest and legitimation from the opening scene. In a terrific panning shot across a massive, moribund east London landfill site, a voiceover, culled from one of the Communist Indianer Filme, works with and against the image to stridently conflate the ideas of frontier conquest, American capitalism and ruthless displacement with current speculative land-grabs in the East End of London. The mythologised tracts of contemporary London stand in for the historic Unassigned Lands where the remnants of a splintered resistance eke out a hounded existence in a rapidly diminishing social space; a space where surveyors, surrounded by "security", chart "the hitherto unmapped territory" of potential capital investment. Gazing out over the land for investment opportunities, the chief surveyor (in an assuredly pompous performance by Robin Laine) propounds the real meaning behind the reductive "civilization/wilderness" binary: "Look at the lay of this great land. Who would have thought that one day we would attach value to this wilderness?"

The film-makers have stated that the main concern of *Trail of the Spider* was to allegorise and question the "the shifting and shrinking space for collective social and political agency, self-determination and dissent" in an urban reality increasingly dominated by large-scale urban gentrification. "Sugar-coated" promises of community "regeneration" cannot hide the fact that what is really occurring is gentrification on an unprecedented scale. The prosaic reality of rampant property speculation is dramatised near the conclusion of the film, when a contemporary, fictionalised "land race" on an open tract of land in London's East End is compared (through the insertion of archival photographs) with the Oklahoma land race of 1889. The event saw Indian squatters forcibly removed from land that had been promised to them so that white settlers could "compete" for plots of land. The conflation of these narratives of speculation and enclosure, with all the legalistic and judicial apparatus that profits from them, nakedly reveals the consistent current of brutal, competitive self-interest that lies behind capitalist accumulation strategies. Displacement, advanced marginality and the ruthless disposal of public assets are the necessary contingencies of this totality.[13]

Hardt and Negri usefully theorise representative democracy as a "disjunctive synthesis" that simultaneously "connects and separates" citizens from the social body.[14] In this context resistance is typically either forced to the margins or defused through legalistic, reformist channels. In both *Polly II* and *Trail of the Spider*, Kirschner and Panos acknowledge and question the problem of recuperation and mediation. But rather than merely contemplating their own alienation, their creative practice emerges from praxis in everyday struggles against gentrification in east London. Most of the people in the film are friends or people they've met through activist campaigns in Hackney. They met Floyd (the Man with No Name) during the Broadway Market occupation,[15] and a prior friendship was cemented with John Barker ("Doctor Dynamite"), whose experience with the Angry Brigade in the early 1970s adds a critical, self-reflexive dimension to an intimately staged campfire scene (the dialogue concerns the potential of sabotage in the face of repression and retreat).[16] Meanwhile, Marnie's impassioned speech (singer/performer Claudette Bonney in a great performance) is partly based on Spirit, a local Jamaican shopkeeper and neighbourhood friend, who is facing eviction orders in a rapidly gentrifying Hackney. David Panos described a packed-out screening of *Trail of the Spider* in Hackney as "somehow recreating the reception to the Spaghetti Westerns in Jamaica and other post colonial countries".

In an aesthetic register that confronts the ossified conservatism of high modernism, and the mindless quotation of postmodernism, the film also brushes popular genre conventions against the grain in an attempt to engage and rearrange the audience's experience and knowledge of history. This way of working with history isn't mere source material for a reified and institutionalised art practice; instead historical forces are represented in such a way that they provide a genuine motivational connection to the possibilities of social change. As Nietzsche said: "We need history, but not the way a spoiled loafer in the garden of knowledge needs it."[17] If Nietzsche's sentiment is true for history, it is also true for a contemporary urban reality in desperate need of radical transformation.

* First published in *Mute*, 11 November 2008.

Nowhere, Somewhere, Far Away:
Where the Hell is Hackney Wick?

INTERVIEW WITH LEIGH NILAND BY SALLY MUMBY-CROFT

SMC: There is a plethora of photographic representation and documentation of the area – how do you think your use of more painterly traditional fine art techniques can reveal perhaps more about the changing landscape?

LN: I don't really know that they can reveal more about the changing landscape. A photograph is a moment of truth, a snapshot in time. A drawing takes longer, and the challenge is to get the information down – no cold, shaky fingers, no ineptitude in the line. Information is edited and added to the composition depending on mood and how much time you have. Whistler's etchings along the Thames are charged with atmosphere – imbued with the enchantment of his mind, on a particular evening, at a certain time in place in his life. I wished to do that with the subject of Hackney Wick. His work depicted the beginnings of the Industrial Revolution, I wanted to think I was here to see the end of it and wanted to employ similar techniques to do so.

SMC: Do you think the relative slowness of drawing, painting and printmaking compared with for example photography or writing impacts on your understanding of the place's diversity in a way that differs from the media's representation of East London?

LN: What comes to mind are some of the encounters I had while out drawing in the landscape. The Travellers at Waterden Road were going to be relocated to a new encampment and I wanted to draw the site before they were. To stand outside their chain link fence and photograph them would have felt invasive. I stood outside and drew, usually for an hour or so. Some of them were curious and came out to see what I was drawing. I don't think they'd have had the same curiosity had I been using a camera; photography is at once more familiar and confrontational, whereas I was there long enough for them to take the time to approach me. Sometimes a few young men would come out and stand with me – explain what was what, tell me a little anecdote, flirt, whatever. I got to meet the people who moved through the space I was depicting, hear stories about what I was drawing: "That building used to be a furrier…"; "You forgot to put in that bit there…"

SMC: What role does memory and reflection play in your prints

eigh Niland, East Cross, 2008

and drawings?

LN: The drawings were intended as a memory even as they were being made. When the project to draw the buildings started, there was no end date and I wasn't even aware it was a project. It was simply that I was intrigued by and kept visiting the Wick to make drawings and I wasn't sure why. It was 2003 and there was no inkling that the Olympics were on the horizon. These buildings looked a lot like home (New England) to me. We have woollen mills and other mill buildings in Boston, Portsmouth and along the Connecticut River from the same era so Hackney Wick looked somehow familiar. So it started as a memory of home, it became my home, and when the Olympics were announced my project began to take on purpose and urgency because the Wick as it was would soon be, and now is, a memory.

SMC: You lived in Hackney Wick for over five years. Now you are based far away; how do you reflect on your relationship with such a rapidly changing place? Can you now say what initially drew you to drawing and recording the Wick?

LN: I lived there for about eight years. My circumstances at the time decided my move back to the USA; my visa expired and I didn't have much of a choice. Plainly speaking, I think what drew me to draw the Wick was the lonesomeness of the place. I can now see that the Wick looked visually how I felt when I was there initially – a tad dismal. I felt this way for a combination of reasons: being far from home, the slight culture shock of a foreigner, not knowing anyone – the general adolescent/quasi-adult depression that can come with being 20 something.

Drawing on the Wick soon became what I wanted to do, it gave me a reason for being there, an employment for my interest, which became founded (however unfounded it might have begun) when the Olympics were announced to be coming to town. My task was set. Suddenly I had to put the pressure on and draw all of these buildings before they were gone. I was in the right place for the right window of time, excited to bear witness to such an historic change.

SMC: You work with screen prints, etchings, mezzotints and lithographs. Are you aware of the link with the history of print manufacturing and production in the site you are depicting? It seems that the area is not only a source of inspiration but also a practical resource as you use local printers and even your sculptures are made from materials collected on site – could you talk a bit about this link to the texture and materiality of a place? Does your work in the area articulate a kind of poetic of place?

LN: Once I became aware of this

history and context it was important to incorporate it into the project. The "Ode to the Blue Haphazard" posters were a way to link my printmaking to the industrial printing business of the area. I had 5,000 CMYK posters printed to give away to the public and shopped around different Wick printers for the best price. My only stipulation being that they had to be printed in the Wick on recycled paper stock and placed on a blue pallet. Each poster contained a haphazard arrangement of details of gouache observation drawings of Hackney Wick, including a pallet, a yellow dumpster, details of buildings and buddleia, a blue skyline profile. The haphazard placement of images on the poster correlated to the arrangements of objects within the Hackney Wick landscape. Placed without care for aesthetics, compositions occurred purely for reasons of utility or simply that these were discarded items that were forgotten and neglected.

Presented as a whole with posters stacked on a pallet and wrapped in clear plastic the piece looked like something that might have been part of this Hackney Wick landscape. I placed this pallet on White Post Lane and invited passersby to a "free, take one" tribute to the space. This project was meant to be a tribute to a place in keeping with the spirit of that place, with regard to the aesthetic, material, imagery found in that place and then displayed in and given entirely to the public of that place.

The broken glass sculpture *Glass Man* came from smashed car window splashes on the Hackney streets in the mornings that I thought were so beautiful to look at – yet so ugly in their story. I gathered sweepings of glass over time, rinsed it and sifted through it until I had enough to build a man I'd often sketched in town. The works were about the street, made from the street; these were the materials I had to work with.

SMC: In reference to your sculpture made of glass and the nature of observation, would you say your practice is socially engaged?

LN: Yes, I would say that *Glass Man* is very strongly socially engaged. When I arrived in the UK I had no work permit so I volunteered as a studio assistant at Core Arts, a charity for adults experiencing mental illness. This opportunity was what really got me started in my arts career, as art could only be a hobby back home in the USA (where one had to make money!!!). I loved working at Core Arts and saw another way.

I soon found a job (UK permanent residency granted!) at Hackney 180°, which was an art charity for homeless at St John-at-Hackney Church. My duty was to set up art materials so people who were coming in for a hot meal could sit and draw if they wanted. We had a studio with materials provided for them to use if they were more serious about it. Through this social work I found myself in contact with a very broad swathe of the Hackney community. We later worked in conjunction with Crisis Skylight studio, a homelessness charity in London.

It seems since then the world has thrown itself into make-money mode; the push is on to end street homelessness by 2012 and many of these "meaningful occupations" projects have been discontinued. I feel fortunate to have met and got to know and make artwork alongside the "service users" and colleagues I have come to care so much for through these charities.

SMC: What made you want to start the Wick-centrics portrait project? Why this title? How did you choose your subjects and why did you feel it was important to paint these characters? Where did you set up the studio?

LN: My studio space was within the Eton Mission adjoining St Mary of Eton Church, with the kind permission of Vicar Alan Piggott. I shared the studio space with painter Jaime Valtrierra, who organised weekly figure drawing sessions in his venture the "Mission Arts Club". We were facing eviction because the building was slated to be developed into luxury flats in time for the Olympics.

2009 was a year of "last hurrahs" as far as art projects went in that space, and a lot of interesting people passed through. Hackney was so characterful, as far as people go, that a walk down any street was eye candy to a painter. Making a "Wick-centric" portrait project brought some logic to the selection of who, where and why were chosen to be painted.

Each sitter was told to "come as you are or how you would like to be portrayed" to sit for a three-hour portrait at the Eton Mission. Other painters were invited to come and paint as well; for a £5 note apiece we could afford to pay the sitter a little something to make it worth their while too. The ten sitters were: fellow studio mate, mime artist Madalena Pinto (whom I posed next to an eviction notice that was posted outside the Eton Mission for development works slated to begin); artist Hilary Powell; Ingrid Z, Director of the Residence Gallery; Snoozie Hexagon, director of the Elevator Gallery; the Eton Men's Club snooker players Willie and Des, who'd been playing snooker at the Eton since the 1970s; Ralph, the drummer of Hackney Boots; Laura, the fiddler of the Hackney Marshins; Wick Ward councillor Christopher Kennedy; photographer Stephen Gill, who greatly influenced my work; and Iain Sinclair, author. "Wick-centrics" because these were

Leigh Niland, Willie and Des - Eton Men's Club snooker players, 2009

people somehow centric with the Wick, Wick the centre of the project, a cross section of the community that I encountered, all perhaps slightly eccentric – or at least interesting to look at, talk to, paint.

SMC: Tell me about the Hackney Wick tourist booth and your motivation for setting it up. In the current context of official Olympic souvenir stands in the area do you think you'll be back with "Postcards from Nowhere" during the Games?

LN: I would like to come back for the Olympics and set up some jubilant display. The tourist booth, exhibited along with the "Ode to the Blue Haphazard", was meant to be a jubilant tribute and finale to a lot of rather lonesome, if not dismal, drawings I'd amassed. My father had an old t-shirt a buddy had given him from a little known town in California called Niland, with a picture of a desert island and lone palm tree on it, which I kept thinking about. I started to think about the notion of paradise and the anti-paradise. I began to put ideas down into a sketchbook and there came a flow of other project ideas to go with it: team-style pennants, t-shirts, postcards – a team colour scheme had to be picked. I thought it was a completely obnoxious project and tried to ignore it but the idea just grew stronger until I just had to go for it in order to move on in my thoughts.

"Where the Hell is Hackney Wick?" was something I asked myself when I initially passed through the area on the 276 bus travelling to work at Core Arts. I thought it was a bleak looking no-man's-land. Nobody got on or off the bus, or even looked out the window as the bus just hurtled through from Stratford to Homerton. I was struck by the peculiarity of this place, completely enamoured by the (non)aesthetic. But with the announcement of the Olympics coming to town, the landscape began to change dramatically. Heaps of earth from the London to Brussels tunnel would build computer-generated rolling hills atop the industry-tainted marsh, transforming the non-destination into World Destination #1 for 2012. No one had heard of Hackney Wick. Would they call it Stratford-upon-Lea for the occasion? Surely they can't keep a name meaning "worked to death": Hackneyed.

SMC: Was it possible to remain uninvolved politically in what has come to be a contentious space?

LN: I consciously set out to be uninvolved politically and to draw the space as matter of factly, as Pliny might have related a diary entry. To me, I felt I was in the right place at the right time to witness a change. I'm just really curious about the extreme dynamic of change I have been given the chance in life to witness. The advantage was that it wasn't my back yard – yes I lived there but I felt like more of a visitor long term. Sub-currents definitely began to arise as to who is this space for? Are residents being replaced and priced out? What types of behaviour are acceptable in the regulated vs unregulated landscape? What kind of thoughts occur to a person walking through an industrial wasteland vs those that occur to that person walking down a wending, model-type train-set pathway? I don't envision being attracted to draw in the new regulated landscape on any long-term basis, though I had thought while drawing the sites that it would be interesting to draw them after the Games as well from the same vantage point.

SMC: What impact do you think the Olympics, and the change from an unregulated to an increasingly regulated landscape, has on the people you worked with while living in the Wick?

LN: The impact has already been that we have fairly effectively disbanded in general. Studio mates have relocated to spaces in Peckham, New Cross and elsewhere. Some lived in squats or affordable apartments, others who kept their boats on the Lea and are getting (re)moved along.

Some of the arts charities I worked with have folded due to funding cuts and so there is currently no place for the homeless and vulnerably housed who used to come and use the studio and materials to work. I left the UK when my own employment with them subsequently ended in 2009. I suppose these are to be attributed to the overall economic down turn and not to the Olympics. It's hard to rationalise such opulence on one hand and such neglect on the other.

David George, from Dissolution Series, 2009

David George, from Dissolution Series, 2009

David George, from Dissolution Series, 2009

The Outdoor Room

JUDE ROSEN

Let memory reinvent us from fragments
before they are set in stone.
It was a coming home, the first relief
of seeing green, wild and wet, stretching
endlessly, screened by tall trees as windbreaks.

Cycling into the wind along Homerton Road,
on the left, a plaque of remembrance and straight ahead:
a knot of flyovers and the familiar fear
and boredom they evoke, no longer seen
through a child's eyes from a suburban car.

On the right a new wood replanted,
new trees springing up, still thin but thickening
while on the other side, the land recedes
to the vanishing point, a sweep of unkempt grass,
its business carried on furtively: unseen

birds nesting, seeds spreading, burrowing worms,
ladybirds alighting, open terraces
to amble aimlessly on, unenclosed land
between the pit and discard beyond the city
walls and the bland unravelling of Essex.

Let the marshes recreate us as they are
our recreation, in solitude and in unions:
in cycling and sporting clubs, Sunday football leagues -
also women's - in defence of Lammas Lands
and the cultivation of gardening societies.

Let memory reinvent us honouring this place
scoring us into the marsh's sediment.
Set the stones in the ground, not on a grave,
to mark an outdoor room that makes us feel
at home in the city and we shall be…

A Fragment from the Long Poem
Reclamations: Voices and Narratives from the Olympic Zone

Rebecca Court,
Olympic Site
CPO, 2010

DISPLACEMENTS

THE OFFICIAL BODIES HAVE CALLED THE OLYMPICS A "CATALYST" FOR THE TRANSFORMATION OF THE "WASTELANDS" OF THE LEA VALLEY. IN THIS SECTION, THE VOICES OF SOME OF THOSE THAT WERE LEFT OUT, CLEANSED, IGNORED, AND DISLOCATED BY THE RE-DEVELOPMENT ARE HEARD. MEMORIES OF THE CLAYS LANE ESTATE, THE MANOR GARDEN ALLOTMENTS AND THE BOATERS COMMUNITY ARE CONJURED AS A FORM OF REVENGE AGAINST THE CAREFULLY PLANNED FORGETFULNESS.

Alessandra Chilá, Looking towards the Olympic Village from Cadogan Terrace, London, 2007, from the series Olympian Visions

An 11-mile fence encloses the Olympic Park construction site. Biometric hand and iris scanners have been installed for workers accessing the site. Military helicopters patrol overhead whilst anti-terror attacks and rescue operations using hostages, grenades, guns and real munitions, are rehearsed for a range of security measures in the Olympic Village. "Secured by Design" schemes are being applied to the construction of venues and buildings in order to reduce crime and security risks.

Whilst the above description might be associated by some with a war zone, the enclosures and violence perpetuated on the land and existing communities, have produced instead the greenest Olympics ever, the largest urban park and playground in Europe.

Alessandra Chilá, Lower Lea Valley, London, 2007, from the series Olympian Visions

The Olympic Park will be sited in the Lower Lea Valley, an area which comprised allotments, football pitches, wildlife habitats, a traveller site, a varied range of industrial units and local businesses, scrap metal yards, a bus depot, a church that hosted 12,000 people weekly, free playing fields and housing for people on low incomes.

The London Olympics will instead offer one of the biggest shopping malls in Europe, corporate businesses, a grand swimming pool and other sport infrastructures, highly secure green areas, riverside housing, bars, restaurants and a manicured landscape.

Alessandra Chilá, Channelsea River, London, 2007, from the series Olympian Visions

Between 160 and 200 boats mooring in the many canals and rivers of the Lower Lea Valley are used as water-based homes. The cost of a license to continuously cruise is approximately £600 per year, representing for many people an affordable way of living.

New rules and a highly expensive fee will be introduced by British Waterways affecting the continuous cruising license. The purpose is to control and reduce the number of boats clustering the waterways whilst allowing other visitors to moor in time for the 2012 Olympics.

In a statement issued to the Guardian magazine by Sally Ash, head of boating at British Waterways, she states: "The only way we can do this is through price, and some people will have to suffer."

Alessandra Chilá, River Lea Navigation, near Hackney Wick, London, 2007, from the series Olympian Visions

In the spirit of "the greenest Games ever", fishes and newts will be gathered into nets and "reversed" into cleaner waters, rare birds will be given new nests, bees and moths will be caught and moved to alternative habitats to save them from being crushed by bulldozer during work on the Olympic site. Upon completion these creatures will then be transplanted back to their new homes, "wildlife refuges", in the finished Olympic park.

Meanwhile, 300 members of the longstanding Clays Lane housing co-operative have been evicted, 250 gypsies and travellers have faced removal from two decades old official sites. To none of them has it been promised that after the Olympics they will move back to their own homes or natural environment. Perhaps the "right to return" attaches better to fishes and bees than to human beings.

Through the Blue Fence to the Emerald City:
From the Contested to the Envisioned Public Realm

JULIET DAVIS

Re-establishing connection between the divided sides of the Lower Lea Valley was said to be one of the key spatial drivers for the Olympic Legacy Masterplan Framework (LMF). This assertion built on studies which identified the historic divide between the inner London boroughs of Hackney and Tower Hamlets from the outer London boroughs of Newham and Waltham Forest as a significant factor influencing deprivation and a lack of strategic investment in this area. The emphasis on connectivity in the LMF echoed the broader urban policy discourse of "urban renaissance".[1] It was also viewed as a vital prerequisite to attracting private place-based investment in the future beyond the Olympics. In the 2009 version of the LMF, visualisations are used to communicate information about how these connections would be made and also what sorts of lived environments might be created in relation to them. In the process, they address questions of how regeneration is conceived by urban authorities and their operatives and what this means for the lived spaces of occupants and users that are the subjects of large-scale redevelopment processes.

The Blue Fence: an enclosure and a land acquisition process

When it was first erected, the chemical blue fence around the 2012 London Olympic site attracted both interest and reaction. Tactics for demonstrating resistance to the new enclosure and consequently the inability of local residents to gain access to it included lambasting its colour, pushing it into the background of a graffiti image or digging through it to reveal its thinness as a masquerade. By means of stencils, transfers and paints, views were articulated. One showed pounds, dollars and euros disappearing into a black hole labelled "OLYMPIC DEATH PIT". Another showed the five rings of the Olympic logo hanging from a gallows. A third depicted the five Olympic rings in the form of linked handcuffs suspended over a shower of "stolen" pounds and dollars, below which a label read "A CRIMINAL WASTE". These were just three of the visualised opinions caught on separate walks along the Olympic site's perimeter in 2007. They were necessarily fleeting as Olympic Delivery Authority (ODA) operatives were engaged in a continuous repainting and repairing process, working around the eleven-mile boundary with tins of Dulux High Gloss Water Resistant paint. This devotion to the maintenance of the projected image of a pristine blue surface highlighted the broader purposes of control and exclusion with which the fence, and indeed all that it contained, had been invested.

This was in sharp contrast with the time-worn walls of the urban fabric just beyond it and the many opportunities this offered for expression and reuse. In Hackney Wick, many of the textured brick walls of Victorian and Edwardian factories were overlaid by graffiti works, a testimony of their frequent contemporary occupation by artists and other creative industries. Sweet Toof's signature "teef" and gums, which sometimes appear alone against a post-industrial backdrop, but also often appear in the painted mouths of one eyed faces and macabre figures by fellow artist Cyclops, were one such example. A powerful outcome of one collaborative endeavour by this pair ran beside the Lea Navigation, directly facing the blue fence beside the Wick. Gummy toothed marine monsters attached to a cord with clothes pegs swam, smiled and seemed to exchange their own brand of menace with the fence.

The contrast between the prohibitive purpose and controlled image of the fence, and the ability of these artists to appropriate recalls Henri Lefebvre's conceptualisation of the production of space as a triad of "representations of space", "representational space" and "spatial practice".[2] According to Lefebvre, social space is shaped in the context of relations between these – between dominant understandings and instrumentations of how cities should be and lived interpretations of city spaces by its everyday users. He defines "representations of space" as imposed conceptions, while "representational spaces" denote "the dominated – and hence passively experienced – space which the imagination [of users and inhabitants] seeks to change and appropriate".[3]

Street art was just one small manifestation of the way in which Hackney Wick was lived and had been appropriated. Artists, along with a range of creative and other small-scale industries, attracted to the area by some of the lowest rents in central London and the underused building fabric, had over time transformed the old associated meanings of industrial era factory buildings and yards. The LSE Cities Programme MSc studio and muf architecture/art, in their respective 2010 studies of Hackney Wick and Fish Island, recorded 610 studios. Later an additional 300 different creative industries and 97 service industries were identified, ranging from printing businesses to car repairs, construction product supply and small-scale fabrication to catering. Although many were isolated businesses gathered together ad-hoc, which utilised their own supply and distribution networks, it was clear that compatible uses and working practices had also "agglomerated",[4] leading to the establishment of a number of subsidiary and/or mutually beneficial services such as cafés and galleries. The mix and density of spaces of work and business presented an alternative view of the common strategic rendering of the Olympic site and its fringes as chronically deprived, characterised by residues of disconnected "past uses" and as mono-functional – necessitating therefore a comprehensive redevelopment.

EDAW Architects' 2007 land-use analysis of the Olympic site, forming part of the application for outline planning permission for the Olympic and Legacy proposals, suggested that most of the 230 hectare Olympic site and its western and southern fringes was zoned light industrial (class B1). In fact, a wide mix of uses was accommodated on the Olympic site, as in Hackney Wick, until mid-2007, suggesting that analysis by land-use category was insufficient for understanding the distribution of actual use, let alone the micro-scaled social and spatial interconnectivities between uses. The 208 businesses included scaffolding pole suppliers, glass manufacturers, metal distributors, a smoked salmon producer, newspaper printers, waste recyclers, set building workshops for the Royal Opera House, a Halal butcher, numerous second-hand car part dealerships and a wig manufacturer. These uses provided approximately 5,000 jobs. Residential use formed a small proportion of the total area, but encompassed nonetheless a variety of types, from Traveller pitches to a gated, private residence (1,500 residents). The site also formed a base for cultural groups such as the Ghanaian Pentecostal church known as the Kingsway International Christian Centre (KICC) and traditional East End "caffs". Open space uses included allotments, an informal market occupying the bowl of a former dog-racing track and club grounds for cycling and athletics. As in Hackney Wick, although the site was physically fragmented, uses such as the car repair industry clustered together and some small-scale amenities were shared.

The winning of the Olympics in 2005 rendered as impossible any planned regeneration strategy that retained elements, if not all, of the existing topography of use and built fabric within the site. Occupants of the Olympic site became subject to the Compulsory Purchase Order (CPO) managed by the London Development Agency (LDA) from mid-2005 to mid-2007 and became engaged in lengthy processes of "negotiation" over relocation possibilities and compensation. In late 2005, the Secretary of State for Communities and Local Government announced that a public inquiry would be held before deciding whether or not to confirm the CPO. The inquiry was held between May and August 2006. The LDA alleged that by the time the hearing commenced, 90% of the land designated for the Olympics was in its possession and that 70% of all existing jobs on the site were safeguarded through successful relocation processes. This suggested that only a small number of individuals were objecting.

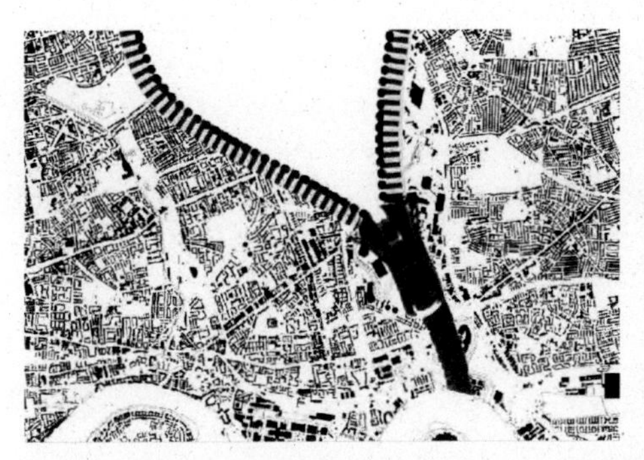

Figures 1 and 2. KCAP, Alles & Morrison and EDAW, Reconnecting the Lea Valley diagram and Draft illustrative perspective of the area near Pudding Mill in Legacy (both produced for the LDA, 2008)

Despite this, the Planning Inspectorate's official report on the public inquiry reveals that objections to the CPO were received from across the site – from each of the residential groups, the allotment holders, several Lower Lea Valley-based environmental pressure groups, sports groups, cultural groups and more than 100 businesses with occupancy and/or ownership interests in the site.

The issue of connectivity figures high in the LDA's statements of case for the CPO.[5] The observation is made that a "dominant feature of the Order Lands is transport infrastructure", which is viewed as both an asset and a potential catalyst for the development of far higher levels of space for employment, habitation and services than the site currently provided. Simultaneously, fragmentation at the local level is viewed as one of a number of primary depriving impediments to this, and one which Olympic and Legacy plans are poised to address. Connectivity was thus understood to relate to conceived development futures, to potentials and envisioned benefits that bore little relation to the specific contexts and scales at which people already lived and worked in the area. Some of the representations made by users at the public inquiry and in the context of face-to-face interviews forming part of this research suggested alternatives interpretations of the value of connectivity for the specific of users living and working on the Olympic site and at its Hackney borough fringe.

Though the LDA's plans suggested that future Olympic site occupants would be advantaged by infrastructural and environmental improvements, businesses Rooff Group Ltd and Harrow Green Group Ltd expressed concern at the public inquiry being shunted out "to areas where they would be separated from their client base and subject to poorer communications than their present sites provide".[6] A similar concern was presented in an interview with salmon curers H. Forman & Sons, who succeeded in settling a deal with the LDA literally moments before its director was due to present an objection at the public inquiry. He argued that good connections to central London were crucial for his firm as the relative freshness of his food products gave him an edge over competitors.

Some users objected to being removed from the regeneration process, which they argued was taking place organically. Two small-scale land owners, A. Hussain and A. Rashid, argued at the public inquiry that as they were already active in regenerating their sites they saw "no reason why the lands should not be returned to the Objectors who would be perfectly capable of redeveloping the site"[7] in accordance with local strategies and in the process realising more value for themselves than they would be likely to through the LDA's compensation programme. In spite of such objections to being relocated at all, the main issue for a number of groups appeared to be having space to use without financial compromise rather than relocation itself. In interview, a key representative for the Eastway Users Group, a cycling group which also succeeded in negotiating a deal in advance of the public inquiry, claimed that "all I needed to know – and all any rider needed to know – was that they were going to get a facility where they could do their sport".[8] This statement highlights Lefebvre's contention that although "the producers of space have always acted in accordance with a representation... the 'users' passively experienced whatever was imposed on them inasmuch as it was more or less thoroughly inserted into, or justified by, their representational space"[9]. This conceptualisation was borne out through this research in the sense that the most forceful objections were made when proposed change appeared to affect spaces materially, not necessarily as physical locations but "as lived".

Although the redevelopment of the site was contingent on the outcome of the public inquiry, influencing its outcomes were the success of the LDA in acquiring most of the land already and the unmovable dates of the Games. The need to have the Olympic Park complete by July 2012 virtually obliged the LDA to deliver a vacant site in July 2007. The hearing concluded in the LDA's favour and the deadline was met, despite negotiations with several user groups remaining incomplete. Key in formulating this decision was the following notion: "The Lower Lea Valley has all the attributes of an area lacking in investment. Environmental quality is poor; movement across the area is inhibited; employment has a narrow focus; unemployment is high and there are numerous signs of marked deprivation."[10] Interpretations of due process and the "public interest", as Imrie and Thomes argue,[11] were essential to the formulation of this conclusion and outcome. Transforming the site's accessibility from other locations and within itself required the capacity to intervene in the spatial organisation of the site on a far bigger scale than the plots of any of the existing land owners. The strategic value with which that increased connectivity was associated overrode objections on the grounds than none presented an alternatively viable way of creating the same degree of long term "benefit" or value.

Occupants of Hackney Wick, though not subject to CPO, nonetheless experienced changing conditions influencing their use of land in roughly the same timeframe. Although with the announcement of the CPO the future for occupants of the Olympic site had a least a degree of certainty, the development future of Hackney Wick appeared to become less certain, given a curious combination of continuity in the structure of land ownership and built form, and likely evolution of local authority land-use strategy for the area. Businesses in Hackney Wick reported difficulties in renegotiating leases with landlords hoping to use the adjacency of the Olympics and the prospect of re-zoning to leverage maximum returns on their assets once the opportunity arose. Long-term uncertainty, combined with the shorter-term prospect of increased rents provided incentive enough for businesses in Hackney Wick to begin to relocate. Between 2007 and 2009, more than 50% of the printing industry in Hackney Wick relocated. Far from remaining as an enclave of complex mixed-use development, which new local connections might have assisted in intensifying, the initial effect of planning for the 2012 Olympics and Legacy for these industries was disconnection.

The remainder of this chapter examines the conceptions of legacy that began to be made manifest in the LMF in late 2008 and early 2009. In this regard, I respond to Lefebvre's challenge that "if architects (and urban planners) do indeed have a representation of space... [w]hose interests are served when it becomes 'operational'?".[12]

The Emerald City

Figure 1, usually the first to be shown in verbal presentations of the LMF, communicates the team's conceptualisation of the disconnection difficulty with which the Lea Valley was associated. It depicts the Lea Valley as an open zip, which the LMF project is endeavouring to close. The LMF suggests that improved physical connections would be enabled by and also symbolise "joined up" decision making – facilitated by the unusual governance structure developed to realise the Olympics and Legacy masterplans. They would serve to "open up" a marginal territory to the forces of renewed economic development. They would also form the spatial fabric of renewed and new "communities".[13]

This is clearly a tall order, both conceptually and practically.

In interview, architects from KCAP and Allies & Morrison argued that the different roles that connectivity was expected to play in transforming the site's long-term prospects were often in conflict, as they implied connections on quite different scales and between quite different entities. For example, while features such as the six- to eight-lane A roads running along three of the site's edges, the Northern Outfall Sewer, the huge new cut of the high-speed rail link to Europe, the tangle of the valley's rivers, thick lines of parallel train tracks passing across the site to Stratford and the new slip road into the Stratford City shopping centre were "major instruments of connectivity", regarded by the LDA as important assets for the future, they were major barriers to pedestrian movement, visual eyesores and potential ongoing deterrents to either investors or inhabitants. In addition, the connective tissue required to enable a Games event to function was quite different from that required to service a complex piece of mixed-use city joined at its edges to existing neighbourhoods. Thus, architects claimed that though the Olympic Games plan was intended to form a crucial underlay of infrastructural investment and a "catalyst" to development, it actually exacerbated given conditions of disconnection with which the pre-Olympic site was associated. How to begin to piece in compact, locally well-connected development against and between such monumentally divisive structures? How, further, to create human links across the site between existing, small-scale urban fabrics such as Hackney Wick and Leyton?

The perspectival view in figure 2 is one example from the range included in the LMF, which focuses on how masterplanners imagined that a new public realm network would be animated. It depicts a busy street, full of the clutter of signs, people and activities. Qualities of street life reminiscent of historic parts of east London are linked with ideas about the potential form, architecture, use and materiality of high-density new development. This image is evidently not a photograph, nor is it a wholly accurate perspective. The images that are collaged together are of real buildings and real people – however, they are rendered as imaginary "representations of space". Looking closely, there are a number of features that render them challenging. First, how often have you witnessed such eclectic public realm uses in the context of new commercial developments? It seems improbable that shops as specialised or as low key as those suggested by the signs on the right would occupy new, presumably premium-value, commercial buildings. Second, scale: look how big the children on the left are next to the white van. The scale of the tower is masked by situating it in the distance and ensuring it occupies only a small proportion of the overall view. Third, use:

what are the relationships between the users of the public realm and the users of the depicted buildings? Are they the same? A conception of chaotic, cosmopolitan urban space is represented as the ground level public realm. However, the buildings only suggest residential and commercial uses. Where and how might cultural institutions – for example, the churches, mosques, synagogues and temples that characterise diverse neighbourhoods throughout the rest of east London, or the shared galleries of Hackney Wick – find space to appropriate, or fashion their "representational spaces" here? And, if one assumes that this would be challenging, how realistic is it to depict the public realm as though it would be capable of absorbing aspects of existing Leyton or the Wick?

When I raised some of these questions with David Roth, it emerged that he was dissatisfied with the images – predominantly owing to an approach which, he claimed, had been imposed by the LDA, rather than originated within the masterplanning team. The LDA, as it transpired, had rejected a number of images that his team produced in which they endeavoured to communicate qualities of a genuinely dense urban and/or more culturally mixed-use building environment. The LDA wanted the people in the views to suggest London's ethnic and cultural diversity and literally reflect their political emphasis on the project's social credentials and its alignment with New Labour policies of social inclusion and equality. However, they appear to have felt that placing symbols such as a minaret in one of these drawings would be inflammatory, suggesting the privileging of one cultural group's interests over another. Perhaps, additionally, including such spaces would suggest that these spaces would still be possible to deliver in the context of the land value uplift which the masterplan was intended to facilitate. Designers were obliged only to include people shot by the LDA's photographer. They were not allowed to populate images with people who might appear to LMF readers as "deprived" or who were engaged in activities that anyone else could construe as detrimental to health or to a wide range of legitimate uses of the public realm. For example, "you can't have someone drinking a beer", Roth claimed. Nor were they allowed to portray the proposals on rainy days as this would impact negatively on the "mood" of the representations. The perspective projections, to use Kester Rattenbury's term, are "media constructions", "representations of space" which may not only not look quite like this in future reality but will almost certainly not look like this at all.[14] The interests that are served are predominantly those of the LDA's as they endeavoured to make their representation appear relevant to all their stakeholders. For Roth himself, they were representations of "political control" and ideological "decorum", contemporary equivalents of Sebastiano Serlio's "Tragic Stage Set".[15]

Conclusion

In different ways, the land assembly process, which directly impacted on existing users of the Olympic site and its fringes, and the early stages of reimagining the site in accordance with "Urban Renaissance" principles, have been problematic in depicting how existing, lived realities are seen, valued and represented. The land assembly process led to a failure to acknowledge the value of particular representations of concern by Olympic site users and to literal dislocation. The LMF, at least in its 2009 iteration, produced a dislocation of a different order – between the imagination of connected, regenerated communities and the social and spatial fabrics of east London all around it. Simply taking the outward signs of deprivation out of the images of the Olympic's urban legacy suggests a failure to really grasp, or at least publicly acknowledge, the relations between the conditions that create spaces of different sorts and prices and the different values – positive and negative – connected with these. In addition, in spite of proffered participatory opportunities, it suggests an unwillingness to make the connection between "representations of space" and the jobs that users do in remaking the city over time. If the 2009 LMF's perspectival drawings are anything to go by, there is a good chance that spaces of connection will not create intensification opportunities that build on how the edges of the site are currently lived, but create the possibility for their disintegration as higher land values, generalised notions of what regeneration should consist of and the redevelopment pressures they endorse force existing occupants out by a number of means. Before lines are fixed in 2012, the following questions need to be addressed: What is already there? How do the people who are there understand their situation and their prospects? How can these perceptions and representations be conceived as catalysts to renewal alongside and in connection to big Olympic gestures?

Forced Evictions:
Legacies of Dislocation on the Clays Lane Estate

CRAIG HATCHER

Introduction

In 2005, the London Development Agency (LDA) issued what has been described as the largest and most controversial compulsory purchase order (CPO) in British history.[1] Over 1000 individuals were forcibly evicted from their homes or businesses in the Stratford area of east London to make space for the Olympic park over the two years that followed. In justifying the need for the evictions, the then Secretary of State for Trade and Industry, Alistair Darling, emphasised that "the Games represented a unique opportunity to secure benefits on an unimaginable scale which could not be realised in a less damaging way".[2] The use of such a legal tool was rationalised by appealing to the broader public interest. It was considered that the benefits of hosting the 2012 Olympic Games for London and the UK as a whole, together with the associated process of regenerating one of London's most deprived areas, would offset the enormous upheaval the evictions would have on the residents and business owners affected by the CPO.

The successful and timely planning of the Olympics has depended on the use of what has been described as an "aggressive method of acquiring property – namely, compulsory purchase".[3] Here, I introduce this contentious legal tool and highlight how its effects are felt disproportionately by those with "weaker" property rights, such as tenants.

Compulsory purchase as a legal tool for development

Compulsory purchase enables developers, under the direction of the state, to acquire large expanses of land in a short space of time. As a legal tool, it avoids the need for developers to undergo the long and laborious process of purchasing individual parcels of land piecemeal only when that land becomes available to purchase by agreement of the owner. On the contrary, compulsory purchase provides the legal means for a state body to purchase land without the consent of its owners. It is the state's "legislative omnipotence" that legitimises and enables the act of compulsory purchase and the subsequent expropriation of property from an individual whether they agree to this or not. The act of compulsory purchase by the state is still open to challenge (from a UK perspective at least) and individuals who are directly affected by compulsory purchase –

those with a vested interest in the land – owners or occupiers of the land – have the right to have their objections heard at a public inquiry.

Compulsory purchase sits uncomfortably with law's high regard for private property.[4] Malloy and Smith note that: "individuals are given property rights as part of democratic political structures, as a means of promoting citizenship, and as a vehicle for advancing economic development."[5] The effects of compulsory purchase on a property owner are therefore qualified by what is known as the "principle of equivalence". This principle ensures that owners are put back into a position where they are no worse or better off than they were before the event – before their property was expropriated.[6] Although owners of a property lose the material space they live in as a result of compulsory purchase, those owners are still, nonetheless, compensated to the extent that they are put in a financial position so that they can purchase, and become an owner of, another property. The principle of equivalence only recognises the owner's fungible interest, however, and not the owner's sentimental or moral value towards the property. The owner's attachment to the particular area through their social connections or personal history, for example, is not considered. Compensation is calculated on the basis of the commodity or exchange value of the property whereas sentiment and personal attachment are conceived as irrelevant factors in the eyes of the law.

The European Convention on Human Rights (ECHR), incorporated into domestic law by virtue of the Human Rights Act 1998, confers a right to property: "every natural person or legal person is entitled to the peaceful enjoyment of his possessions. No one shall be deprived of his possessions except in the *public interest* and subject to the conditions provided by law and by the general principles of international law."[7] Tom Allen argues that "public interest is interpreted broadly to the extent that "it is difficult to imagine how a redistribution would not serve a public interest in some way."[8] The case of *James v United Kingdom* centred on the meaning of public interest in the ECHR.[9] Judges in the European Court of Human Rights did not accept that: "the transferred property should be put into use for the general public or that community generally, or even a substantial proportion of it, should directly benefit from the taking."[10] Therefore, "public interest" is interpreted generously in the UK together with other signatories to the ECHR. Public interest does not necessarily assume that the public will have a right to use or enter the property or that it will remain in the public domain: the bar for satisfying public interest is set low and is attainable through the indirect effects of economic and profit-orientated developments.

Benjamin Beach, Clays Lane was Here, 2011

Large-scale regeneration projects in cities instigated as a result of a successful bid to host a mega-event, such as the Olympic Games, have relied heavily on the use of compulsory purchase powers. Cities that host these mega events "push urban regeneration at a more rapid pace than 'normal' development... so it is possible to achieve infrastructure developments, relocate people and create new centres of housing, commerce and cultural activity within an accelerated time-scale".[11] Developers therefore see compulsory purchase as an effective method of expediting the process. Wilkinson argues, however, that mega-events have a "tendency to displace groups of citizens located in the poorer sections of cities".[12] These groups are less able to form community groups or protect their interests unlike more dominant ones that mobilise support against such developments. In particular, past mega-events have resulted in landlords forcing low-income tenants out of their homes in favour of a new social class of residents that pay higher rents or, alternatively, housing is made available for lucrative short-term lets made available for tourists and organisers visiting the event.[13] According to a report published by the non-governmental organisation, Centre on Housing Rights and Evictions (COHRE), for example, approximately 1.5 million people were displaced in the run-up to the Beijing 2008 Olympic Games in order to make space for the physical structures required for the Olympics.[14] Tenants were particularly affected by the displacements as they were not entitled to compensation, unlike property owners.[15]

Other cities that have hosted past Olympic Games have also used compulsory purchase as a tool for development. In Athens in 2004 new compulsory purchase powers were introduced specifically for the event in order to expedite the expropriation process. In Atlanta, in preparation for the 1996 Olympics, compulsory purchase powers were also used largely in respect of public housing estates.[16] Sydney is a useful example of a city that applied only a light-touch approach to compulsory purchase, but it was tenants who still experienced the brunt of the Games: private landlords evicted tenants in order to provide short term accommodation for tourists visiting the city.[17]

London 2012 and the Clays Lane estate

Before its demolition in 2007, the Clays Lane estate was nestled between the green open space of the Lea Valley cycle track and Hackney marshes to the north and Stratford's commercial centre to the south. Originally built in the early 1980s as a housing cooperative for single people, the estate housed over 400 residents in a mixture of four-, six- and ten-bedroom shared houses and some single-occupancy bungalows.

The CPO was served on the residents of Clays Lane (together with other residents and businesses that were located within the area ear-marked for development) on 16 November 2005, four months after the International Olympic Committee announced that London had won the bid to host the 2012 Olympic Games.[18] The CPO was made under the powers of the Regional Development Agencies Act 1998 (RDA 1998) and the Acquisition of Land Act 1981 (ALA 1981).[19] The RDA 1998 empowers the LDA, as an "acquiring authority", to compulsorily purchase land in pursuing its "purposes" as the regional development agency for London.[20] The "purposes" of the LDA include furthering the "economic development and regeneration" and promoting "business efficiency, investment and competitiveness" in London. Such economically targeted "purposes" highlight the context within which compulsory purchase is conceived – the law of compulsory purchase is structured in order to attract capital investment to cities.

A public inquiry was initiated by the objectors of the CPO in May 2006. These objectors included some of the residents of Clays Lane as well as other residents and businesses affected by the CPO. In his decision, the inspector appointed by the Secretary of State declared that the area the CPO encompassed was used inefficiently and desperately required regeneration.[21] With particular reference to Clays Lane, the inspector said:

> The overt sense of community and the value that many residents put on their homes and their surroundings is foremost in my mind. Their loss will be a substantial one. However, I find the anticipated benefits of the legacy and the catalytic effect of the Olympic Games to be a more forceful factor.[22]

While sympathies were expressed over the loss of the community as well as the demolition of the residents' homes, the CPO was still regarded as a proportionate interference of the residents' rights. The benefits that the Olympics would bring through the regeneration of Stratford as well as the event's long-term legacies were too important to forego for the sake of the residents of Clays Lane and the other individuals it would affect. The decision to use the legal tool of compulsory purchase on the residents of Clays Lane was therefore based on proportionality. The Secretary of State balanced the estate's use value for the residents against the land's potential exchange value. As Don Mitchell notes: "[I]f a built environment possesses use value… but that use value threatens what exchange value may exist or may be created then these use values must be shed."[23] The "public interest" test applied to restrict any arbitrary use of compulsory purchase is geared towards the potential exchange value of land rather than use value that the land may have had for the residents of Clays Lane.

The law of compulsory purchase order from a UK perspective places a limited re-housing obligation on the "acquiring authority" (the LDA). Re-housing is provided for under s.39 Land Compensation Act 1973 (LCA 1973), which notes that:

> where a person is displaced from residential accommodation on any land in consequence of the acquisition of the land by an authority possessing compulsory purchase powers… and suitable alternative residential accommodation on reasonable terms is not otherwise available to that person, then… it shall be the duty of the relevant authority to secure that he will be provided with such other accommodation.[24]

The "relevant authority" is the local housing authority. In the case of Clays Lane, this was the London Borough of Newham. The local housing authority is ultimately responsible for re-housing tenants affected by compulsory purchase if no "suitable alternative residential accommodation" is available. There is no further reference in the LCA 1973 as to what "suitable alternative residential accommodation" means, and there is also little case law on this issue. In the case of *Savoury v Secretary of State for Wales* (1976), tenants who were subject to a CPO requested to be re-housed together in the same area.[25] The Secretary of State for Wales confirmed that 50 per cent of the tenants would ultimately be re-housed in the same area but could not guarantee that the remainder, or all of the residents who requested to move together, would be re-housed there. The tenants sought to set aside the CPO on the basis that the Secretary of State for Wales failed to satisfy the "suitable accommodation" criteria. This was dismissed and it was held that the Secretary of State had satisfied the criteria by offering reasonable accommodation to the residents regardless of whether it was in the same area as the other tenants. The concept of "suitable accommodation" was therefore based on housing tenants individually and there was no obligation on the "relevant authority" to house tenants as a group.

In *Savoury v Secretary of State for Wales* (1976) it was seen to be just and equitable that each *individual* was re-housed in suitable accommodation and that the residents could not expect to be re-housed as a group in the same area. Joseph Sax indicates how the law has a tendency to treat property as individual parcels of land separated from each other and therefore:

> What is missing is the question whether there is some entity consisting of all the pieces taken together, a community, the interest of which are neglected in any such item by item approach. The current law does not agonize over such an issue... The interests of a community have no formal status; they are not, for example, property rights. In the law's eye, they are only sentiment.[26]

There is no mechanism in law for instigating a movement of a group of people affected by a CPO and living in geographical proximity to each other to a new location. Property is, instead, conceived as an individual, freestanding commodity.

A large proportion of the public inquiry focused on the residents of Clays Lane request for a "community move". This also formed a key point of discussion during the interviews I conducted with a group of residents from the estate in the summer of 2010, three or more years after they were evicted. Several respondents lauded the community ethos of the estate and the social networks they had formed. They commented on how since the evictions they had "lost the sense of community" and the social connections they had enjoyed in their former homes. One resident told me that "Clays Lane had certain unique features, you know, networks of support, social community... by and large, people thought it was a sociable community." It was apparent that the residents valued the community ethos of the estate, but were also keen to highlight that Clays Lane was not perfect. There were problems between residents such as noise issues and verbal and physical fights. One resident highlighted the dual nature of the community:

> Clays Lane was not an ideal community, sometimes you come across people and they were like "oh yeah, I've heard about Clays Lane, marvellous, wonderful place". They're disillusioned. I'm just telling you the reality. I'm not going to try and paint a picture which is not true. It has good things in it, it was a sociable place there were some good people there, and yeah you have problems when you're mixing a lot of people like this, but what the hell!

A community was a valued resource, but this did not necessarily mean it had strong social-bonds. Another resident summarised this aspect nicely: "Yes, even if I didn't get on with them [the other residents], it was still a community!" Another resident reported that the relationships he had formed with other individuals during his fourteen years on the estate were relatively superficial. He was, however, comforted by the fact that he was surrounded by people whom he could talk to if he wanted to: the community was a resource he could call upon. This was recognised as a unique feature of living on such a large estate with people from similar backgrounds. The estate only accommodated single people, which some respondents believed made it a more open and sociable community: "[F]amilies often operate separately. They have their own lives, they know other families with children and so on… single people maybe have a greater impetus to get to know people just by virtue of the fact you haven't got anyone else to share your time with."

Despite there being no obligation on the LDA, or indeed the local housing authority, to re-house individuals as a group or a community, the LDA and the tenants entered into negotiations to try and effect a community move. The residents noted that the LDA offered potential sites for a large number of residents to move to another site together. This would have involved constructing a new estate and there was the potential for residents to become involved in the design process.[27] The residents interviewed, however, considered these sites to be in marginal and undesirable areas of London compared with where Clays Lane was located. One resident expressed her dissatisfaction with a site proposed by the LDA : "[N]obody wants to be stuck between the sewage works, a chemical plant and the airport. We were emphatic about that".

The community move, therefore, got off to a bad start and at the same time other residents who were not part of these negotiations were in the process of moving out of Clays Lane into self-contained flats. The estate was gradually emptying, to the concern of some residents who, in principle, wanted to be part of the community move, but feared they would not be re-housed should the community move eventually fail: a prospect that began to look more likely. This concern was exacerbated by the fact that a group of residents (mainly international students) had been informed by the housing association that owned the estate and the LDA that they had no recourse to public funds and therefore could not be re-housed. This was later highlighted as an erroneous interpretation of the law as this specific group of residents was in fact entitled to be re-housed as housing association tenants but not as local authority tenants. Indeed, guidance for residents in such a position (as well as legal practitioners) seems to be particularly opaque. A leaflet produced by the Department for Communities and Local Government states: "If you are genuinely made homeless [by compulsory purchase] but you do not qualify for re-housing contact your local housing department immediately as they *may* still be able to help."[28] There is no affirmative responsibility on the local housing department to provide housing if that individual does not "qualify". The issue arose in this particular context because of the transfer of Clays Lane ownership from its tenants (the estate was initially a housing cooperative) to a housing association in 2002. Under the cooperative's original constitutional rules, residents were accommodated loosely on the basis of "housing need". The cooperative did not apply the strict criteria that housing associations often apply. With this wide interpretation of "housing need" and its extremely low rents, Clays Lane was popular with international students.

The combined fear of not being re-housed should the group move fail, and confusion over some residents having no entitlement to re-housing, resulted in some residents withdrawing from the community move and switching to viewing self-contained flats organised through the LDA. A three-way division also formed within the group that wanted to move as a community owing to differences of opinion over the vacant development site proposed by the LDA. Two of the residents interviewed from the community moved earlier than some of the others so they could be re-housed in self-contained flats: "I kind of gave up on that idea [the community move]. I was panicking. I thought 'I've got to get myself re-housed'. It seems a bit selfish but if we were just going to argue and bicker about what we were going to do, I didn't want to be part of that."

In organising these moves, the LDA negotiated with housing associations to provide individual self-contained properties for the residents. The residents selected properties through a choice-based system: residents would view one property and if they decided it was not suitable they could look at another property, but if the second property was not suitable they would have to accept the final property or lose their right to be re-housed.

The division with the community move occurred at the same time as the public inquiry was held and the LDA raised this formation of different factions during the inquiry. The LDA dismissed the residents' preference to move as a community labelling it as "co-op nostalgia".[29] The LDA believed that the residents were hankering after a lost time when Clays Lane operated as a housing co-operative: "[E]ven the nostalgia will fade over time and principles of the organization that once brought and held the community together will have little relevance even if the estate were retained."[30]

The LDA reinforced its sceptical attitude towards the community move by questioning the validity of the community and commenting on its fragmented nature:

> [I]f everyone were to have their way, most residents would leave the so-called community, and those that are left would choose to live apart in 3 separate groups. It should not come as a surprise because it reflects the complexities of human relationships, but it should sound a note of caution when claims are made that the community at Clays Lane should be preserved in the public interest. So, given their choice of relocation, the community, as it is called, would fragment. There is nothing to suggest that the Clays Lane community warrants protection in the public interest.[31]

Ultimately, the community move was a failure. Approximately 40 individuals[32] from Clays Lane were moved into self-contained flats on an estate in Bethnal Green, east London but the residents I interviewed were unclear whether some form of "group move" was facilitated by the LDA or whether residents were housed randomly in an estate that had vacant housing. One resident interviewed noted that he happened to be re-housed in a block of flats where other former residents from Clays Lane were living, but he was unaware of this until he moved in:

> Resident: There was an accidental group [move] – there's three of us in this building... we weren't close friends, I did know them, but we

weren't big chums.
Author: And do you like the fact you are with other people from Clays Lane?
Resident: Yeah, it did help. There were some friendly faces, I knew someone in the area – it made it easier.

Conclusions

Compulsory purchase has been used extensively and globally in an Olympic context. As a legal tool, it allows public bodies to acquire vast amounts of land in a short space of time without the consent of those who live and work there. This resulted in a considerable amount of displacement from the Stratford area of east London in relation to London 2012. The law behind these displacements is not applied equally, however; some groups in society, most notably tenants, are targeted or notice the effects of compulsory purchase more than others.

Through interviewing the residents of Clays Lane, it also became apparent that the compulsory purchase process, and in particular, re-housing, is structured only to recognise individuals and fails to account for "community" or group moves. This is despite an emphasis on "community legacies", which clinched the Olympic bid for London against other cities in 2005. During the public inquiry, the LDA appeared dismissive of the residents' call for a community move, labelling their request as "co-op nostalgia" and referring to the "so-called community". It appears that whereas the law that governs compulsory purchase fails to recognise the "community" *per se*, the LDA, which applies the law, has a particular version of what is a "community". Clays Lane failed to exhibit these characteristics and was therefore unworthy of protection in the public interest.

Clays Lane Live Archive

ADELITA HUSNI-BEY

Clays Lane was a fully mutual housing cooperative established in 1947 to address the lack of housing for vulnerable single people in east London. It was located on the top of a small hill, the former West Ham Tip landfill, and consisted of 57 shared houses and 50 self-contained flats. Up to 450 contractual tenancies were available for single persons aged between 18 and 59. Tenants were required to purchase a £1 share in order to become a member of the cooperative, entitling them to attend and vote in the annual general meeting, elect or stand for the management committee, participate in the cooperative's affairs and receive its services. Making its residents full stakeholders in the estate was an attempt to establish a form of direct democracy and communal responsibility, towards one another and the upkeep of the buildings. Clays Lane was designed to engender a strong local community – its motto was "A community, not just a housing estate". Demolished in 2007 to make way for the Olympics, nothing remains to commemorate this social experiment. Those who lived at Clays Lane were treated as if they could be disposed of, relocated and dispersed without significant consequence. The violence of this action was masked with an impressive amount of data, charts, surveys and questionnaires which legitimised the eviction process and the erasure of this community.

The Clays Lane Live Archive is a participatory research and development project with ex-residents of the estate. It seeks to visualise the disjuncture between the language of bureaucracy and lived experience by simultaneously questioning the official rhetoric of regeneration and the rhetoric of community held by Clays Lane. Works based on the language from the bureaucratic materials used to evict residents are interwoven with subjective records of lived experience.

A series of "mini-projects" makes up the archive: an audio-history of the court case, narrated by Julian Cheyne, along with tens of thousands of pages of legal documents; John Sole's collections of hand-drawn architectural drawings of the site, which span a ten-year period; a set of posters, CDs and paraphernalia donated by the band Dead Dog Mountain, based on the estate; a selection of intimate photographs shared by Katie Stubbs; a hand-saw mindmap, which displays the relationships between the ex-residents; and a full set of *The Wire Newsletter*. Also part of the archive is the compulsory purchase order used to acquire the land, official ODA publicity material, and the Fluid Survey and Inspector's Report.

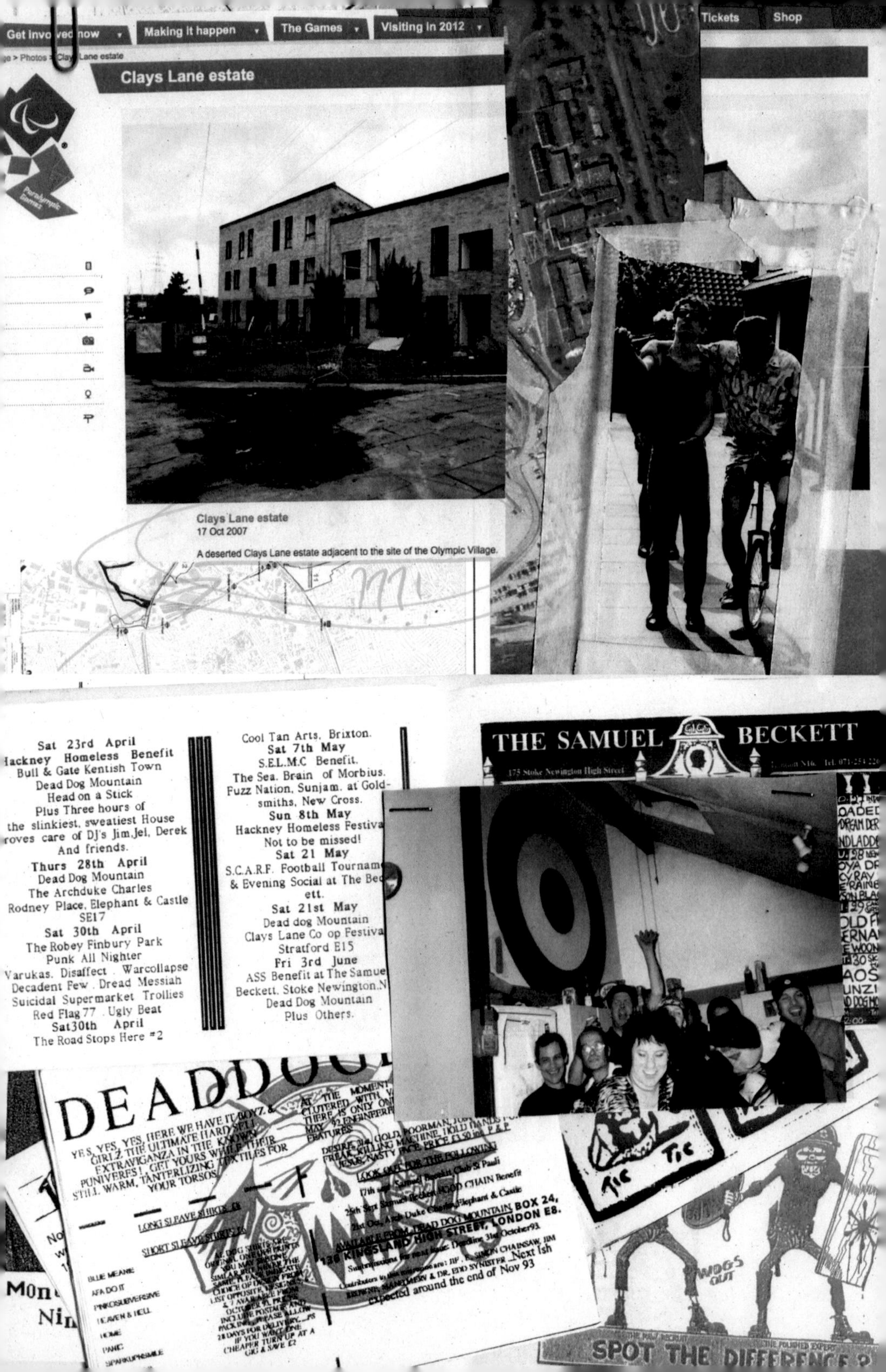
Get involved now
Making it happen
The Games
Visiting in 2012
Tickets
Shop
Clays Lane estate
Paralympic Games
Clays Lane estate
17 Oct 2007
A deserted Clays Lane estate adjacent to the site of the Olympic Village.
Sat 23rd April
Hackney Homeless Benefit
Bull & Gate Kentish Town
Dead Dog Mountain
Head on a Stick
Plus Three hours of
the slinkiest, sweatiest House
roves care of DJ's Jim,Jel, Derek
And friends.
Thurs 28th April
Dead Dog Mountain
The Archduke Charles
Rodney Place, Elephant & Castle
SE17
Sat 30th April
The Robey Finbury Park
Punk All Nighter
Varukas. Disaffect . Warcollapse
Decadent Few . Dread Messiah
Suicidal Supermarket Trollies
Red Flag 77 . Ugly Beat
Sat30th April
The Road Stops Here #2
Cool Tan Arts, Brixton.
Sat 7th May
S.E.L.M.C Benefit.
The Sea. Brain of Morbius.
Fuzz Nation, Sunjam. at Goldsmiths, New Cross.
Sun 8th May
Hackney Homeless Festiva
Not to be missed!
Sat 21 May
S.C.A.R.F. Football Tournam
& Evening Social at The Bec
ett.
Sat 21st May
Dead dog Mountain
Clays Lane Co op Festiva
Stratford E15
Fri 3rd June
ASS Benefit at The Samue
Beckett, Stoke Newington.N
Dead Dog Mountain
Plus Others.
THE SAMUEL BECKETT
175 Stoke Newington High Street
DEADDOG
YES, YES, YES, HERE WE HAVE IT BOYZ & GIRLZ THE ULTIMATE HARD SELL EXTRAVIGANZA IN THE KNOWN PUNIVERES! GET YOURS WHILE THEIR STILL WARM, TANTERLIZING TEXTILES FOR YOUR TORSOS
LONG SLEAVE SHIRTS
SHORT SLEAVE SHIRTS
BLUE MEANIE
AFA DO IT
PINKOSUBVERSIVE
HEAVEN & HELL
HOME
PANIC
SPARKUPHSIBLE
LOOK OUT FOR THE FOLLOWING
AVAILABLE FROM DEAD DOG MOUNTAIN BOX 24, 136 KINGSLAND HIGH STREET, LONDON E8.
expected around the end of Nov 93
Next Ish
TIC TIC
WOGS OUT
SPOT THE DIFFERENCE ?

ALL HANDS ON DECKS
ELVIS HAS JUST LEFT THE BUILDING
SQUEEZING THE EVENINGS PLEASURE GRAPES
SHERMAN AT THE CONTROLS
PHAZEMASTER J (TRANCE MAFIA)
HORTON JUPITER
+ SPECIAL MYSTERY GUEST CAPTAIN SMILE
IN THE MARSHMALLOW LOUNGE : DECKMASTER TRIP
LIVE P.A. BY FALCO
MENTAL FLOSS
PROJECTIONS BY JOE SANTOS
10 DALY COURT, CLAYS LANE STRATFORD
SATURDAY 6TH NOVEMBER 1993
11.30 P.M. ONWARDS UPWARDS INWARDS & OUTWARDS
(DONT FORGET TO BRING THE GAFFA TAPE)
PULLED OUT AT THE LAST MINUTE)
Burning down the
House
6th Nov. 1993 midnite til
1, 2, 9 & 10 Daly Ct. Clays Lane, Stratford
4 Sound Systems - DJ's
Kicking off with Fireworx at 11pm

CLAYS LANE CLOSE
18 - 30 4 Bed

[illegible]AT IS A HOUSING CO-OPERATIVE?

[illegible]ousing Co-operative is different from other types of Housing such [illegible] Council or privately owned or Rented property because it operates [illegible] the premises of <u>COMMON OWNERSHIP</u>, this means that <u>YOU</u> are [illegible]sponsible for the upkeep and maintenance of your home as well as that [illegible] the Co-operative.

[illegible] you move into your room you will be required to purchase two £1.00 [illegible]res, and only then will you be a <u>Full Member of Clays Lane Housing</u> [illegible]<u>operative.</u> All members in the Co-op have an equal say in how the [illegible]e is run, and each member is expected to play a part in the Co-op. [illegible] levels are kept low because the members of the Co-op do much of [illegible] work that a private landlord would do such as rent collecting,

Clays Lane Housing Measurements
floor area, volumes & window areas
floor area
volume
Total
P-Person
Total
P-Person
Total
4 Person House
Bedroom
36·04
9·01
Kitchen & Sitting
16·60
4·15
6·72
1·68
2·01
0·50
10·37
2·59
17·92
3·77
25·89
12·94
9·02
46·32
23·16
3·82
1·91
8·78
4·39
2·77
1·38
6·57
3·18
1·53
0·76
3·51
1·57
33·72
16·86
90·87
Wire
A newsletter for the Clays Lane Community
Issue 15
February 2002
IS THIS THE BEGINNING OF THE END?
Security of tenure
Allocation policy
Co-op living
Maintenance
Management
Finance
Personal control
Ideology
Choice
Support and mutuality
Existing issues
Co-operative living
Sense of Community
Unique character
Clays Lane
3823
POLICE

ondon was successful in its bid
on and are supportive of the broad endeavour.
NCES OF CPO FOR CLAYS LANE RESIDENTS
members instructed the Executive Committee, prior to the transfer of
the task of gaining accommodation suitable for a group of people who
continue in some kind of co-operative endeavour or relationship. Clays
community, as with any community there are similarities and there are
s, these characteristics are the strengths to which the Office of the Deputy
nister refers when it talks about sustainable communities.
ane residents are being placed in the position of taking an unreasonable
the cost of the enforced move. These costs are not only financial, though this
nsideration; they are also transgressions of our rights under Article 1, Article 6
rticle 11 of the Human Rights Act and are noted in our objections to the
removal from our homes
ulsory Purc
concomitant
s of freedom
d to make g
believe th
tremely adv
sident and C
At the behest
survey of the
group that m
move as a gro
to move as a g
undertaken b
FAIR DEAL
FOR
YS
AYS
ANE
WANTS
ITS
OUSING
CLAYS LANE
THE REAL
OLYMPIC
VILLAGE
NO G
FO
THE L
KEEP YOUR
PROMISES
LDA!
Jason Prior of EDAW explained that the residential impact would be relatively small.
He explained that the Clay Lane Estate in Stratford had been placed in danger but
there are preliminary plans to move it into Stratford City or accommodate it in the
Olympic village. He also said the same of some student accommodation in the area.
He also noted that there were two separate communities of travellers in Hackney an
Newham who would both require new sites to be found for them.
More crucially Gareth Blackall of the LDA explained that 350 local businesses woul
potentially have to be moved by the plans. He explained that these were being
riorities of the LDA were to tr
vay area, but failing that, they
fort had been made to ensure
here would be absolute
o be close to certain
table, there would inevitably
sed Olympics.

Scenes from Public Consultations

MARTIN SLAVIN

The Games are promoted by a large-scale publicity offensive which overplays the beneficial outcomes of the project as a "catalyst for regeneration". It promises a positive and widespread boost to the local urban economy in the sectors of employment, tourism, construction, housing, transport, sports, leisure and culture. But as the government's own *Game Plan* report suggests, these benefits turn out to be marginal at best, mainly transient, hugely expensive and often negative:

> We conclude that the quantifiable evidence to support each of the perceived benefits for mega events is weak. The explicit costs of hosting a mega event should be weighed very carefully against the perceived benefits when a bid is being considered, especially given the high risks attached. The message is not: 'don't invest in mega events'; it is rather: 'be clear that they appear to be more about celebration than economic returns'.[1]

By reading about the impact of the Olympics in previous host cities it becomes clear that this mega-event follows consistent and evolving forms of implementation which continue to marginalize and exclude the more disadvantaged and insecure members of local urban populations with the least access to social capital.

In this context public consultation turns out to be a shallow charm offensive; a gaggle of professionals trying to persuade people that their plans will cleverly solve chronic problems of local underdevelopment and neglect that have taken decades to arrive at their present condition. Focused consultations have taken place with local groups affected by relocations. Responses from them varied from indifference through positive engagement to hostility. Among other things, members of groups such as the Clays Lane Estate residents, the Travellers, the Eastway Users Group and the Manor Gardens Allotments felt that their expressed needs and positive suggestions were misunderstood and/or ignored; that Olympic development professionals were working to an inflexible agenda; and that agreed outcomes were not adequately delivered.

I have taken photographs at several of these public consultation events. The captions give details of these encounters.

Kevin Sugrue, Chief Executive of development consultants Renaisi, urges Hackney Wick residents to grasp the business opportunities which the Olympics will bring. 31 May 2006

Members of Hackney Marsh Users Group questioning Hackney Council staff who are promoting the Olympic project at a Hackney Wick consultation. 31 May 2006

Anne Woollett (back to camera) of Hackney Marsh Users Group questioning Richard Caborn, Minister for Sport (centre). Her critical attitude towards the broken promises not to use Public Open Space on Hackney Marshes for the Olympics displeases Caborn's ministerial aide (far right) and Meg Hillier MP for Hackney South and Shoreditch (left).

The Planning Inspector in session at the Olympic Compulsory Purchase Order Public Inquiry. 1 Aug 2006.

I submitted my objection about impacts on those with privately rented homes to the Olympic Compulsory Purchase Order Inquiry based on my paper "Displacement of Private Tenants". To which I received the following response from David Rose: "I am not convinced that the experiences of former Olympic cities around the world, with different social contexts, administrative and regulatory mechanisms and specific characteristics, has any material bearing in anticipating social outcomes in the Lower Lea Valley. There is no direct evidence to support the proposition; and the LDA has taken account of the experience of other host cities.
Here the actions of the LDA are supported at all levels of Government and one of the lasting benefits of the Games will be the provision of a significant number of affordable housing units. Any pressures on land values and accommodation, arising from the Games, have to be considered in the context of the very substantial benefits that the project will bring, not least; improvements to the environment; enhanced community facilities; more efficient infrastructure; and increased employment opportunities to complement the new housing provision."[2]

Planning Decisions Office. Julian Cheyne of Games Monitor looking at maps of the London Olympic site in the Olympic Delivery Authority Planning Office in Stratford. 14 Feb 2007

"Three Games Monitor romantics paid a visit to the ODA Planning Decisions Team office in Burford Road, Stratford on St Valentine's Day [2007]. We wanted to view the new Olympic Planning Application which is contained in 53 document folders containing hundreds of individual documents, plans, drawings, etc, numbering in excess of 10,000 pages. It is difficult to determine the exact number of documents from the website as many refer to different aspects of the application. The documents should soon be available to the general public in a set of dvds at a cost of £25 plus postage and packaging or in hard copy at a purchase price of £500.

We were shown into a kind of short corridor the size of a walk-in cupboard, with a couple of bookcases, a small table, two chairs and a small counter on one wall. Another planning Valentino was already studying a set of documents when we arrived.

ODA PDT staff were helpful if slightly embarrassed by the short, narrow space we were jammed into. We were told that originally this area was supposed to include a neighbouring corridor but this had been disallowed on health and safety grounds. No other rooms were available."[3]

Reg Parrott (L) and Bill Colley talk about how best to deal with their forthcoming eviction from Manor Gardens Allotments. 2 July 2006

Julie Sumner challenges Gareth Blacker (right), head of Land Acquisition at the London Development Agency about the reasons for demolishing the unique site of Manor Gardens Allotments. 25 Nov 2006

Tree Nursery Consultation Anne Woollett of Hackney Marsh Users group looking at plans for the new Travellers site on Hackney Marsh. She is trying to discover how many trees are to be cut down to accommodate this development.

Local Councillor Christine Boyd telling Katy Andrews from Walthamstow that she should not be expressing her criticisms of the Olympics at a Hackney Wick consultation.

Sceptical listeners at a "Your Games, Have Your Say" PR event in Hackney. A plan of the Olympic site lies on the table.

Westfield Poster. Stratford shoppers trying to make sense of the recent view of construction continuing behind the hoarding. 3 Jan 2010

Athletes to Zucchini:
An A–Z for Manor Gardens Allotments

JULIETTE ADAIR

A is for athletes, architects and aspiration. On 6 July 2005 the London Olympic bid is announced to have succeeded. There is dancing in the streets. Lots of people are happy. An urban wasteland, a toxic site, will be regenerated. There will be new transport, new energy and wonderful new sports facilities. Property prices will shoot up. This is a cause for dancing. In particular it will be good for local kids. It will inspire them. The world's athletes will be coming to Hackney. Perhaps there will be a local hero(ine). That would be something.

And for allotments. The next morning, at Manor Gardens Allotments, Hackney, Hassan is making an omelette. He picks chives and marjoram to flavour it and throws rice to the pigeons and the magpie, which watches from the fence. His friend, Reg, brings spinach and some ripe tomatoes. Together they chop the veg and put out some plates on the table under the vine-covered arbour. As Hassan starts to cook the egg, Julie arrives from the plot next door. They do not speak as usual. Hassan throws the egg shells on the ground and the birds peck at them.

Have you heard the news?

B is for bombs, bridge, and bulldozer. The number 30 bus had its roof blown off. The Hackney bus. Hassan listens to the news on a radio powered by a car battery. He came to London from Cyprus. He does not wish to live with violence again. Every day he cooks lunch for his friends, and some extra in case there are visitors.

To get to the allotments you turn left off Waterden Road just after the bus depot. There are two gates. You have to unlock and relock each one behind you. The second is high and laced with barbed wire. No parking, it says, including Sunday. Then you cross the bridge. The River Lea flows underneath it, its banks black and printed with the feet of moorhen and mallard. Sometimes there are swans or cormorants and, just occasionally, the blue flash of a kingfisher's wing.

On the far side of the bridge is another kind of world. Bluebells and later red hot pokers surprise you with colour in the high grass. The old gravelled track has grass down the centre. You can leave your bike in the hedge and no one will take it. The birdsong and the wind in the plum trees along the bank and the wide sky, all these things and something else: the air of quiet industry, the sound of a spade hitting a stone as it is sunk into the earth, the smell of a bonfire. A place distant in time and space is brought into the present here.

Manor Gardens Allotments is on the east marshes in Hackney. It is right in the middle of the proposed site for the 2012 Olympics. It is to be levelled to make way for a concrete footpath: a glittering white motorway for pedestrians entering the Olympic Village. I am to be given a plot and a mission to make it as beautiful as possible in the time left. Perhaps, then, it will be just a little harder to bulldoze.

B is also for blossom and beating the bounds. In spring the plum trees which completely cover the steep bank down to the river are covered in blossom. The season is short. I missed it, just catching the last blooms on the last tree. Perhaps I will get to see it next year. It will be the last chance. The London Development Agency (LDA) is planning to take ground level right down to the water: it's about twenty feet, perhaps more. The plum trees will go, every one.

In May, the Green Party encourages people to Beat the Bounds. This is the old ritual of beating with sticks on the margins of common land to reassert the public right to use it. They walk the boundary of the Marshes. It feels poignant now, important and ineffectual in equal measure. This year it rains like it used to – heavy all day. But they still go ahead.

C is for cauliflower and compulsory purchase order. The notice is up on the gate at the back of the allotment. It's a gate out into the wilds of the nature reserve. The grass is already high. There is no sign that anyone makes the effort to undo the wire holding the gate shut or that anyone has a key to the rusty lock. Still the notice is there. Is anyone aware of it? Does it count as Notice? We have to be given notice by the end of April or else it cannot be served until September, the end of the growing season. We have one year from the time notice is served. So it makes all the difference. Everyone is hoping for an extra summer here.

(Later I am told that Reg often goes out that way walking to the bus stop on Ruckholt Road through Bully Point nature reserve. He reports on the number of rabbits in the warren out there. The rabbits seem to be closing in on the allotments as their land is gradually bulldozed and the foxes, normally good at keeping the rabbits in check, have vacated altogether.)

Julie shows me a cauliflower grown by Reg. I take a photo and when I look at the print, I notice how tenderly she holds it – as if it were a small baby and she's moving aside the leaves as you would a blanket hiding a delicate face. What a beautiful cauliflower. The leaves are generous and stiff, the heart clean and firm.

D is for digging. We get our allotment on Easter Monday. It used to be worked by an old man in his 80s called Sam. It's a beautiful plot. The fruit tree is white with blossom that day and old roses climb across the green house roof and over an archway into the plot. I want to say garden, but I don't know if anyone calls a plot a garden. The paint on the fence and the greenhouse is layered: turquoise, lime, dark green. It has an unassuming beauty. It needs a bit of shoring up and the glass in some of the panes and on half of the roof is broken. We pull out the broken panes and put them in a crate to take to the dump later. We replace them with corrugated plastic. I would love to do it in glass, but for such a short time it seems too expensive. We also mend a hole in the roof of the shed. The children spread seeds randomly before we've got the beds ready, but maybe the plants will come up anyway. We dig about half the plot, pulling out clumps of grass that have established themselves amongst the marjoram and wild rose, trying to trace the bindweed deep down and pull it out. We are all happy. Digging makes us content.

E is for eviction.

F is for feverfew, flowers, forage, football and fig trees. When the rain stops and they decide that it is really summer, Hassan and Reg will spread towels over the reclining car seats and lie under the fig tree. For now they prune the lower branches so that one can walk underneath without spearing an eye.

"It's the last time," Hassan mourns. We'll be out by next year.

"And will it be worth planting a new one on the temporary site?," asks Reg.

Fig trees take their time about getting established. Like people.

G is for grow your own food campaign. Reg is famous for growing his lettuces early. He knows a lot about how to grow vegetables, having come here as a boy with his father. Now he is in his 70s. He has had his plot for 53 years. He brings some young lettuce plants for Julie to plant in her plot.

The Mayor, in acknowledging that transporting food over long distances increases greenhouse gases, has promised to support schemes to boost locally produced food. East London is apparently a food desert when it comes to the number of people growing their own. He says, "I want London to set a standard for other cities around the world to follow in reducing its own contribution to climate change. How we deal with food will play an important role in this." Quite. But, Ken, phrases about left and right hands come to mind.

H is for hands, heartsease and harvest.

Mimi Mollica, from the series Manor Garden Allotments, 2007

I is for involvement. Also, identity, immigration and integration.

J is for jerusalem artichokes. It's possible that we have too many cooks. Iona and I plant sunflower seeds along the south-facing fence. Two weeks later there is a row of plants at least a foot high. Wow! I say. They did well. It turns out that our neighbour Ali gave Matt some Jerusalem artichokes and he planted them, having no idea that we had put in the seeds. They will be high and beautiful with nasturtiums sprawling at their feet. "Fartichokes," says Matt – which the children love.

K is for kite flying and kohl rabi.

L is for laurel and lammas land. At the front of our plot, among the Chinese lanterns and the mombretia, a laurel has sprouted. I wonder whether to pull it out. If I don't, in a short time it will overwhelm all the other plants and even the fence. The Olympic plant will be stamped out in gold, silver and bronze to decorate the winners. And in this guise it will dominate this plot whether or not I pull it out now.

One of the places the LDA is thinking of moving us to in on Lammas Land in Waltham Forest. Lammas Land is land held in trust by the council for public use. The new Lammas Land Defence Committee has formed to protect the marshes from changes of use. No one would win from moving the allotments onto this land. Apart from the fact that the proposed new site is currently polluted with asbestos and rubble from the Second World War, our move there would be temporary. Open space which is currently a wonderful green amenity for everyone would be lost while its value as allotments is limited as well.

L is also for lollo rosso, leeks, lemon balm, larkspur and list. Julie sends me a list of all the vegetables, flowers, herbs and wildlife that she has on her plot. Such diversity on one small patch.

M is for muck. At one time Hackney was crammed with horses. There have been large stables in the area for hundreds of years. The Lea Valley Riding School sometimes takes manure up to the allotment in trailers and gives it out for free. I was tempted to put this under "U is for urban regeneration", because what better symbol is there of recycling, reuse and reinvigoration? Muck into veggies and harmonious multiculture. Certainly more productive than a concrete path. It puts me in mind of line from a poem by WB Yeats – surely the laureate of the plot holder – "Love has built his mansion in the place of excrement." For the next line, see under "S is for sheds".

N is for newts and nature reserve. On the far side of the allotments is Bully Point nature reserve. It is a remarkably peaceful, litter free and relaxing place. Mown paths allow one to wander through it and admire its wildness. There has always been a pond there with a large population of Great Crested Newts. When the Stratford/Channel Tunnel rail link was built, the pond had to be moved. Great care was taken and English Nature's guidelines for relocating these protected animals were followed. A grant was obtained and volunteers mobilised to do the work.

What will happen now? I have not, as yet, heard what the LDA plans to do with the newts. Will there be another nature reserve established? Will English Nature's (extensive) guidelines be followed this time?

O is for open days. The open day in May is wet wet wet. It rains hard, almost non-stop all afternoon. Still, nearly 100 people come. Lots of people have made food using produce from their plots. Elif makes traditional Turkish börek: a pancake cooked on a metal plate using spinach and spring onions. There are barbeques and cakes and herbal teas. The local paper reports how the visitors are amazed that it is all free. The atmosphere is warm and relaxed despite the weather.

Matt has got a generator and set up his telly and DVD in the community shed – for the purpose of showing a film made by St Etienne about Stratford and Hackney, and featuring Manor Gardens, called *What Have You Done Today, Mervyn Day?* It shows an area rich in history but a bit of a ghost town. There is a shot of the bridge to Manor Gardens over the River Lea and close ups of some sunflowers, but no shots of people. It is beautiful but elegiac. I feel that it kills off the allotment community prematurely. Our next open day is on 2 July 2006. This time we have food cooked by the Moro restaurant owner, Sam Clark, who is also a plot holder. The plots will be that much more luscious than they were in May.

And omelettes. The LDA told us: to make an omelette you have to break eggs. This community is one of the eggs.

P is for pathways, perpetuity and peas. My daughter, who is six, doesn't like peas. Or she didn't until Sunday. She moans about going up to the allotment, but we persist. We take some fish with us to barbeque and go to see what the hot weather has done to the plants. As soon as we arrive, she is excited. Everything has grown so much since we last came up – and she hasn't seen it since the open day in May. Spinach, beetroot, sunflowers and calendula are all doing wonderfully. Our sole surviving pumpkin has quadrupled in size and seems rabbit-proofed in its water-bottle tube.

She suddenly claims to have planted everything herself and no-one wants to contradict. We find some strawberries. The strawberries really were planted by the children just after Easter when we first got the plot. Now there is a small bowlful of ripe berries: the first fruits, literally, of her labours. And then there are peas. We have a crop of about a dozen mange tout. For beginning veggie gardeners, this is exciting in itself.

"I'm going to take some round to Julie," Iona says.

On the allotment, a six year old can roam alone. The joy of this is felt all round. A few minutes later, she returns, twice triumphant. One, she has found the way to Julie's plot and back. Two, she has tasted peas fresh from the pod – and loved them. Julie has made her a present of a good handful of pods. Iona carefully opens one each for us and eats the rest herself.

Q is for quiet.

R is for river, reed bed, restaurants and robins. A robin is nesting in an old dustbin on Adile's plot. One by one we creep in to look at the chicks. The mother follows Adile around because she does so much weeding and turning the earth. Hassan nick-names the bird Adile.

Now the six chicks are flown but she still takes food to them in the tree.

S is for sheds, seed swapping, and the speaker of Hackney. An unsympathetic eye saw Manor Gardens as little better than a shanty town. Our sheds are colourful and composed of reclaimed timbers and other materials that no-one else considered useful. Each one is different; some, indeed, are held together by little more than faith and the plants they support. But this is what the French collage artists called bricolage: things put together in an immediate, trial and error way – creative and resourceful. We are bricoleurs; we are sole and whole because we are rent.

T is for toxic, tree nursery, toads and treading. I have heard that Hackney Tree Nursery is also threatened by the Olympic upheavals. The travellers' site on Waterden Road may be relocated there. Clearly, a new site must be found, but on green marsh land? And where will the tree nursery be allowed to put down its roots again?

U is for urban regeneration and urtica.

V is for villages.

W is for wheat, walking and the Wick. Ali tells me about his first gardening joy. His grandfather had a farm in northern Cyprus. All the ploughing was done with oxen – everything by hand. When Ali was five his grandfather gave him a little bag of wheat and let him plant it himself. He dug the ground and raked out the rows. Then he threw down the wheat. He gestures now, showing me how abandoned he was. He covered over the soil and went back to Nicosia for the winter with his family.

The next spring he returned.

"I was amazed," he says. "The plants were so high, I got lost in them."

They harvested and ground the corn into flour. They made cracked wheat – bulghar – and bread. For several months the family ate the food that five year old Ali had grown.

His plot hints at his early experience. It is teeming. Among the potatoes and onions, Jerusalem artichokes, carrots and everything else is a profusion of self-seeded fennel and poppies, and a mass of fragrant coriander. Ali's sister-in-law also has a plot and he often helps her when she's too busy to get up there. He is still feeding the family. In the week he drives a lorry transporting biscuits. Sometimes he brings Jammy Dodgers for tea.

Albert is 86 and has lived all his life on Hackney Wick. His dad sold fish on a stall at Ridley Road market. When he was six his mum sent him from the Wick up to the market to do the shopping. He paid for the groceries in fish from his dad's stall. He got two large bags full, heavy things like potatoes, and set off home. But the buses were on strike. Instead of telling his dad about this, he walked. It's a good way from the market to Hackney Wick – I'm not sure of miles; they always seem difficult to calculate in a city – but for a six year old it was a marathon. I wonder if the strike he remembers was the General Strike in 1926. The timing would be right. For Albert, the story is mainly about the row that his parents had when his dad got home: a row that happened in the 1920s still blazing in Albert's memory.

X is for exodus, excavate, ex.

Y is for yarrow. Milfoil, Thousand Weed, Bad Man's Plaything. And it has many other names. Good for staunching wounds and stopping nosebleeds. Reputed to help with measles and baldness. Also used as snuff.

And youth.

Our Olympic legacy – what will it be? What sort of landscape will we leave and what will it say about our values?

Z is for zucchini. Barbequed by Hassan, one of Rick Stein's food heroes, zucchini concludes this A–Z and leaves a lingering sweetness on the tongue.

Revisiting The Community Shed

THOMAS PAUSZ

Between November 2007 and January 2008 we conducted a series of interviews with Manor Gardens Allotments gardeners in east London. These interviews were made into a self-published limited edition book called *Revisiting The Community Shed*. The gardeners had been evicted from their plots and the allotments demolished to make way for landscaping on the site of the upcoming London Olympics. The initial aim of our questionnaire interviews was to ask for architectural information in view of a physical reconstruction of the "Community Shed" – a self-built centre of democratic dialogue, parties, and afternoon naps which for us constituted a significant example of allotments' vernacular design.

At about the same time, planners and local authorities were also sending questionnaires to the ex-plot owners. These official multiple-choice questionnaires aimed to gather information about the facilities (such as the size of the sheds and plant beds and water points) needed in the new "ready made" site to be *designed for* the gardeners. A critical look at these documents showed that they reduced the history of the disappeared gardens to ground plan dimensions and lists of functional facilities. The formulation of questions implicitly denied the cultural significance of self devised spaces in the city and the unquantifiable losses such as the quality of neighbourly relationships, the international culture of the gardens and an invaluable sense of ownership and belonging.

In these planning documents the reduction of language to a purely factual tool at the expense of its poetical and significant dimensions (memories, wishes) subtly enforced a reduction of the disappeared place to a picket fence around a patch of green: no place in the text boxes for the many stories and anecdotes we had heard about life in the former Manor Gardens. To re-establish the balance we decided to adopt but subvert the format of the written questionnaire to trigger memories about the use of the Community Shed, embedded in its architectural features. Thus we hoped to revive not only the building's shape but also some fragments of the gardeners' experience, and the "psychology" of the place.

The second reduction of the questionnaire format happens when the answers are read and "turned into data" by the administration. It was important to us to avoid this de-personalisation. To try and render the multiple voices and accents of the people we were interviewing in the final book we conducted a typographic experiment, giving all interviewees a specific font devised from their handwriting and what we knew of each "character" interviewed.

FURNITURE INSIDE

What furniture and objects were kept inside the shed?

Table Bench Chairs Bookcase Railway Type Bench

see 18 (furniture)

One table
3 CHAIRS
One SOFA
2 BENCHES WITH LOTS OF CUSHIONS

One table and 4 chairs

Old net curtains, old sofa cushions in brown and orange colour, a table and a few more formal chairs for the committee and a writing desk. A notice board. And quite a lot of junk.

There were some easy chairs & a sofa

Chairs, tables

Chairs, Table

Please describe in detail one piece of furniture of your choice.

Bookcase with 3 faded jigsaw puzzle boxes- a few grubby books and pots, general detritus of years of neglect. Grubby papers in piles

SOFA-BEIGE-3SEATS OLD + COMFORTABLE

seats around the walls

An old squashy sofa with most of outer covering peeled off so you could see the sponge below. It was low with blankets over it: but quite comfy.

Nothing stands out in my mind.

Bonifica

JUDE ROSEN

It is a promise inherent in the earth
that the planted will sprout, the green grow back:
the rubble from the war laid on the back
of the marshes, borne by them in the postwar years,
now hidden beneath grass, visible only
in the foxholes and stripped-back undergrowth.
But now the black poplars, those ancient statues
that mark the city boundaries, are being
blotted out, eleven football pitches cleared
to make way for a mammoth car park.

It is the premise running through the river
that it will flow and flush away
the cumulation of what stays still, cleanse itself
in its ritual daily washing, disperse sawdust
from the mills, and effluent of later industry
renewing the water quality, and sustain
the flight paths of birds and spawning grounds -
glimpse their traces in Grebe Close, Bream Street –
the Lea banks and floodplains, the sponge that keeps
Hackney afloat, damp but inhabited.

It is the claim of land reclamation –
this *bonifica* – that it makes good the land,
removing heavy metals, toxic waste -
radioactive thorium - mining
to remediate, cleaning up no-man's land.
But by clearing Clays' Lane courts and alleyways
they've displaced the transient who lived there long
having found safety on the city edge,
wiped out the cycle track to make way for Sport,
and Manor Gardens' cultivation's gone.

Now they have started work on the language:
a bonifica of words: branding *silver* and *gold*,
London, *summer*, *2012* so a few
can name the city and the date, while those
who make good the waste cannot use these words.
Now they threaten a suit for the offence of writing
fiction: seeking to ban *Olympic Mind Games*,
so the language will be cleaned up, along with the mud
on the tidal sweep of the Lea that will be expunged
with other misfits, and impounded.

A fragment from the Long Poem *Reclamations: Voices and Narratives from the Olympic Zone*

an Stradtmann, from the series Manor Garden Allotments, 2007, Courtesy of Troika Editions

Jessie Brennan, The Cut (Detail), 2011

Jessie Brennan, The Cut (Detail), 2011

Jessie Brennan, The Cut, 2011

Boaters
A Series of Portraits and Short Stories

MAN CHEUNG

Steve, 10 June 2011

Sometimes we know where our lives are heading and how our plans will work out. My own life seemed channelled one way from early on, but the currents that carry us all forward run deep and they run strong.

Our school was the sort where kids had the upper-hand and teachers were not inspired to teach. You could remain uneducated if you tried hard and our class in particular was often held-up as an example to the rest of the school. Like most of my friends, I left at fifteen with no qualifications and started full time as an apprentice carpenter. I was paid £20 per week for three years, which was less than the money paid on the Youth Training Scheme introduced in 1983, but at least my employers let me attend Barnsley Technical College to formalise my training.

Carpentry work paid ok when I qualified, and I soon found more lucrative employment working on new housing sites. People often say to me, "Oh, I would like to be a carpenter", and I answer, "well it was good enough for the son of God", but the truth is carpentry can involve a lot of monotonous repetition and hard work. Try hanging doors all day for four months or knocking 20,000 lost-head nails into flooring every few days, on your knees, and see what you think about carpentry then.

I slowly and painfully adopted my dad's strong work ethic (for dad, work was the defining role a man could have in life) and saved for a deposit on a run-down terrace house in Barnsley (at a time when people like me could actually afford to contemplate owning their own house) and spent the next year renovating it in between jobs. I realised, aged twenty, that I should have tried harder at school as it dawned on me that this was the beginning of the rest of my life.

I fell in love at 24, sold my house, got married and moved away to the sunnier climate in Cambridge where my wife encouraged me to do an Access to Higher Education course. When our relationship ended I returned to Barnsley with the money I'd made from the sale of my first house and bought another run-down terrace house. I spent six months renovating it and six months living in it before letting it and setting off for university halls, where I intended to capitalise on my new academic qualifications. My university choices of Cambridge, Leeds and Keele were based on my idea of kudos, proximity to my home town and a mention on the Alan Partridge show, respectively, that, and an over-riding desire to meet girls and get out of Barnsley.

I got to know plenty of girls at Keele, all of whom I loved in my own ridiculous

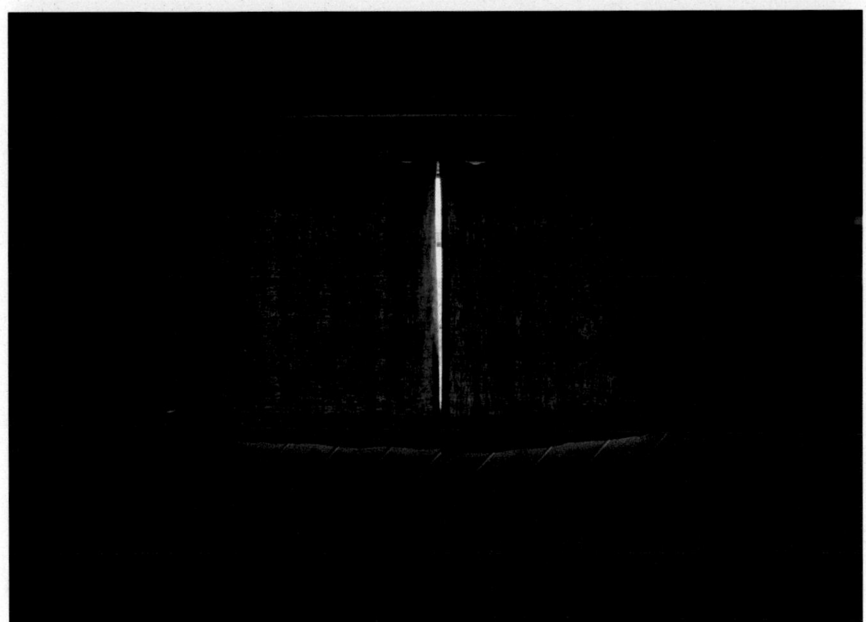

Man Cheung, Steve, From the series Boaters, 2011

way, and in my third year studying history and psychology decided to apply to do a PhD in developmental psychology. I won the PhD place and a graduate teaching assistantship to pay for it and left Keele with a doctorate in psychology.

In the meantime the terrace house I'd let was slowly trashed by a tenant who'd fallen into a serious drug habit. I cleared the house of junk, did the repairs, redecorated and – unwilling to stay in Barnsley or let it out again – sold it before moving to Manchester. I completed a post-doctoral research post working with young children, and then spent a year wondering what to do next. This was the time off I'd promised myself and it turned out to be the most unhappy period of my life, when I drifted pointlessly without purpose from pillar to post.

Soaring property prices meant I could no longer afford a place of my own without a fat mortgage hanging round my neck again; disillusioned with the academic process, I fell back on what I knew and did what I could afford with the money I had. I bought a narrowboat shell, materials and equipment and spent a year fitting out my new home. It was the best year's work I've never been paid for. And unbeknown to me, life cruising the waterways of England turned out to be the best life I could have chosen. I loved the self-sufficient low impact life onboard – it fitted so well with my desire to lead a greener existence.

I began to enjoy the many daily challenges to subsistence I encountered, such as obtaining water, fuel and other services or carrying out the ongoing upkeep required to keep a narrowboat engine and on-board systems running properly. This close, causal contact between what I did and how I lived had been missing before.

You lose certain things when you slow life right down but you gain other pleasures that are surprising, like the bubbles I could feel pushing through the hairs on my body as they fought upwards through long-cooled bath water, or a swan, normally the worst of birds, gently nudging my arm that lolled over the edge of the boat as I lay in the prow in the dark warm summer night.

The countryside is stunning from the canal and you see the best side of the towns and cities you travel through. Two years passed with just me and the ducks and I started to fantasise about travelling the world as I undertook the hard, six-week cruise from Manchester to London, where I intended to sell my boat and get out of England.

When I arrived in London I was amazed to find a vibrant, diverse and friendly community of like-minded boaters cruising the capital's waterways. I had never found a sense of a community like this anywhere I'd lived before. The boaters in London come from all walks of life and many consider themselves river-gypsies. It dawned on me that I had become a river-gypsy too, and that this was another beginning of the rest of my life.

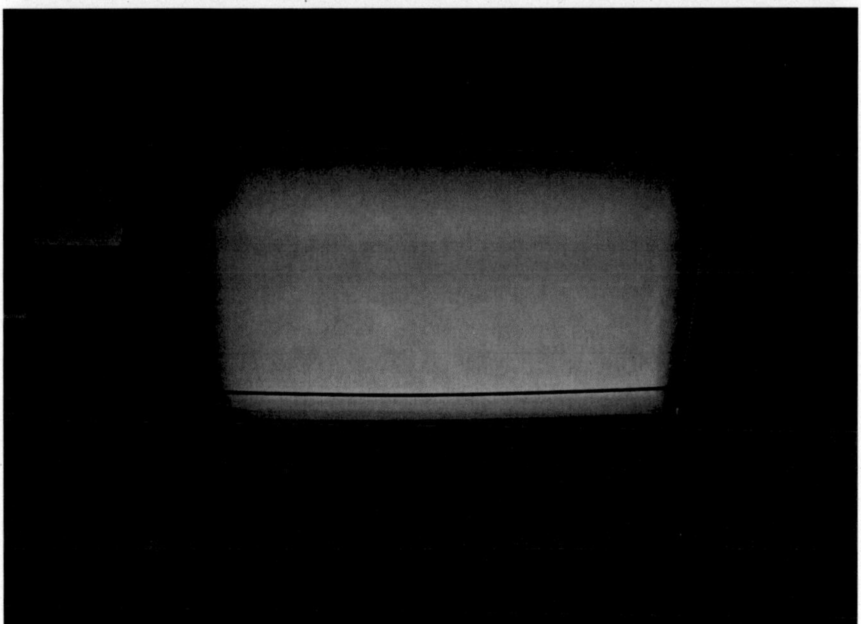

Man Cheung, Rebecca, From the series Boaters, 2011

Rebecca, 23 September 2011

Having lived on a narrow boat for three and a half years I have grown to love and respect the network of canals and rivers across the UK and particularly London. I specifically love the diversity of the people who use the canals, the juxtaposition between urban and rural and the remains of a once bustling and still very evident and important industrial history.

I never welcomed the Olympics to London; I believe such events cost an obscene amount of money for just a few weeks of enjoyment. I understand how the revenue from such events can help boost the economy however is the Olympics the answer? If we did not spend the money building the Olympic site in the first place would we not be better off in the long term? I unfortunately don't know the answer to that.

Something I do know the answer to is that the Olympics arriving in London has resulted in under represented communities being destroyed or at risk of being destroyed. This began with Gypsies and Travellers being forced out of their homes and from the site where the Olympic park now stands. Boaters have since been targeted by British Waterways' introducing new and unreasonable rules to a community who live a quiet and resourceful life on the canals and rivers of London.

Some boats were even used to sell the Olympics in one advert. "Look how diverse VISA and the Olympics are?" said the advert – while the powers that be were actually trying to get rid of and destroy our diverse community.

What will happen to the Olympic site after 2012, will it really be used? I again can't answer these questions and I suppose only time will tell what the 2012 Olympics will really bring to London, however I can say one thing, that my Olympic "journey" so far hasn't been a good or welcome one.

Hackney Cut Enfield Lock

ANDREW BAILES

Footpath Closure: Ground Investigations

...and not those carried out by your psychic geographers, tamed lunatics unleashed to care for *the community. It is sad, to see them go, the encroachment upon a space made public by neglect - "in need of redevelopment" - where amateur fishermen fry burgers on an open fire, pull tiddlers from the River Lea or Lee Navigation. To the east it is being parcelled up, closed-off, bought-out, regardless of any inconvenience; to the west of the river's canal the public investment's corporate shadow buys up and knocks down red brick factory buildings to install great crescents, nine-storey apartment blocks grandstanding, or better, making an amphitheatre of the emptying site, with huge potential views, finding their way into property and* Guardian Weekend *property supplements, magazines. And before the planners, the yellow bulldozers, the cranes: the salaried Graffiti Artists marking territories less a declaration of occupation than an urban echo of the foresters' mark in white paint - this too will be weeded-out, thinned-out - the latest, white teeth in pink gums, pre-empting the chewed bricks of the cement-works, as self-confident and vacuous as a corporate logo: ODC Cyclops. White Hart Field Weekes Field Morris Field Arena Field, where a landscape artist crazed with his own power and influence has employed two bright yellow pneumatic JCB diggers to build a step-pyramid of topsoil, and unbuild and rebuild a step-pyramid of topsoil. Until someone asks them to stop, or asks "why?"*

There is some new bureaucratic consensus that insists that the possibility of an Olympic Park exists, has always existed, beneath the industry-scarred and blitz-cleared landscape, a landscape where a river cannot hold onto its name, slips and shifts identity with the tide, is channelised and abused, finds itself dead-ended and worse, becomes an empty name, goes nowhere. These rivers and roads have been, are being, and will be walked by more ambitious poets, poets with agendas, politics. I am neither for nor against, am merely recording, awaiting further instruction/inspiration. Fictionalising as I fall asleep - the Great Squat; the battle for the Greenway Bridge, Machine-Gunners in Mystic Pill Boxes. Looking for an opportunity to assassinate, again, having missed before: Blair, Bush, Putin. Fuck, even Seb Coe will do, for starters - boyhood hero athlete usurped by Tory today. A dream of occupying a privatised space, not insurmountable but definitively FENCED. Will he approach with caution, tear his trouser-leg on wire-topped wall, trespass? The most likely threat, after Thames Water (the company, not Thames Barrier's failure, inundation): private security, with or without dogs, or the innocent aggression of the burners of stolen mopeds and motorbikes next to the brick-breakers and concrete-makers of the Northern Outfall Sewer/Greenway. Illegitimate car-breakers in training, riders around canal-path and rough-and-ready off-roaders three to a bike, no silencer no helmet. No Hard Hat No Boots. The Independent State of Hackney Wick. We welcome those who seek asylum: be it political, ethical, economic, industrial or plain psychological: Hackney Wick: Welcomes Careful Asylum Seekers. Defensible.

Hackney Cut

Her bob-cut hair barely brushes against her fine sharp nose and she brushes it back against her eyes, a light brown fringe falls back in place. She walks alone, small against the buildings in the City's silence, pulls a dufflecoat collar closely against her exposed nape. It seems empty, the City, though she cannot tell for sure. Behind blinds and curtains noises and movement suggest life. Down by the canal now, small knots of teens light cigarettes, brag into phones and plead for a touch, a small gesture of familiarity - they touch knuckles on greeting and departing, converse in French, in Spanish, in languages carried across from Africa, India. A lone white youth, acned, darts across from a doorway causing her to briefly break stride.

There's nothing happening, as far as Capella can tell. She feels reassured, hopes for continuity. She doesn't know where she walks, whom she may be bound toward, whether all is as she left it. A canal boat passes peacefully down the centre of the Cut. Coots cluck and scurry back to nests under eaves and arches. Ripples pool out and reflect back from kerbstones. Capella breathes in deeply, steps onto the glassy surface and submerges rapidly, the green water closes over the brown strands of her hair.

He waited outside at the tiller as she changed in front of the stove into a check shirt and dungarees, tied the shoulder-straps around her waist as a belt and wrapped her hair in a dry towel. *The Riverboat* captain wants to talk about his life, hauling coal, wood from the canalside, wherever it can be had. More of it and easier to find these days. Talks of using horsepower again, encouraging the take up of more traditional means of transportation. He notices that Capella sleeps, watches her small breasts rise and fall beneath his shirt, tucks a blanket under her chin and steps up the three wooden rungs to the deck, starts the biodiesel engine. Purrs down the quiet waters and under Lea Bridge Road's arch into the evening's welcoming gloom.

Zed Fontema, finding his way back through the part-lit streets, pooled by oily, deep shadows, approaches his Hackney Wick flat crabwise, perched on kerbstones to avoid the small lake formed by a burst water-main at the junction.

The flat was cold, dark. He flicked a match alight and in the flickering darkness lit two rings of his gas stove, looked briefly at the folded laptop computer. His sturdy walking boots sat in the two small pools of their own shadows, oily black from the road loitered in the corners of the room.

The Riverboat was loaded to the gunnels. Coal, mostly, but, Capella discovered later, a large cache of small arms wrapped in oily cloth made up the rest of the cargo. The boat travelled at a steady, sturdy walking-pace, pushing out the fresh popcorn smell of bio-diesel into the air, dirty water back into the canal. Capella would get out and walk on the canalside for an hour or two most days, increasingly, as her relationship with the captain deepened into a comfortable silence, she would indulge in long meaningful reflections, entirely personal to herself, and pass hours in a long-limbed ground-eating reverie.

Zed is walking along the towpath that flanks the River Lee or Lea Navigation. Birds dot the banks of the reservoir, gulls spot the sky which opens out above Walthamstow Marshes, one-hundred and eighty degrees of blue wonder, gull-spotted, louring clouds. He approaches Hackney Wick, where, attached to a lamppost he discovers the following document. With one foot on the kerbstone, one foot in the gutter he crouches at the foot of the lamppost and reads of

> Development in the area bound:
>
> to the north by the Eastway (part), A12 East Cross Route (part) the River Lea, the northern and eastern boundary of East Marsh, New Spitalfields Market, Ruckholt Road and Temple Mill Lane;
>
> to the east by Temple Mills Lane, the Lea Valley Overground Railway Line, land to the east of Leyton Road, Angel Lane, part of the Great Eastern Line until Stratford Regional Station, the Lea Valley Overground Railway Line and a section of the northern part of the Stratford development site;
>
> to the south by part of the northern boundary of the Stratford City development site, the southern section of the rail loop which connects the North London Line and the Great Eastern Line, the main line railway and land on the eastern banks of the Waterworks River, the Greenway (part), High Street Stratford (A11), Rick Roberts Way and including land to the east of Canning Road, west of the North London Line, and south and west of West Ham Station, the land between Bow Back River and Barbers Road and part of the Great Eastern Line;
>
> to the west by the A12 Blackwall Tunnel Northern Approach Road (part) the River Lea and the River Lea Navigation (Hackney Cut) and

> land on the western bank of the River Lea to the east of the A12 East Cross Route.

He continues walking. The startled coots' feet flap lazily, shaking water from beaded grass blades, been-in-the-bath-too-long feet. Woodsmoke from canal boats scents the air, reflects in the oil-stained, litter strewn surface. Two graffitists compete: the pink teeth versus ODC. Zed reserves judgment, allows the Olympic Delivery Authority to decide.

> I give notice that the Olympic Delivery Authority is applying to the Olympic Delivery Authority (as local planning authority) for planning permission for: Application 1 - 07/90010/0UMODA.
>
> The Olympic and Legacy Transformation Planning Application is for development in connection with the 2012 Olympic Games and Paralympic Games and Legacy Transformation involving:
>
> Earthworks to finished levels, sports, leisure and entertainment venues within class D2, (including ancillary service areas); Olympic Cauldron; open space and circulation areas (involving soft and hard landscaping and associated structures); under and over bridges;
>
> Utility structures (including wind turbine, pumping stations, electricity substation, telecommunication masts), Channel Tunnel Rail Link cooling box, an Energy Centre (including a Combined Cooling and Heating Plant and biomass boilers);
>
> Construction of buildings for use within classes A1, A2, A3, A4, A5;
>
> Construction of a building for use as the International Broadcast Centre/Main Press Centre and Multi Storey Car Park;
>
> Erection of a perimeter enclosure for the period of the works;
>
> Temporary coach parking areas.

It is nearing completion, nearing the time when temporary coaches will permanently occupy both pavements outside the flat, but Zed is not bothered by this, aware that the action has moved to where the International Broadcast Centre catches the mild morning sunshine as Capella Byrne clings to the top of a container of low grade radioactive waste, on its way from Sizewell to Sellafield trundling along the North London Line past Stratford, below Homerton and through the gapped sycamore trees that canopy the railway line.

The pantogaph sparks above her arched back as Capella's spread arms grasp cold steel, evaporating the dew that falls from the overhead lines. She brings in one hand, then the other, clutching them to her chest a moment and then breathing sharply into her net driving gloves to resume her hold. The train takes a corner, and the scarred Olympic landscape careens into view, swinging beneath her as the train gains pace.

Two cars behind, Broom, *The Riverboat* captain, clutches anxiously at an emptying bottle of vodka, crouching beneath the steel canister containing the high-grade, Top Secret Government Documents Midnight Express stuff. He thinks he can hear its half-life atomic clock ticking.

> In the period following the Games, the Legacy Transformation Phase involving:
>
> Partial deconstruction, demolition, dismantling and construction of venues to form legacy sports, leisure and entertainment venues, servicing facilities, car parking, vehicular access and ancillary works for use within classes D1 and D2; and of over and under bridges and buildings and structures (including telecommunication masts);
>
> Engineering earthworks involving the reconfiguration of levels, and the laying out to provide permanent public open space (including outdoor sports facilities, play facilities, cycle circuit and ancillary facilities), allotments and sites for future development; and
>
> Erection of perimeter enclosure.

The undoubted benefits of perimeter enclosure in defining public open space became clearer to Capella as the train hurdled under and over bridges, she free now to sit upright, the pantograph having been lowered, a powered rail serving the same purpose beneath the train. The electricity that drove the train shut off and it rolled to a halt. No driver leapt from the cab, there being no driver. For Reasons of Security. Capella uncoupled the last few empty carriages and the driving carriage. She and Broom pushed them a few yards away from the Keystone. Then both sat and looked at it. Capella's phone rang.

Connections to host utilities.

Zed had had to wait until the lights went out, too long, until he'd known for sure that he could leave the flat and couldn't do shit about it now no matter what happened. That felt better, after so long, to be without the nagging feeling that every action contained, implicitly enacted the moment of its own destruction. This, at least, felt better than that. He had switched the power off, and Broom and the Chick had either coasted their deadly cargo to the point on their map marked X, or they hadn't. With a piece of luck, he would be near enough to see it happen, or to be one of the very few to know what it was when it happened to them. Or

> Bulk earthworks to finished levels and associated remediation (including stockpiling of materials); demolition of existing buildings and structures (including areas of hard standing); clearance of vegetation and felling of trees; and, the erection of perimeter enclosure (Detailed Planning Application).

It would be over before anybody knew of it, at all and forever. Though dusk was falling, it wasn't all dark from the Greenway. Zed topped the Victorian Outfall Sewer, crossed the bridge at Old Ford Locks, and ducked into the Pill Box.

> Notice is hereby given that the London Development Agency ("the Agency") on 2 March 2007 made a general vesting declaration under section 4 of the Compulsory Purchase (Vesting Declarations) Act 1981 ("the Act") vesting the land described in the Schedule to this notice ("the Land") in themselves as from the end of the period of 28 days from the date on which the service of the notices required by section 6 of the Act is completed. The Agency will in due course tell you the date on which the service of the notices was completed.

Zed pulled down the periscope and peered through it. He could see over the cleared land from the Greenway clear to City River, where it ducks around to meet the River Lee or Lea. He could see the raised railway, and the team pushing borrowed sleepers up underneath the steel cylinder containing the spent uranium fuel, rolling it gently in its cradle then swiftly steering it onto a second cradle formed by the pneumatic arms of two commandeered JCBs. Zed mused again upon just how flexible your unregistered illegal immigrant labour is when presented with the concept of overtime.

> On the first day after the end of the period referred to in the first paragraph of this notice (the "Vesting Date") the Land, together with the right to enter upon and take possession of it, will vest in the Agency.

The two JCBs turned in perfect unison, their poisonous cargo swung smoothly out and down onto a smaller version of the railway carriage that Capella had ridden in on, which ran on narrow-gauge tracks parallel to but lower than the raised North London Line. Zed lost sight of it then, but visualised in his mind's eye the carriage being swiftly propelled into the vast underground spaces where five decades worth of electrical cable and machinery had been hurriedly hidden.

Olympic Moorings

Downstream from Enfield Lock Boris's Erection pushes itself from the polluted mud that bounds the Olympic Cauldron. Capella is thinking of that, and of the poisonous cargo she had helped to unload there months before Lakshmi Mittal even mentioned the steel, his desire to put his name to something more profound and permanent than Queen's Park Rangers' brief Premier League sojourn.

Standing on the narrow deck of *Swiss Cheese* Broom pulls on the throttle again and she swings out gradually from the flooded dry dock. All the other boats face south, their engines ticking over and their crews saying their farewells, see-you-soons as they pull into the centre of the river and head downstream, toward the Olympic site. It is the day before the Opening Ceremony. There is something in the air, hints and suggestions. Broom wants nothing of this, he has tried his best to avoid all knowledge. He still feels that his fingers have been burned, that he can excuse himself one more protest, another demonstration. He deserves a quiet life. Some of the boaters are seeking sanctuary on the Stort. Broom hopes to follow them, to risk *Swiss Cheese*'s uncertain engine.

> Given the likelihood of exceptionally high volumes of boats travelling southwards along the Grand Union Canal and Paddington Arm into London, we envisage the need for a form of controlled zone for at least all or part of the period mentioned above. This is likely to run from Little Venice through the Regent's and Hertford Union Canals and for some distance up the River Lee Navigation, probably to around the Lea Bridge Road area.

A Thames Tug fronts the Diversionary Force. They are approaching Lea Bridge Road. The cutter on the front of the Tug's steel-grey battleship's prow, a scissor intended to close upon the below-water barriers and propeller entanglers, is carefully lowered into the water, adding its own small wake to the Tug's wake, a great shifting wall of green water.

Two narrowboats travelling in tandem fire the first of their emergency flares. Red smoke drifts from the riverside where one of the canisters has lodged, another smokes and splutters in the canal, having bounced from the high brick side of Lea Bridge Road.

> Casual mooring will not be permitted along the towpaths within the controlled zone. This is to keep space available for operational, patrol and police boats, and obviously to facilitate boat movement or to keep the stretch clear for safety and security reasons.

The patrol and police boats swing into action a little too late, nudging the steel running strakes of the Tug's sides and bouncing harmlessly off. The lookout on the mid-deck of *Diversion Ends* has spotted the armed police contingent overlooking the bridge. There is no sign of anyone going for their guns as yet. The visored cops peer into the smoky red gloom below, deafened by the roar of the Tug's powerful diesel engine running at full throttle, exhaust fumes and flare-smoke choke them. A push and a roar and the boats are through and under the bridge.

The Diversionary Force turns into the Bow Back Rivers, having fought their way through Old Ford Locks. They would never have made it but for the covering fire offered by the machine-gunners in the Pill Box. They had kept the bridge overlooking the locks clear until the last boat had passed through. The lookout on *Diversion Ends* saw the hand-grenade tossed in there by a uniformed soldier, the burst of smoke, flame and rubble. There could have been no survivors.

The floating barricades and concealed entanglements that reach across and beneath the duckweed-green surface of the water underneath the towpath's steel footbridge drifted apart in the wake of the heavy Tug's steel scissor. They have had to deploy the water cannon, firing duckweed and canal water at the armed groups on the banks, then sheltering inside the reinforced steel of their engine rooms as bullets ricochet around them, breathing teargas through their neckerchiefs and sleeves. Capella had better deliver her ultimatum soon.

In a few minutes Zed's Yacht has sunk into the watery tomb of the Thames Lock at St Katherine's Dock and Zed is watching the great weed-encrusted gates swing open onto an acre of angry Thames. Out there he can see the ragged Royal Regatta that fights to keep formation as the buffets from a strong southerly gale spit unseasonal hail in their faces, as the waves and their own wakes break about their bows. A few damp streamers and spluttering braziers, a brace of soggy courtiers are all that mark their successful arrival, their having travelled afloat all the way from Windsor to the Tower Of London where Pomp and Circumstance await their Prince. Zed pushes on the throttle and the Yacht steams in to engage the enemy's flagship.

> We have several demands. We also wish to convey a sincerely intended warning. We have concealed a container of spent uranium fuel rods beneath the Northern Outfall Sewer, and we have planted enough explosives to disperse the material over an area broadly defined by the perimeter enclosure of the Olympic Site. We have no wish to use this device, and offer it only as a surety of the seriousness of our demands. As a consequence of this, a video file describing the type of device, its location and the means of defusing it will be sent in a gesture of goodwill, once we have secured a suitable exchange for this information.

Peter Green is sweating in the driving seat of the Olympic Services truck as he listens to Capella's voice through the mobile phone link that Zed has set up alongside the Yacht's public address system. The Royal Barge should be broadside to the Yacht now. From the Barge's high white side, has all gone to plan, the young Prince in all his finery is about to be lowered into the wild river in a lifeboat, all alone.

> We ask that you hand over the heir to the throne. He will be kept in one of the state rooms on this vessel, which will then withdraw to a secure location, from where we will issue our demands. Please do not attempt to approach this vessel, either through force or through subterfuge, while we make this exchange.

He pulls at the sodden armpits of his Olympic Services sweatshirt. He wants to take the damn thing off. It's too hot. No-one's around.

He had checked the truck over, climbed in and started it, pulled it out of the shed where the load of mining explosives had been waiting for him and driven through the perimeter enclosure with the most perfunctory nod from the armed guards. The courtyard next to the Greenway bridge had emptied at the first sight and sound of the Diversionary Force's attack. Peter had parked the truck, as planned, beneath the bridge, then sat back to listen.

He looks over his shoulder at the pallets of neat, innocent wooden boxes before pulling the tight sleeves down over his hands and reaching inside the sweatshirt, his bare fore-arms running against the sweat pooling above his belly. His elbows push out and as he pulls the neck hole up and over the end of his nose his left elbow jogs the detonator behind the headrest of his seat. He had hoped that the thing had not been wired in.

Henrietta Williams,
Olympic Village,
2012

AFTERMATHS

VISIONS AND PROMISES OF "LEGACY" HAVE BEEN WIDELY USED TO LEGITIMISE THE 2012 GAMES. THESE TELESCOPED CONCEPTIONS OF THE FUTURE ARE IN STARK CONTRAST WITH THE DAILY EXPERIENCES AND EXPECTATIONS OF THOSE LIVING UNDER THE OLYMPIC SHADOW. IN THIS SECTION, DYSTOPIAN RENDERINGS OF THE FUTURE ARE JUXTAPOSED WITH CRITICAL ENGAGEMENTS WITH THE TANGIBLE, IRREPARABLE LEGACIES ALREADY APPARENT IN THE AREA SURROUNDING THE OLYMPIC PARK - THE NEGLECTED PERIPHERY.

Future Orientations:
Utopia and the 2012 Olympics

ROWENA HAY AND DUNCAN HAY*

Not far from here at the base of another tower, people sit watching screens amongst piles of mouldering paperbacks. The street outside is empty, and a bruised sky threatens sleet. A group of young men and women are rushed through to the lifts and ferried in excited ones and twos to the viewing platform 22 floors above. From there you can see the whole site: a network of cranes, gantries and unfinished concrete that stretches away into the distance. Inside, computer-generated renders hang on the walls; a white surface curves organically into a pale blue sky, touching the ground only lightly as if tethered merely by the curtain of reflective glass that cascades from its underside. The prow describes a parabola that is pent with energy, whilst in the foreground, their shadows casting crisp shadows on the pale stone, people stroll around a reed-edged pool, as if unaware that at any moment the whole gull-like structure might flow, extend, flex its pinions, and take off.

The 2012 Olympics represent a radical change in the urban fabric of east London. In the official discourse of marketing materials, economic projections and developers' master plans, the project is presented as one which will lead to positive change in the area, and which promises a better future for the city. Such an ambitious redrawing of the London landscape must inevitably entail contradictions and ambiguities: the bright, aseptic future of the architects' computer models contains a strongly utopian undertow, which contrasts strongly with not only the reality of the Olympic developments, but also the visions of the future that have served to shape the area over the preceding decades.

In this essay we focus on Holden Point, a 22-storey tower block of sheltered housing on the Stratford side of the Olympic site, which became the location of the Olympic viewing platform. It has played a role in creating a particular image of the Olympic site for visitors and residents and embodies the starkness of the contrast between the huge investment in the Games and the lack of investment in the deteriorating estates that surround it, and which we built on the basis of the promise of a better life for their prospective inhabitants.

Newham's Olympic Park Viewing Gallery was built in 2005 as part of London's bid for the 2012 Games. The gallery, which sits on top of Holden Point, 64 meters off the ground, offers a panoramic view of the Olympic Park. From this height one can't help but admire the sheer scale and ambition of this vast construction project.

On cue, an aerial photograph of the construction zone flashed onto the screen. At the centre, emerging from a nest of scaffold, cranes and trusses, was the unmistakable oval of the main stadium. From this vantage point it resembled a broken eggshell, dropped from orbit into the mud. "As many of you will know", Johnston continued, "as part of the data-gathering activities that are a routine aspect of the LOC's activities, our scientists have been conducting a magnetic survey of the site by low-orbit satellite. This process was finally completed last month, and this – he said, advancing the slide – was the result." The photograph was replaced by a meshwork of glowing blue lines resembling a topographic map. For the most part, the lines were equidistant, but close to where the stadium was on the previous slide, the contours changed and the lines were closely knotted. At the bottom of the image were the words: "STRATFORD MAGNETIC ANOMALY-ONE (S.M.A.-1)"; across the top right, in crude, red capitals, "CLASSIFIED".

The atmosphere of expectation in the briefing room was palpable. Even to the unscientific eyes of the assembled press, it was obvious that something unusual was happening to the planet's magnetic field.

The success of London's winning bid rested on the notion that it would have a lasting impact on "the communities" of East London, "who will be touched most directly" by the Games.[1] The Olympic village will not only provide a bed for 17,000 athletes and officials during the games but a "lasting legacy of essential new housing for East London" with 2800 new homes, 1379 of which will be "affordable".[2] Westfield Stratford City, which is Europe's largest urban shopping centre, will provide more than just "bricks, mortar, fabulous shops and restaurants"; it will also be "instrumental in helping us transform the lives of our residents by providing them with employment and jobs that they can turn into fulfilling and rewarding careers".[3] The Olympic park will be transformed into some "250 acres of new parklands created from former industrial land by the Olympic Delivery Authority providing a colourful atmosphere for the London 2012 Games and beyond" as well as a "haven for wildlife and plants, with new habitats created for species including otter, kingfisher, grey heron and water vole".[4]

The old men say that soon after the site was noticed the change began to be visible. It became grey and gleaming everywhere, in the first spring, after Stratford ended, so that all the country looked alike.

The land began to sprout pylons and street lamps; patches of concrete emerged from the scrubby grass, their edges slowly converging until the whole expanse was paved. Presaged by the arrival of swarms of yellow-jackets with hard hats and theodolites, rabbit paths widened and split into roads, and the brown earth was carved into chasms through which engines on steel rails roared. So that there was no place which was not more or less grey; the roads were the greyest of all, for such is the nature of tarmac when it has been driven on, and by-and-by, as summer came, the former fields were thinly covered with the dust that had spread out from the excavations and construction works.

In the autumn, where toxic berries had formerly fruited, hedgerows incubated embryonic retail opportunities, bursting free of tangles of bramble and hawthorn in shocks of plate glass and neon. The trains came and went; where ponies grazed, soon there were to be equestrian events; upstream the waters were to clear, silt brown, to blue, to white; where towpaths provided uneven habitat for walkers and uncertain cyclists, there would be velodrome and track. As the winter came on, the sleet fell on the muddy ground, and across the valley strange and bulbous forms grew and split, overripe, like pumpkins left rotting in the rain.

According to Newham Council the Olympics is a "once-in-a-lifetime" opportunity "to speed up the regeneration of the area", to provide "hundreds of jobs and business opportunities before, during and after 2012", to "improve transport networks", and to "inspire people to participate in sport and healthy lifestyles".[5] Holden Point is a local authority owned housing block built in 1969 to provide sheltered housing for elderly people living on low incomes in Newham. The tower is located within a small housing estate right on the edge of the Olympic site. It is in a bad state of disrepair and suffers from a high level of deprivation. People living in the area (particularly older people) suffer from low income levels, barriers to housing, services and amenities, high crime levels, low quality housing, poor air quality and a high number of road traffic accidents.[6]

The Olympic project can be seen as the continuation of a model of regeneration promoted by governments since the 1980s that see private initiatives, leveraged with public money, as the answer to social and economic problems.[7] The East End of London was the testing ground for this sort of regeneration with developments like Canary Wharf, the ExCeL Centre and the O2 arena. The replacement of the area's industrial base with the rapid expansion of global financial services and the knowledge economy has created significant wealth for knowledge workers in the financial services and jobs in creative industries, technology and IT.[8] However, the idea that the wealth created through "economic growth based on increased property values" will "cascade to the poorest" and alleviate poverty and deprivation has not rung true.[9] Evidence suggests that socially excluded communities, the majority of whose members live in social housing stock, are "functionally disconnected" from macro-economic trends and "do not appear to be feeling any benefits at all from the new economy".[10]

"At first we assumed that this must be an outcrop of ferromagnetic rock, but the geological structure of this region makes this highly unlikely. It warranted further investigation. Our first team found nothing. Just the usual admixture of heavy metals and methyl isocyanate residues. They drilled into the surface to take a core sample. At around 10 metres, the drill stopped. So they started to dig. What they discovered made them send back to base, for a bigger team, with heavy-duty excavation equipment. What they discovered is the reason that the LOC decided to hold this press conference."

The screen changed once more. It showed a man in a hard hat and high-viz, standing at the bottom of a broad, deep crater. It was night, and the pit was illuminated by the bright-white glare of metal-halide floodlights. Next to him was a sleek form, partially submerged in the earth. Though everything around it was caked in mud, the object itself was spotless, and seemed to emit a pale light. Its surface was impossibly smooth, and appeared to be fabricated from a single, seamless sheet of material, so perfect that even in photograph it played tricks on the eye. It was as if the object itself resisted the attempt to hold upon it. Fins projected from what appeared to be the rear of the object, its fuselage pocked with air intakes and vents. On the nose cone, beneath a small biohazard symbol, was inscribed the legend: "UNION CARBIDE".

In Docklands, the result of eight and half square miles of development, which operated outside normal planning laws and the local democratic process, was a tax-payer bail out of Canary Wharf in 1992 because it was "just too big to fail".[11] The ExCeL centre, a huge conference and exhibition centre on Royal Victoria Dock, seems "purposefully cut off from its surrounding (very poor) communities and is virtually inaccessible on foot".[12] Even when this model of development has been specifically targeted at the poorest neighbourhoods, as in New Labour's Housing Market Renewal policy, it is questionable as to "who actually might be benefiting".[13] The regeneration of housing estates through compulsory purchase orders, demolition and redevelopment worked to move working-class residents out in favour of more affluent residents with an "elite cafe culture sensibility" and a higher rent potential.[14] This is all the more worrying when there is a significant gap between compensation for compulsory purchase orders and affordability of new homes, or when "affordable rents" are set below market value but still remain out of reach for working class people.[15] From this point of view the representation of areas like Holden Point as an area of "urban decline" is deeply problematic and may not correspond with the "lived view" of the residents.[16]

The stigma associated with social housing such as Holden Point is actually rather new. After the Second World War there was a severe housing shortage in the UK. The lack of housing production during the war years, and extensive bombing of many of the UK's major cities, took their toll on the quality and quantity of housing available.[17] This was particularly acute in the East End of London, which had been very badly damaged in the bombing raids of 1944 and 1945.[18] The solution was an extensive local authority building programme, and a million new-build council houses were planned for construction over a seven-year period. The provision of housing can be seen as part of the formation of the welfare state, alongside health, education and social security.[19] At this time social housing was of relatively high quality compared with the private rented sector, and therefore an aspirational tenure catering for working class households and white collar workers in what was a "much more differentiated sector" than it is today.[20]

It is in this context that modernist housing blocks like Holden Point were developed across the East End. As early as 1943 the County of London Plan sought to "sweep away and rebuild a huge area... forming a corridor some one and three-quarter miles long and three quarters of a mile wide between the London docks and the regents canal".[21] The introduction of a green belt to limit city growth, a government subsidy introduced for every additional storey built, combined with a need to replace and rebuild crowded slums led to the development of blocks of flats rather than family homes and "from the mid 1950s to the mid 1970s mass housing became the vogue".[22]

One and a half million social housing units were built using industrialised techniques in high-rise blocks "fitting neatly with the political commitment to rebuild and the post-war technocratic approach to 'machine living'".[23] The early days of modernist housing estates were met with hope and embraced by families who were moving out of run-down overcrowded conditions into flats with modern amenities.[24] Unfortunately many of the housing estates were built without attention to design and used poor quality building materials: "[T]enants found themselves uprooted into a hurriedly built system built flats lacking amenities, environment, lacking in fact anything except a roof and four walls."[25] A fatal gas explosion at Ronan Point in 1968, a tower block just three miles north of Holden Point, killed five people, and "almost overnight the high-rise programme was abandoned".[26]

Many of the criticisms of the modernist housing project were about its lack of consideration for the social organisation or cultural life of a community and "the imposition of universal design solutions on communities who had no say, or ownership, over the outcomes".[27] The slum clearances of the post war period were not unambiguously good: although there were serious housing issues and overcrowding, modernist housing estates did not on the whole live up to their "promotional claims".[28] However, it would be too easy to write off the whole modernist project without making the same mistakes again. As Loretta Lees highlights in her study of tenants' views of the Aylesbury Estate in Elephant and Castle in London, many residents value their homes and resist the way the estate is labelled as a hotbed of crime and social degeneration.[29]

I do not know whether science would benefit by these brief notes if they could be published, but I shall not take the responsibility of divulging one word of what is written here on account of the abomination described. Though horror and revolting nausea rose up within me, and an odour of corruption choked my breath, I remained firm. I was the privileged or accursed, I dare not say which, to see that which lay me, smoke-blackened and reeking, transformed before my eyes. The streets, the buildings, the very flesh and ligaments of London itself that I had thought to be unchangeable and permanent, began to melt and dissolve. I know that the city may be separated into its elements by external agencies, but I should have refused to believe what I saw. For here was some internal force, of which I knew nothing, that caused dissolution and change.

Here too was all the work by which the city had been made repeated before my eyes. I saw the form waver from slum to gentrified estate, from fashionable shopping district to deserted precinct, the city dividing itself from itself, and then reunited. I saw London descend to the hovels from whence it ascended, and the heights go down to the depths, even to the abyss of all being.

The light in the sky had turned to blackness; not the darkness of night, but the negation of light. Objects were presented to my eyes, if I may say so, without any medium, and for one instance I saw a Form, shaped in the dimness before me, which I will not farther describe. But the symbol of this form may be seen in ancient sculptures, and in paintings which survived beneath the lava, too foul to be spoken of… as a horrible and unspeakable shape, neither city nor wasteland, was changed and made visible, and there came finally death.

*Fictional extracts procured with no small assistance from Arthur C. Clarke, Richard Jefferies and Arthur Machen.

Laura Oldfield Ford, Savage Messiah

UTION
RN OUT THE
YUPPIES
SAVAGE MESSIAH
ELEKTRON TOWERS

Laura Oldfield Ford,
Savage Messiah

FORD CITY
LOOTED
ESTROYED

Legacy Now:
SPACE's engagement in Olympic Legacy

ANNA HARDING

From autumn 2005 SPACE until spring 2012, SPACE artist support agency has held Legacy Now, an annual symposium to raise awareness of the potential impact of the Olympics on the creative sector and Hackney, to provide a forum for artists and policy makers to come together to influence the inevitable change that the Olympics will bring to east London.

To ensure that our large portfolio of studio buildings supporting artists at the Olympic edge remain on the new map, SPACE engages in all forms of debate informing emerging policy and practice. Since 1968 SPACE has championed the role of artists in society - and in urban regeneration. We have had studios in Fish Island next to the Olympic site since 1983 at Britannia Works in Dace Road when there were few other takers for large industrial premises. The building quality (solid, high ceilings, great natural light) and cheap rent, made these some of London's prime studios, also the finest industrial buildings in an area we share with builders' merchants, ice cream van depots, printers, manufacturers of Harry Potter's spectacles, of sofas and smoked salmon.

Hackney Wick Fish Island has recently blossomed as a creative enclave in adversity. Spontaneity and being under the radar are key appeals of Wick Fish Island as it has come to be known. As Jean-Francois Prost, our Canadian artist in residency, described at Legacy Now 2008:

> What draws many people to London, myself included, is the undetermined aspect of London. There is something about the way it functions and is built that breeds creativity, space to live and create things. This space is fundamental, something that you cannot define. It's essential to keep this spontaneity for and after the Olympics.

Can a new shopping mall and acres of new flats compensate for the loss of this undetermined space? Will young people still be able to slip into empty buildings and hold raves hosted by Gash, or hone graffiti skills along the canal without an official commission or designated site?

SPACE has contributed to east London's regeneration for decades, our own worst enemy. Our first building in 1968, Block A at Saint Katharine Dock, was home to the creative hipsters and happenings of its day. This huge building was leased from the Greater London Council after mass dock closures threw up acres of unused space. SPACE today is one of the largest occupiers of industrial premises in east London, with 750 artist tenants in studios in nine London boroughs. We support an art industry, one of the few growing areas of London's economy with essential space for artists to work, often for uncertain returns.

As part of our policy of supporting artists to contribute to neighbourhoods where they have studios, in the 1990s SPACE helped Hackney deliver its Single Regeneration Programme with public art commissions in Hackney Wick. We also worked in Bow with Tower Hamlets Housing Action Trust, Circle Anglia, British Waterways and other partners, wrote the Tower Hamlets public art strategy and ran the Bow Festival from 2003 to 2005. SPACE was also an active member of the now defunct Fish Island Business Club.[1] We continue our sense of civic duty, using our planning and legal expertise to advocate to ensure that space will be available for future creative communities.

In 2007 Councillor Christine Boyd introduced me to Alan Piggott, the wonderful vicar of St Mary of Eton, the UXL team at Eastway Baths and Tom at the Trowbridge Centre. We met that summer to discuss working together as organisations interested in the future of this area about to be affected by the Olympics. A series of meetings led to a community-led Hackney Wick Festival, with SPACE helping constitute and manage the festival in 2008, passing the baton to a festival committee. Hackney Wicked emerged also in summer 2008, with SPACE artists opening studios at our Britannia Works, Bridget Riley and Eastway Studios. Wick Creatives more recently emerged as a regular meeting point for creative tenants of Wick Fish Island, hosting information exchange with regeneration agencies. The future of Hackney Wick and Fish Island has been a major preoccupation for 7 years now, we hope it has been worthwhile.

The Legacy Now symposium was inspired by a conversation with Jude Kelly, cultural programmer for the original Olympic bid at a big meeting in 2005 at Stratford Town Hall. We discussed that the Olympic legacy began the day the Olympic decision was made and we should make this an urgent rallying cry, as a rush of property speculation was bound to affect the creative enclaves of East London.

Our first Legacy Now in November 2005 examined the implications of London's Olympics for artist studios in east London, and considered models and precedents to steer development in a beneficial way. Jaap Schoufour, city planner from Amsterdam, presented his visionary scheme set up with 2.5 million Euros from the City of Amsterdam, enabling artist groups to self-organise, convert and manage substantial premises. If only we had such trusting and visionary civil servants in London to let artists spend funds intelligently! Dave Wetzel of Transport for London proposed taxing infrastructure built underground, by Crossrail and Eurostar, as a financing mechanism for community infrastructure. Frances Hollis presented her PhD research on work–live as a key design type for creative people, with a long history in east London.

Since 2006 the London Borough of Hackney has sponsored Legacy Now in a productive partnership. A particular for the borough has been on ensuring the Olympic Broadcasting and Press Centre provides a tangible legacy for residents of the borough through employment and training opportunities. The 2006 Legacy Now symposium "Visioning a future for the Olympic International Broadcast Media Centre" focused on the opportunity presented by this 1.25 million square foot shed. The audience included many east London media companies, invited to see how together we could influence the project for maximum benefit to those living beside it well beyond the weeks of the Olympics. Questions included: Can we ensure that local people and creative sector benefit, that affordability and suitability are built in to the spec from the start? Can the media centre grow Olympic-class talent in arts and media? Can transparency and accessibility be built into a broadcast media centre? How can we ensure it's not soul-less, hidden behind barriers, turning its backs on local people? How can local young people engage in and be part of this, rather than be alienated outsiders looking in? Can the media centre offer east Londoners world-class opportunities after the world-class athletes have left town?

Looking to see what we could we learn from other media parks, Richard Pearce of TCN, developer of Hilversum Media Park, explained that a public-funded national museum was key to their scheme and a large commercial anchor tenant in Sony. Urban Splash developers, Ralph Luck, Head of Properties at the Olympic Delivery Authority, and award-winning Hoxton new media agency Lateral, and the youth media training project UK SoundTV (a SPACE/Hi8us/Circle Anglia partnership based in Bow) all contributed and enabled participants to suggest futures for east London creative people and organisations in the IBC/MPC. The collective vision was for the Olympic broadcast media centre to focus on its potential to harness the passions of young people; bring benefits to the area; and incorporate future patterns of global distribution of news information. Suggestions were to design and build it in collaboration with a consortium of end-users, including higher education, workspace, training providers and media agencies; create a hub for connectivity; be a model "Smart City"; include an "innovation lab" to support entrepreneurial and media advancement and interdisciplinary initiatives; attract groundbreaking private–

public partnerships; and be user driven, with emphasis on public access. These ideas were disseminated widely and informed thinking of bidders and agencies involved in the future of the premises.

Legacy Now: Global Meets Local at the London Olympics in February 2007 opened with SPACE artist in residence Jean-Francois Prost comparing the different legacies of two important events in Montreal: the 1967 Universal Exhibition, seen as one of the most successful exhibitions, was compared with the 1976 Olympics, whose legacy was considered very negatively. People remembered the Olympics as a deficit, an empty experience. Prost advised: "If you want participation in the future it will stem from first impressions." John Hopkins, Head of the ODA Design Team rehearsed the government's legacy plans as if he really meant it. Jude Woodward, Mayor Ken Livingstone's senior policy adviser, explained how the Mayor's office under Ken had approached the Olympics:

> The Olympics offers us a chance to really grasp what is our city and what makes it what it is. London is in a new category, it's a World City. If we let London fall behind we will pay a cultural and economic price. We have the opportunity to communicate what London is really like, not just Buckingham Palace and The Tower of London, that the world is welcome here.

Adam Hart, Director of Hackney Cooperative Developments, has contributed some of the most impassioned and poignant commentary to Legacy Now year on year:

> We built our culture not on the wealth of our city but in the wealth of our imperial past that leaves us with a diverse population. What's the pay-back? Where has this energy come from? These are the things that will change in the next few years. Trickle down economics doesn't work; let alone trickle down cultural policies. We live in a society where social mobility has almost stopped.

Micheal Pyner, Director of Shoreditch Trust, asked critical questions: Is there finance once we move into the post-Games changes? There is land value, but what else? Artists can be the brokers for how people engage with developments and space after 2012. If the space is throbbing with local people after 2012 then the Olympics will have been a huge success.

Hackney Councillor Guy Nicholson explained that there is a memorandum of understanding between the Mayor of London and the Treasury stating that all the money being invested by the lottery into the Olympic Park is paid back over a 30-year term by realising the financial assets generated by use of the land. Do we campaign to say we will not be paying that money back, as it will be crucial to bring affordability to this area after 2012?

"Legacy? What Legacy?" in 2008 included artist Laura Oldfield Ford, who said:

> I don't see the changes that have been brought about by the Olympics as in any way progressive. I see the regeneration as basically a corporate land grab, an attempt to privatise public space, and public housing. Privatise a lot of areas, and use public money to do it. Hackney Wick, Stratford, those were not empty spaces – people lived in those spaces, worked there. Many people have been evicted so what was genuinely a vibrant area – these buzzwords that developers like to use "vibrant" or "multi-cultural" it was genuinely that – but attempts are being made to eradicate and impose instead a bland yuppie monoculture.

In 2010 SPACE collaborated with the Architecture Foundation on Legacy Now Plus: Interim Uses Suggesting Permanent Outcomes – looking at imaginative, improvisational, temporary uses to flourish as a way to shift mindsets and encourage more interesting outcomes. Some young European architecture practices participated and speakers included Emily Miller from Meanwhile Space, which finds creative uses for empty shops to regenerate town centres; Andreas Lang of public works presenting the Wick Curiosity Shop; David Powell, consultant and participant in several of our Legacy Now symposia; Juliet Davies and many more, with a subsequent 2 day programme at the Architecture Foundation. Interim uses proposed included campsites, allotments and swimming pools in skips.

In 2011 SPACE commissioned an important related project, "The Cut", an oral history and art project about the area surrounding The Cut canal running between the Olympic Park and Wick Fish Island. A team of artists and oral historians engaged first-hand with canal culture past and present, forgotten industries and stories from the area, which was a centre of innovation a century ago, drawing attention to the importance of ordinary people's heritage and a history of radical change in this area. Three artists made new work, oral historians recorded interviews, a newsprint publication and an exhibition were produced, and Ken Walpole headlined a lively debate.

Did we make an impression?

I question the wisdom of having invested so much time in planning consultations,[4] advisory meetings, briefing endless consultants who are on fat fees – but felt we had little choice but to engage as proactively as possible. Can the interests of artists ever be a serious long-term consideration for developers and landowners unless by political obligation or financial incentive? Our stand on the importance of this creative district seems to have helped change mindsets from imagining that artists would just move out, to seeing them as kick-starting the next phase of regeneration, but we should be careful of what we wish for.

LTGDC's parting shot before it was abolished was to develop outline planning for the Hackney Hub, a large creative workspace-led mixed development on land it had assembled around Hackney Wick station. The management proposal in the planning application compares the development to high-end office suites in Angel and Shoreditch, rather than anything that the creative sole traders in this area would want or could afford. This scheme was informed by consultant Tom Fleming's advice to LTGDC to move Wick Fish Island from "pioneer artists' community" to "arts & creative district: a centre for production and consumption". He advised that a "mixed ecology" was essential, which required "hygiene factors to be developed – business support, skills and market development". The successful delivery would then lay the ground for "London's globally-facing media cluster & innovation centre for social innovation", assuming eastward migration of creative industries from Hoxton area, rebranded Silicon Roundabout, clean technologies just needing space to perch a laptop, the new salvation for our economy.

Kick-starting regeneration is about creating opportunities for developers to exploit for profit. The release of industrial land through land assembly and compulsory purchase orders for regeneration is profit-motivated, not quality of life or community-motivated. The public benefit test used by planning authorities places far more emphasis on economic benefit than on taking into account the effect on community.[5] But compulsory purchase powers could equally be used for community benefit – such as buying the freehold of a studio building so that artists can make a contribution to society and afford to work, or premises for community use. As private housing generates highest profit to developers, "creative industries" are only likely to have a future in this area if they help a developer secure planning gain. High-rise and low-specification maximise profits, a familiar story in London's history.

Councils have turned a blind eye to unauthorised uses, leaving temporary windows of opportunity for the young and improvisatorial. Unregulated raves, canalside graffiti and boat-dwellers add "vibrancy" while they can, hanging on to some of the last edge places still available.[6] Canny landlords waiting to unlock the goldmine engage with the artist community to create interest and maximise profit. Cultural diplomacy greases palms. Arty tenants on short lets, some rent-free, animate spaces awaiting redevelopment – SPACE included with The White Building project. SPACE's Dace Road landlord set up a company letting unofficial live-work space on short leases to artists and cafés operated by laid back Australians who provide good coffee and atmospheric space for developer and architect meetings.

Brochures from LTGDC, London Borough of Hackney and British Waterways court developers with "artists' impressions" of a future vibrant "creative hub" or "quarter", festooned with waterside cafés and marinas. The Lower Lea Valley Waterspace Strategy, for example, launched in November 2011, suggests attractive settings and infrastructure to encourage new development. The report's author described at the launch a vision of his family making a visit from Hampshire if the area became a visitor destination in its own right. I queried the logic of high-rise development by the waterside, overshadowing public amenities, and was told bluntly "it's about the land values" as if the sole purpose of the gathering local organisations here was to give our blessing to this approach.

In summer 2010 Design for London invited SPACE to bid for an interim use project to provide a cultural building on the canalside by the Olympic Park, bridging the inside and outside of the park, providing a meeting point for local art community and residents to raise the profile and accessibility of creativity in the area. This project, which became the White Building, in less than two years moved from Design for London at London Development Agency (LDA), via the Mayor's office (the Greater London Authority) to the Olympic Park Legacy Company (OPLC) or the Legacy Company, before going to the London Legacy Development Corporation (LLDC) – all before the venue even opened. The project team moves from one new agency to the next. This project makes us official Olympic legacy beneficiaries.[7]

The 6th Legacy Now symposium at SPACE on 21 February 2012 focused on crossing the bridges inside and outside the Olympic park. Speakers at the 2012 event were Rob Whitehead (Centre for London at Demos), artist Jim Woodall, writer Anna Minton, Paul Brickell (executive director of Regeneration and Community Partnerships, OPLC), Eric Reynolds (founding director, Urban Space Management), Sarah Weir (CEO, the Legacy List), Rebecca Whyte from Stour Space and Jake Ferguson (CEO, Hackney CVS).

Speakers and participants drew up a series of proposals for the new London Legacy Development Corporation with powers extending to the areas surrounding the park:

- Retain and sustain – "if it ain't broke… don't push it out"; develop what's there
- Affordability and value – low cost of space is key to success; value and celebrate social and economic achievements of arts, businesses and community in the Olympic fringe
- Small is beautiful – small organisations do things more quickly and innovatively
- Engage communities – community involvement and stake such as a development trust will result in stronger, successful regeneration
- Cut bureaucracy – without red tape change can happen quickly and cost effectively
- Seek Mayoral Development Corporation commitment to form a creative industries enterprise zone and support this manifesto

I hope that Legacy Now has brought insight together each year from a broad spectrum, and helped the new agencies as they have emerged to understand some of the challenges and passions of this area. We think we have ensured that attention is paid to the creative community and its future.

Beyond the Park:
The Olympic Legacy that is Already Here

OLIVER WAINWRIGHT*

> "Legacy is absolutely epicentral to the plans for 2012. Legacy is probably nine-tenths of what this process is about, not just 16 days of Olympic sport." Sebastian Coe, 2006

> "In this gold-rush land-grab of flexible futures... legacy is all important. It's like reading the will and sharing the spoils before the sick man is actually dead." Iain Sinclair, 2008

London won the bid for the 2012 Olympic Games on an ambitious promise. Unlike any other Games before, the UK capital's bid was based not on two weeks of sport, but on what would come after. London won because of the overwhelming emphasis placed on what the International Olympic Committee (IOC), in all its paternalist grandeur, terms "legacy". In summing up London's bid in 2005, the IOC Evaluation Commission described its Games, first and foremost, as "a catalyst for the re-development of the Lower Lea Valley, a 200-hectare rehabilitation and regeneration project in East London". It noted with firm approval that the Games "would provide long-term benefits for the residents of London, including employment, housing, educational and recreational opportunities".

It would be the miracle cure for the maligned East End and an expedient way of leveraging funds for this long-earmarked site, conveniently positioned at the fulcrum of the Thames Gateway Growth Area and the London–Stansted–Cambridge Growth Corridor, as well as the heart of the Lower Lea Valley Opportunity Area and the collision of four different boroughs. It was the perfect nexus of boosterish acronyms at which to place the largest regeneration project in Europe.

The site was soon consecrated with a fence, cordoned off with an endless ribbon of bright blue plywood, inscribing a vast ring around this newly sacred swathe of land. Only this was more than a fence. It was a billboard emblazoned with scenes of verdant valleys and glistening buildings; Olympic venues embraced by swathes of schools and housing. It was an eleven-mile frieze trumpeting the heroic legacy vision – an image of infinite promise, plastered on an infrastructure of exclusion.

In 2011 the first tangible piece of this legacy fantasy land opened, providing a glimpse into the golden-wrapped future to come: Westfield Stratford City, the largest urban mall in Europe. In its first week of opening, over a million people flocked to experience the sprawling complex of 300 shops, 70 restaurants and a 17-screen multiplex cinema, as well as the city's biggest casino. For 70% of visitors, this is also the official gateway to the Olympics – the world's first official Olympic shopping mall.

Yet just a few hundred metres down Stratford High Street – the misleading name for what is in fact the roaring six-lane dual carriageway of the A11 – several other gateways to the Games have emerged, largely unnoticed. While the world waits with bated breadth to see what the official Olympic legacy will look like – a gleaming new city quarter of 8,000 new homes on the doorstep of the Queen Elizabeth Park – few realise that it is already well under way in Stratford, and has been for some time. In fact, over 3,000 units are already climbing out of the ground. "We've been working here for the past fifteen years," says Julian Stock, founding director of Stock Woolstencroft architects, as we stand at the top of his 16-storey Taylor Place building at the Bow roundabout, looking north-east up the A11 across a startling vision of cranes, scaffolding and glassy blocks that is beginning to resemble the outskirts of Shenzhen. "At most junctions along the road you'll find one of our towers."

This is no understatement. Walking up the High Street from the roundabout, we pass block after block from the Stock Woolstencroft stable. Athena, Aurora, Icona, Velocity, each alluring brand name matched by a tower reaching ever higher, from 17 to 22 to 28 to 43 storeys – the Spirit of Stratford, one of the tallest residential buildings in the UK.

Each also has its own distinctive identity, or rather, number of identities. For this is the kind of architecture, like Westfield up the road, that dissembles and disaggregates its sheer bulk by pretending to be made up of many different parts. One Stratford, a £45 million scheme of 300 units for Telford Homes, completed in 2008, comprises a nine-storey block of brick and bright orange cladding, turning the corner to give way to an elevation of rendered panels in three shades of green, which connects to a 22-storey tower of powder-coated blue metal and back-painted glazing in three further vivid shades of turquoise all framed by two cream-rendered blocks, with bright yellow, red and blue infill panels. It is a fruity concoction indeed, not calmed by the imaginative range of balcony types – from glass, to timber and tensile wire – liberally scatter-bombed across the façades.

The report from the Planning Decisions Unit of the Greater London

Authority (GLA) showered praise on the "palette of innovative modern materials", with a colour scheme inspired by the adjacent river, describing approvingly of how "the pattern represents a linear transmogrification of water and fenestration". The case officer diligently points out that the densities far exceed those set out in the London Plan, but that this can be pardoned by the design quality and the introduction of a new "public" riverside walkway – which has remained gated off ever since.

The same story is repeated further up the street, only on a progressively more bloated scale. It reaches its apogee at the junction of the High Street with Warton Road, a former industrial backwater (and protected as industrial land in the Mayor's Opportunity Area Planning Framework) but now a key route into Stratford City – a fact that did not pass the land-owners by.

The western corner of the junction, allegedly acquired by a local speculator for £27 million in 2006, was then sold on to the Genesis Housing Group for £47 million, a vast overspend for the housing association, after which the only option was to ask Stock Woolstencroft to design the biggest possible development it could get away with. A 43-storey tower surrounded by a slew of ten-storey perimeter blocks, a £300 million scheme totalling over 650 units, is the result – although not without a struggle. In 2009 the Homes and Communities Agency (HCA) was forced to pump in at least £48 million of public money to save the scheme, after the developer went bust. (On the bright side, the HCA also called in AHMM architects to redesign the lower blocks, which emerged with a promising brick treatment, a sober foil to the nearby riot of coloured glass and flimsy metal panels.)

The Commission for Architecture and the Built Environment twice reported "fundamental concerns" over the quantum of development and slammed the design of the tower as "disappointingly generic". Yet it was still consented by the GLA and London Thames Gateway Development Corporation (LTGDC) – within whose boundary this valuable gauntlet of real estate lies, and for whose housing targets such steroidal schemes are a boon.

Over the road, the 28-storey curving glassy sheath of Athena tower forms the other half of this monumental gateway. A £40 million development for the McFeely Group, it is another symphony in green back-painted glass rising from clunky shoulder blocks of blue and grey power-coated metal. Again, every architectural element has been expressed with a new find from the depths of the sample library, double-order white banding framing recessed prefab blue cassettes, with thc uppermost storeys clad in dark grey – in the hope that you won't notice them. The tower pretends to be thinner by being split in two, the glass element strapped to a vast grey slab, whose northern elevation reads as a stacked cliff of Portakabins – now looming over the local primary school playground. The GLA detects such moves as a sign "of the highest design quality", for which breach of density and urban vandalism is again forgiven.

Smothered in a panellised garb of lilac and minty hues, the £24 million, 13-storey Aurora tower stands across the way – which Stock admits now looks strangely "dwarfed" by its neighbours. "It is more the family of Icona," he says, pointing out the 18-storey block right on the edge of the Olympic site, an oval extrusion covered with a tutti-frutti spray of neon balconies, completed in 2008 for Telford Homes.

He talks about these projects like wayward children, each the product of its time, their heights corresponding to market confidence like a bar chart made real. "Architecture has become a bit less shouty since the turn of the century," he admits ruefully, as we pass the most recently spawned offspring, the zinc-clad Velocity tower, also for One Housing, marked for its relative restraint – no doubt the result of its chastened £16 million budget.

But the fundamental problem with Stratford High Street, and the broader legacy within the "Olympic fringe", is not one of aesthetics alone. The vernacular of shouting louder than your neighbour will no doubt continue as more investors flock to Stratford, Hackney Wick and Leyton to build their Olympian icons – even if it is a little surprising that these lurid totems have all come from the same architectural hand. The real issue is that these are singularly mean-minded, inward-looking buildings, gated enclaves of mostly one- and two-bed flats airlifted into one of the poorest parts of London, with no overall vision for the consequences.

"We had very few objections to these schemes," says John Woolstencroft, by way of defence, back in his Aldgate studio. "There is not much of a community there already to complain." Try telling that to the residents of Carpenters Estate, an ailing 1960s council development of terraced houses and three towers, sandwiched between the High Street and the railway tracks, now bordered by the service entrances and bin stores of the new schemes. Long subject to abortive master plans, many of the residents have now been decanted – although their future still remains a mystery.

"It's been going on for ten years," says Lorraine Cavanagh, manager of Carpenters & Docklands community centre. "Local residents have been ground down and they've just had enough. I don't believe it's fair that a whole community is being broken up because of a development that's probably not going to be filled."

One housing group's estate agent, Site Sales, is more optimistic, enthusiastically telling me quite how quickly Velocity sold out and how over 50% of Aurora went in less than four weeks, adding that 40% of the buyers are based in China. "Overseas buy-to-let is a real concern, but as a planning authority we can't dictate how the sales go," says Peter Minoletti, Planning Development Manager at the LTGDC, who has presided over bountiful housing quotas, but gives little assurance that they are making good communities. Each development came with the promise of an active frontage – the corner shops and nail salons that places need to work – and yet, without fail, all ground floor units remain boarded up. And the Section 106 money? It has been spent on removing guard rails, planting some shrubs and laying paving slabs. Up the road, meanwhile, £3 million of Westfield's 106 was spent erecting the "Shoal" sculpture – designed by Studio Egret West to hide the downmarket Stratford shopping centre from Olympic visitors.

"The Olympic legacy is supposed to be about regenerating local communities, helping to sow the seeds for thriving neighbourhoods," says Eleanor Fawcett, head of design at the Olympic Park Legacy Company, and formerly lead for the Olympic fringe at Design for London. "That's the big failure here – these developments haven't given anything back to the area. What's it really going to be like as a place to live in ten years' time?"

Design for London started getting involved in trying to steer the High Street schemes in 2007, by which time many of them had already won planning, creating something of an uphill struggle. "Once the doors had opened, you could never go back," Fawcett recalls. "The precedent had already been set, so it would have been very difficult to defend refusal if it went to appeal." Minoletti agrees: "There was an element of closing the stable door once the horse had bolted."

But how was the horse ever allowed to bolt so far down the A11, reaching with such unbound Pegasusian ambition towards the skies? "You have to think of these schemes in the context of ten years ago," says John East, director of Planning and Development Services at Newham since 2010. "Very little was being built in Stratford and getting development to happen here was an achievement in itself." Many have told me this tale, of the wide-eyed, pre-Olympic Newham, so flattered that anyone would want to build in their borough that they welcomed developers with open arms, spell-bound by visions of soaring glass shards, and egged on by the GLA's boom-time tower fetish.

"It is fair to say that Newham's aspirations have risen in recent years," says East, diplomatically. "Design quality is now at the top of our agenda." At the launch of the Olympic Legacy Supplementary Planning Guidance, his message to developers was nothing if not cautionary: "We welcome you, but if you think we're just another part of the East End and you can do what you've done before, you're better off going somewhere else." Let's just hope they haven't been down the A11 recently.

How far such fighting talk will be demonstrated in action remains to be seen. The High Street has been covered by four master plans – albeit lacking any teeth – and was under the gaze of seven sources of design critique, including Newham's own independent design review panel since 2007, yet still these schemes made it through – as have many others, still to come. "People should be more prepared to stand up and refuse applications on design grounds," says Fawcett. "At the moment, planners simply don't have the tools at their disposal to insist on really good places."

One development that hinted little had changed was the demolition of virtually all of the Sugarhouse Lane conservation area buildings, south of the High Street, to make way for Ikea's 1,500 unit Landprop development by Tunbridge Wells architect, ARC-ML – with little evidence of what would come in their place. The only part of the design revealed was a hulking 40-metre timber tower, modelled on the Olympic torch and topped with a "halo", soon to glow above this flat-pack Scandinavian version of a suburban Tesco town.

The announcement of the Mayoral Development Corporation, which, like the Docklands model, will have development and planning powers over the whole of the park and Olympic fringe area, brings some hope of joined-up thinking. If run properly, it might once and for all clarify the quagmire of conflicting design advice and procedural confusion that has led to such a compromised situation along the High Street, and finally raise the bar on quality and ambition for what the broader Olympic legacy can be. But it will only work if the current planning practice of ad hoc interpretation from manuals of vague platitudes – alongside the flagrant flouting of statutory designations – is exchanged for open and accountable enforcement of a truly democratic plan.

Legacy may well have been "epicentral" to the plans for 2012, in the words of Lord Coe. But so epicentral that the periphery has been crucially overlooked, left with a fractured landscape of bloated buildings, vacant streets and magnified social division – the irreparable legacy beyond the park.

* A version of this text was first published in *BD*, 21 September 2011.

Stratford Façade
A Death Mask

ALEX SPROGS

Stratford Facade addresses the redevelopment along Stratford High Street in relation to the Olympic Games and Westfield Shopping Centre. Stratford High Street falls under the remit of "High Street 2012", a project which groups together individual sections of London's streetscape from Whitechapel to Stratford under one branded banner. The traditional function of the high street as a shopping destination is replaced by its new function as a busy motor route leading to the *über* consumer destination of Westfield.

An impression was taken from the façade of 190a Stratford High Street in March 2011 and cast in plaster. In the tradition of the 19th-century death mask,[1] the facial memento of the deceased, a fragment of London's pre-Olympic urban idiosyncrasy and outmoded commercial enterprise was preserved. Within the short space of three months after making the cast, the façade of 190a had been stripped, rerendered, painted and refurbished – a microcosm of east London's rapid urban renewal.

As a resident of the neighbouring London Olympic Host borough of Tower Hamlets for the last four years, I have observed and experienced the knock-on effect of the Olympic development in my local area, from road widening schemes to the gradual increase in house rental prices.[2] The project was a personal reflection on the transformation of my locality. The plaster casts were produced in a studio in Carpenters Road off Stratford High Street, previously home to many small businesses, including taxi garages, cold-storage units and catering wholesalers, now mostly relocated after the Olympic perimeter fence was established.

The decision to record this built environment by façade, as a cast, was intended to be part of a wider discussion over the impact of urban renewal, and the consequences of, or tension between, what is left behind, what is chosen for demolition and its subsequent replacement. "High Street 2012", in addition to a series of developments by the private sector, is a landscaping and conservation public works project, concentrating on the urban environment immediately intersected by the A11. Initiated by various partner bodies, which include the London Development Agency (LDA), Design for London and English Heritage, the primary objective along this route is to "enhance and celebrate the ribbon of London life that connects the City at Aldgate to the

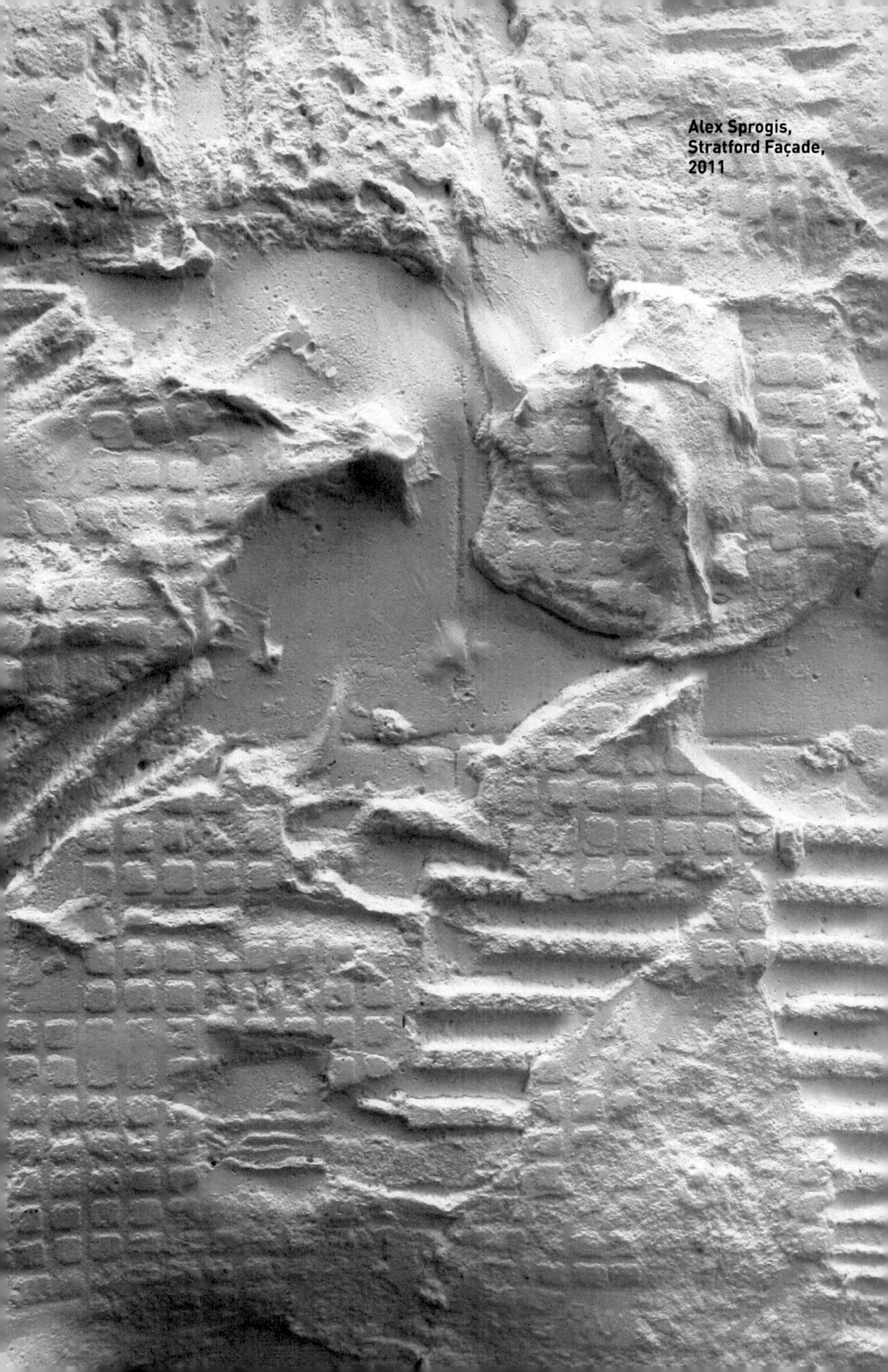

Alex Sprogis,
Stratford Façade,
2011

Olympic Park at Stratford".[3] Selected historic buildings and public spaces along the route are receiving conservation work, including Altab Ali Park in Whitechapel, Wickhams Department Store in Stepney and other prominent buildings. In total nearly 100 buildings across the whole six kilometre stretch will be part of this "street action".

Number 190a was one building that stood out among the new faces on the street. A two-storey brick construction, the old façade was bricked up, framed by a layer of cream-coloured tile beneath the adhesive of subsequent ages of tile and render. I chose the lower corner of this façade to cast in plaster. The cast itself reveals clearly defined marks of age, weathering and disrepair alongside the idiosyncrasies of traditional building technique; it is the labour by hand of the application of render and tile adhesive and even a faint logo on the back of one of the tiles.

To designate a building as "historic" or to evaluate its individual contribution to the "character" of an area requires a set of values that are inherently subjective. The production of the *Stratford Façade* acts as a counterpoint to established values of building conservation. A seemingly arbitrary tiled wall becomes a memento after the "death" of the building, a reminder of imperfection and urban historical context. Like the 19th-century *memento mori*, the resultant cast is an acceptance of this death and the urban cycles of demolition and regeneration. Capturing a brief moment in a process of transition between identities.

Seeing Stratford and the 2012 Olympics through the eyes of homeless young people

PAUL WATT AND JACQUELINE KENNELLY*

This piece presents a series of photographic images taken by young people living in temporary housing in the London Borough of Newham. These represent some of the visual findings from a research project involving a longitudinal, comparative, cross-national study of low-income youth in Vancouver, host to the 2010 Winter Olympics, and London, host to the 2012 Summer Olympics.[1]

During the summer of 2011, the authors used photo-elicitation methods,[2] including photo-journals and accompanying group interviews, to illustrate the perspectives of homeless and low-income young people living in the shadow of the Olympics. In addition to taking part in interviews that explored their views of life in Newham, thirteen young people completed the photo-journal section of the research, which involved them taking photographs of their local neighbourhood. We asked them in particular to focus on the places they frequented and how the Olympics was impacting on these places. Using disposable cameras that we provided, the participants took nearly 200 photographs, most of which they then placed into photo-journals and captioned. The camera-users were a multi-ethnic group of young people including immigrants from African and southern European countries as well as others from Black African–Caribbean, mixed-race and white east London backgrounds. The thirteen young people had been living in their current temporary supported housing for various lengths of time; only two were in paid work at the time of the interviews.

We have written about the photo-journals and interviews at length elsewhere,[3] highlighting the young people's increasingly precarious sense of place in Stratford, an area which is undergoing marked gentrification under the aegis of the Olympics mega-project and other Newham regeneration schemes. Our aim in this chapter is simply to present a small selection of photographs from the project that illustrate the "old" and "new" Stratford as the young people themselves see it. We have provided pseudonyms for the young people in order to preserve their anonymity.

*The authors would like to acknowledge the Social Sciences and Humanities Research Council of Canada for funding this research. We would further like to thank the young people who participated in the project, as well as the staff at the transitional housing centre who facilitated our access to the participants. This project could not have happened without their help. Jacqueline Kennelly would like to further thank her Canadian research assistants, Christopher Enman and Amelia Curran, for their assistance in uploading and scanning the photographs..

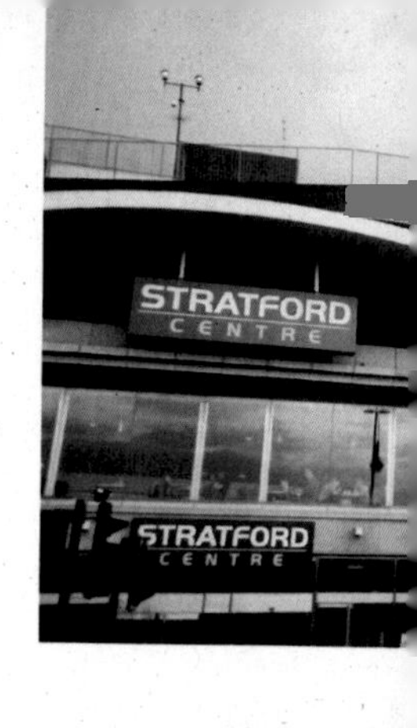

Everywhere you look you see advertisments for new offices to let. Since Olympics it seems everyone has forgotten the demand for housing the homeless.

NEW:

Wow! That's A Change! Will people Enjoy the view?

This image shows a few luxury flats with various bedroom numbers available. Only a small percentage of this if any will go to people like myself. Only the people that can afford it will get it.

westfield – opportuniti

This is one of many stool holders trying to survive but slowly getting pushed away. →

OLD:

The old is never enough what is going to happen to stratford Shopping entRE ??

Just one of the parks in and around newham as this parks are in stratford Im sure they will be reformed but this picture shows you that the parks are in a bad State and have been for a long time.

Parks

The borough should also focu on hygiene and making the environment pleasant and clean.

WOULD YOU LIKE TO ATTEND THIS CHURCH?

I dont think so

Top row: Jessica, Freddie, Michael
Bottom row: Olu, Tehuti, Tiffany, Niamh

OlympicField

BEN SEYMOUR

FINAL SHOOTING SCRIPT

Slate: Text on green SCREEN in the style of the opening shot of disaster-monster film 'Cloverfield':

MULTIPLE SITINGS OF CASE DESIGNATE
<OLYMPICFIELD>
CAMERA RETRIEVED AT INCIDENT SITE UK 447
AREA FORMERLY KNOWN AS HACKNEY

TV static: VIDEO begins: Scared looking man addressing us. Gradually realise we're looking THROUGH A VIDEO CAMERA. Behind his head we glimpse the brick wall of a warehouse or warehouse apartment. [Warehouse apartment style brick tiling in gentrified east end ex-council flat.]

NARRATOR/ROB HAWKINS
(to camera)

My name is Robert Hawkins.
Approximately 10 years ago something attacked the city.

Narrator continues as VO with images of Olympic stadium assembly/invasion, Hackney & Tower Hamlets, London, before and after, etc.

NARRATOR (VO)

If you're watching this then you probably know more about than I do.
They came out of nowhere.
They tore down factories.
They tore down houses.
Driving people out.

For every building they tore down
they threw up fortresses of their own.
At first we thought they were alone.
But then we realised.
They had people on the inside.
Some of us joined them.
The rewards were too great.
It was unstoppable.
It looked like they would take the whole city.
And then one day
even faster than they came, they disappeared.

Olympic torch fails. Stadium begins to ascend

NARRATOR (VO continues)

They left nothing behind but the debt.
And the stadium, of course.
After the bankruptcy they renamed it Stadium Island.
Turned the whole zone into a prison.
The whole place is overgrown now.
But there are still workers inside.
We don't know what they're doing.
We think they are working on some kind of weapon:
Project Legacy.

Cuts back to opening VIDEO:

INT./EXT. WAREHOUSE/STYLE FLAT.

If you find this, if you're watching this,
You have to do something!
You have to, you have to...

VIDEO breaks off. STATIC. Green SCREEN slate as above.

THE END

Structures of Enchantment:
Works in construction and collapse

HILARY POWELL

> "The line smoulders, the rhyme explodes - and by a stanza a city is blown to bits." Vladimir Mayakovski

Amidst the Lumière brother's films of trains arriving at the station and workers leaving the factory was *Demolition d'un mur* (1896) literally recording the demolition of a wall. Their penchant for the "trick" of screening the film backwards (thereby resurrecting the wall from dust) offered a new, reverse perspective on its destruction, pre-empting and illuminating a fascination with the entwined processes of construction and demolition that persists today in everyday curiosity and the operatic spectacles of controlled blow-downs. Recognition of the thrill sits alongside an exploration of demolition's place within the boom and bust landscape of capitalism – for although it may be inescapable that "the visual arena of the city *must* move through concurrent acts of construction and obliteration",[1] what are the motivations and ethics of demolition's symbiotic relationship to archaeology, urban regeneration, collective memory and urban imagination? The project *Structures of Enchantment*[2] revitalises the art of the pop-up book and the tradition of etching to unfold and inscribe a layered past and future of one such site of construction and obliteration – the 2012 Olympic Park – creating an animated archive of transformation and entropy.

In July 2007 2.5sq km of east London land was acquired by the Olympic Delivery Authority (ODA) and cordoned off. Taking an early bus tour of the site was a literal journey through ruins as remnants of car yards and industrial depots lined dusty routes of a now deserted landscape. The digging and demolishing of the Park's "Demolish, Dig, Design" phase was underway in earnest. The Old Testament-esque adjustment of the ODA to Olympic *Deliverance* Authority in the BBC comedy *Twenty Twelve* highlights a dubious enforced redemption in which an edited version of the past and its deletion is encouraged in the name of branded regeneration. Hard-hat photo opportunities of symbolic destructive transformation supported the fallacy of renewal through modernisation and archaeological finds were subject to censorship and absurdism – an early 20th century Pepsi bottle taken off display to protect official sponsors Coca-Cola. The rhetoric of blight and cleansing had to be justified and the off-message past consigned to scrap or hidden archive.

The need for an inverse cartography and politics of value amidst the Olympian copy-writing and myth-making became increasingly clear and I found this in a journey through the Museum of London's Archaeological Services "Standing Building Survey" and around the edges of the Olympic site. If, as Bataille states "…the ground we live on is little other than a field of multiple destruction",[3] I attempt to understand and subsequently recreate such multiple destructions in miniature through my position as "unofficial artist in residence of sorts" on a vast development site on the southern fringes of the 2012 Park.[4]

"Demolition sites: sources for the teaching of construction. Never have circumstances been so favourable for this genre of study than the epoch we live in today".[5] The aesthetic and materials of both demolition site and archaeological archive are my source and resource – from salvaged roof zinc as etching plate to London brick ink and abandoned office stationary used to construct sculptural pop-up and other moveable books.[6] All form an alternative archive of and response to urban change at once indexical, playful and critical.

I was drawn to the pop-up book as the optimum medium in which to experiment with a creative modelling of change. Each turn of the page sets in motion simultaneous collapse and construction as pop-up mechanisms enable a form of what artist Robert Smithson described as "ruins in reverse"[7] in which buildings rise into ruin – constituting a potential future rather than a memory of a past. Within the pop-up pages buildings rise and fall again with parodic regularity in a panoramic and seismic landscape.

It is the pop-up book's association with the fairy-tale gothic and description as "structures of enchantment" that consolidates their potential to critique the overarching myths of progress inherent in London Olympics' seductive spell. In order to disenchant through enchantment the pop-up constructions deal with archaeological and architectural facts to create an alternative urban phantasmagoria. The use of etching to re-present buildings destroyed or imagined continues the lineage of the gothic and sublime – most specifically a tradition of "romantic ruinology" depicting centres of power as ruin. The chemical process of etching reinforces this, as images are created through active entropy (degradation of the metal plate) and composed as a mirror image and double negative.

Just as the Lumière brothers reversed destruction, this project operates in a world of tactile and conceptual reversals and inversions – where the "tricks" of paper architecture offer shape-shifting glimpses of the future out of fragments of the past. These books and etchings offer up landscapes poised on the fluctuating edge of potential and entropy creating a space and time in which "Some enchanted evening, the future is called the past"[8] – and vice versa.

Hilary Powell,
Structures of
Enchantement,
2011

Notes

Notes to Marrero-Guillamón & Powell, "Introduction"

1 Here we are paraphrasing Gilles Deleuze and Félix Guattari, *What Is Philosophy?* (New York: Columbia University Press, 1994).

2 Jacques Rancière, *Dissensus: On Politics and Aesthetics* (London and New York: Continuum, 2010).

3 See Jacques Rancière, *The Politics of Aesthetics: The Distribution of the Sensible* (London & New York: Continuum, 2006).

4 In other words, this is a "distributive whole", as opposed to a "collective whole". See Deleuze, Gilles, *The Fold: Leibniz and the Baroque* (London and New York: Continuum, 2006).

5 This is Mallarmé's formulation in his poem "The white water lily", mentioned in Jacques Rancière, *The Emancipated Spectator* (London: Verso, 2011).

6 There has not been a "movement" against the Games in London, but a plethora of actions of different kinds instead. Without attempting to be in any way exhaustive: for instance, the arrival of the Olympic torch in 2008 was met by direct action by pro-Tibet activists; members of Games Monitor have used the Freedom of Information Act 2004 to make public key documents such as the Host City Contract; the East London Community Organisation (TELCO) led the Ethical Olympics campaign; displaced Clays Lane's residents and Carpenter Road businesses legally challenged the Compulsory Purchase Order they were served; members of We Are Bad collective have been flyposting the East End with subversive messages; the Counter-Olympics Network was set up as a meeting platform for a number of country-wide campaigns including nuclear waste, corporate sponsoring or police watch; and the Occupy Movement camped out on Leyton Marshes to block the construction of temporary Olympic infrastructure.

7 Giuliana Bruno, *Atlas of Emotion: Journeys in Art, Architecture and Film* (London: Verso, 2002), 35.

8 See Stephen Gill and Jon Ronson, *A Book of Field Studies* (London: Chris Boot, 2005).

9 Stephen Barber, *Fragments of the European City* (London: Reaktion Books, 1995), 77.

10 Yi Fu Tuan, *Topophilia: A Study Of Environmental Perceptions, Attitudes and Values* (New York: Columbia University Press, 1990).

11 In the form of Squint Opera's 2009 animation commissioned for the announcement of the design of the Olympic Stadium for the 2012 Olympics in London.

12 Patrick Wright on the methodology of Iain Sinclair, in *A Journey Through Ruins: The Last Days of London* (London: Radius, 1991).

13 W. G. Sebald, *Austerlitz* (London: Penguin, 2002), 24.

Notes to Marrero-Guillamón, "Olympic State of Exception"

1 P. Fussey and G. Galdon-Clavell, "Introduction: Towards New Frontiers in the Study of Mega-events and the City", *Urbe, Revista Brasileira de Gestão Urbana (Brazilian Journal of Urban Management)* 3, no. 2 (2011): 149–55.

2 Giorgio Agamben, *State of Exception* (Chicago: University of Chicago Press, 2005).

3 Some of the examples Agamben provides are financial crises in Germany (1923) and France (1925, 1935 and 1937); the abolition of slavery (1862) and the approval of the New Deal in the USA (1933); or the Emergency Powers Act in the UK, passed in 1920 during a labour dispute.

4 IOC, *Host City Contract: Games of the XXX Olympiad in 2012* (Lausanne: International Olympic Committee, 2005), 2.

5 S. Humphreys, "Legalizing Lawlessness: On Giorgio Agamben's State of Exception", *European Journal of International Law* 17, no. 3 (2006): 679–80.

6 G. Agamben, *Homo Sacer: Sovereign Power and Bare Life* (Stanford: Stanford University Press, 1998), 168–9.

7 Agamben, *Homo Sacer*, 175.

8 IOC, *Olympic Charter* (Lausanne: International Olympic Committee, 2010), 20.

9 James Kenyon and Clive Palmer, "Funding and Sponsorship: the Commercial Impact of the 2012 London Olympic Games – Some Considerations", *Journal of Qualitative Research in Sport* 2, no. 1 (2008), 29–44.

10 Tripp Mickle, "IOC Cashes in on Beijing", *Sports Business Journal*, 13 July 2009.

11 Christopher A. Shaw, *Five Ring Circus: Myths and Realities of the Olympic Games* (Gabriola Island: New Society Publishers, 2008).

12 It should be noted that the contract was only made public following a successful appeal to the Freedom of Information Act. It is available at

www.gamesmonitor.org.uk/node/553 (accessed 27 March 2012).

13 IOC, *Host City Contract*, 4.

14 Mark James and Guy Osborn, "London 2012 and the Impact of the UK's Olympic and Paralympic Legislation: Protecting Commerce or Preserving Culture?", *Modern Law Review* 74, no. 3 (2011): 416.

15 IOC, *Host City Contract*, 23.

16 IOC, *Host City Contract*, 28.

17 Kenyon and Palmer, "Funding and Sponsorship".

18 IOC, *Technical Manual on Brand Protection* (Lausanne: International Olympic Committee, 2005), 60.

19 IOC, "Revenue Sources and Distribution", International Olympic Committee, http://www.olympic.org/ioc-financing-revenue-sources-distribution?tab=0 (accessed 13 March 2012).

20 IOC, "Revenue Sources and Distribution".

21 London Olympic and Paralympic Games Act 2006, 46.

22 IOC, *Brand Protection*, 13.

23 London Olympic Act 2006, 16.

24 James and Osborn, "Impact of Olympic Legislation".

25 The London Olympic Games and Paralympic Games (Advertising and Trading) (England) Regulations 2011, 4.

26 K. Blowe, address to the the Counter Olympics Network on 28 January 2012.

27 "Home Secretary RUSI Olympic Security Conference Speech," Home Office, http://www.homeoffice.gov.uk/media-centre/speeches/Home-sec-olympic-speech (accessed 13 March 2012).

28 Nan Ellin (ed.), *Architecture of Fear* (New York: Princeton Architectural Press, 1997).

29 Pete Fussey et al., *Securing and Sustaining the Olympic City: Reconfiguring London for 2012 and Beyond* (Farnham and Burlington: Ashgate Publishing, 2011), 67.

30 Fussey et al., *Securing the Olympic City*, 67–8.

31 Owen Gibson, "Olympic Security Chief Says Public Will See 'Bobbies on the Beat'", *Guardian*, 19 January 2012.

32 "London 2012: Major Olympic security test unveiled", BBC News, 30 April 2012.

33 Fussey et al., *Securing the Olympic City*, 61.

34 "SBD Award for London 2012 Olympic Park", Secure by Design, http://www.securedbydesign.com/news/viewstory.aspx?id=1449&url=http://www.securedbydesign.com/editable_pages/SBD_1296560660316.html (accessed 13 March 2012).

Notes to Walker, "The Implications of Linguistic and other associations..."

1 David Bond, "Fifa cracks down after beer stunt", BBC News, 17 June 2010.

2 Radio Nederlands Worldwide, 15 August 2010.

3 Other cases of guerilla or ambush marketing include Linford Christie at the Atlanta Olympics 1996 (http://www.flickr.com/photos/danizegtyo/2148251639/) and Andy Murray drinking the "wrong" water at Wimbledon (http://londonersdiary.standard.co.uk/2009/06/a-test-of-murrays-bottle.html).

4 LOCOG, *London 2012's UK Statutory Marketing Rights: Brand Protection* (London: London Organising Committee of the Olympic Games and Paralympic Games, 2011).

5 LOCOG, *Statutory Marketing Rights.*

6 LOCOG, *Statutory Marketing Rights.*

7 "Embracing the Olympic dream", *Business Matters*, http://www.bmmagazine.co.uk/falling-foul-of-olypmics-act.294 (accessed 1 March 2012).

8 LOCOG, *Statutory Marketing Rights.*

9 LOCOG, *Statutory Marketing Rights*, 37.

10 "London Olympics Bill – Restrictions on the Use of Olympic Words", http://webarchive.nationalarchives.gov.uk/+/http:/www.culture.gov.uk/NR/rdonlyres/2E467472-C10B-40EB-A386-7504ADA25CDA/0/050824Billmythbusters3.pdf (accessed 1 March 2012).

11 "London Olympics Bill".

12 "IP Controls in Place for 2012 London Olympic and Paralympic Games: Association Rights", HM Revenue & Customs, http://www.hmrc.gov.uk/manuals/ciprgmanual/ciprg8040.htm (accessed 1 March 2012).

13 "Great Exhibition 'Faces London 2012 Legal Action'", BBC News, 14 June 2011.

14 "What is the Great Exhibition?", http://www.thegreatexhibition2012.co.uk/what-is-the-great-exhibition (accessed 1 March 2012).

15 LOCOG, *The Protected Games' Marks* (London: London Organising Committee of the Olympic Games and Paralympic Games, 2010).

16 *London Olympic Games and Paralympic Games Act 2006: Explanatory Notes.*

17 Paul Chamberlain and Mark Bateman, "Brand Protection and Ambush Marketing: London 2012", Davenport Lyons, http://www.davenportlyons.com/legal-services/articles/539/ (accessed 1 March 2012).

18 H. Wallop, "London 2012 Olympics: Water, Mobile Phones and Sandwiches could be

Banned", *Telegraph*, 17 March 2011.

19 J. Magnay, "London 2012 Olympics: Government Unveils Plans to Ban Ambush Marketing and Bolster Games Security", *Telegraph*, 7 Mar 2011.

Notes to Duman, "AdiZones"

1 Francis Keogh and Andrew Fraser, "Why London Won the Olympics", BBC Sport, 6 July 2005.

2 DCMS, *Before, During and After: Making the Most of the London 2012 Games* (London: Department for Media, Culture and Sport, 2008), 5.

3 DCMS, *Before, During and After*, 8.

4 "London 2012 Olympic Games Budget Cut by £27m", BBC News, 24 May 2010.

5 "40 Adizones Across England", The Great Outdoor Gym Company, 14 January 2010, http://www.tgogc.com/home/news-and-updates/40-adizones-across-england.html (accessed 27 March 2012).

6 Donald R. Liggett, "Just Let Yourself Play, Enjoying All of the Feelings and Sensations that Come When You Are IN The Zone", in *Sport Hypnosis* (Champaign: Human Kinetics Publishers, 2000), 15.

7 Joe Fernandez, "Adidas to Build London Olympic Venues", *Marketing Week*, 11 September 2008.

8 See Wikipedia, "My Adidas", http://en.wikipedia.org/wiki/My_Adidas (accessed 15 September 2011).

9 "Brown Backs Child Sport Campaign", *BBC News*, 13 July 2007.

10 "AdiZones FAQs", http://www.tynewearsport.org/files/faqs.pdf (accessed 15 September 2011).

11 London Borough of Newham, "Investment Portfolio", May 2010 , http://www.newham.gov.uk/NR/rdonlyres/8AF0D6BC-7A8E-4625-85D1-2083502CB3D5/0/InvestmentProspectus.pdf (accessed 15 September 2011).

Notes to Wynne & Lenskyj, "Symbolic Resistance: Turning the Rings"

1 Helen Lenskyj, *Olympic Industry Resistance: Challenging Olympic Power and Propaganda* (New York: SUNY Press, 2008); Helen Lenskyj, *The Best Olympics Ever?: Social Impacts of Sydney 2000* (Albany: SUNY Press, 2002); Helen Lenskyj, *Inside the Olympic Industry: Power, Politics, and Activism* (New York: SUNY Press, 2000).

2 Chris Shaw, *Five Ring Circus: Myths and Realities of the Olympic Games* (Gabriola Island: New Society Publishers, 2008).

3 George Orwell, "The Sporting Spirit", first published in *Tribune*, December 1945, available at http://orwell.ru/library/articles/spirit/english/e_spirit (accessed 17 March 2012).

4 George Monbiot, "Everywhere They Go, the Olympic Games Become an Excuse for Eviction and Displacement", *Guardian*, 12 June 2007.

Notes to Powell & MacGilp, "The Games"

1 Iain Sinclair, "The Olympics Scam", *London Review of Books* 30, no. 12 (June 2008): 17–23.

2 Peter Ackroyd, *London: The Biography* (London: Vintage, 2001), 760.

3 Wim Wenders, "A Step Ahead of the Times: A Conversation About Photography, Painting and Film with Paul Puschel and Jan Thron Prikker", in *Wim Wenders: On Film* (London: Faber and Faber, 2001), 73.

4 This question was put to me by Anna Hart on a welcome break from the Olympic site while undertaking a project in Archway. See http://www.archwayinvestigationsandresponses.org (accessed 27 March 2012).

Notes to Campkin, "Buried by Stephen Gill and Hackney Wick"

1 Iain Sinclair quoted on Stephen Gill's website, http://www.stephengill.co.uk/portfolio/about (accessed 27 December 2011).

2 Victor Buchli and Gavin Lucas, "The Absent Present: Archaeologies of the Contemporary Past", in *Archaeologies of the Contemporary Past* (London and New York: Routledge, 2001), 3.

3 See *Hackney Wick*, 2004; *Buried*, 2006; *Hackney Flowers*, 2007; *Archaeology in Reverse*, 2007; *A Series of Disappointments*, 2008; *Warming Down*, 2008; *The Hackney Rag*, 2009; and *Off Ground*, 2011. All were published in London by Nobody.

4 Theorist of archaeological photography, Michael Shanks, defines "photoworks" as explicitly interpretative photographs, where the photographer is aware of photography as an act of cultural production rather than of objective documentation: "It is proposed that photography, far from being homogenous, is an unstable category, and that it is better to think less of photographs than of photoworks, with emphasis placed upon acts of cultural production: photowork is then one aspect of how the archaeologist may take up the remains of the past and work upon them. This is the positive moment of critique – finding the creative potential within particular modes of cultural production, a potential to express different

interests in the material past." Michael Shanks, "Photography and archaeology", in Brian Leigh Molyneaux (ed.), *The Cultural Life of Images: Visual Representation in Archaeology* (London: Routledge, 1997), 73–107.

5 See Ben Campkin, *The Regeneration Game* (London: I.B. Tauris, forthcoming); and Michael Edwards, "London For Sale: Towards the Radical Marketization of Urban Space", in Matthew Gandy (ed.), *Urban Constellations* (Berlin: Jovis, 2011), 56.

6 Owen Hatherley, "Ghost Milk: Calling Time on the Grand Project, by Iain Sinclair", *Independent*, 8 July 2011.

7 Interview with Paul Jennings, London 2012 Organising Committee, and Anthony Palmer, formerly Olympic Delivery Authority Filming and Events Manager, 21 December 2011, Canary Wharf, London.

8 This publicly funded archive has to date only been made partially accessible. It is now controlled by the London 2012 Organising Committee (LOCOG), a private company, which is negotiating with the National Archives and the British Film Institute with a view to depositing it with them.

9 Timothy Wray and Andrew Higgott (eds.), *Camera Constructs: Photography, Architecture and the Modern City* (London: Ashgate, forthcoming), 18; and see Robin Wilson, "At the Limits of Genre: Architectural Photography and Utopic Criticism", *Journal of Architecture* 10, no. 3 (2005): 265–73.

10 Correspondence with Stephen Gill, 8 November 2011.

11 "Stephen Gill", http://www.stephengill.co.uk/portfolio/about (accessed 1 December 2011).

12 Raymond Williams introduced these terms in *The Country and the City* (Oxford: Oxford University Press, 1975).

13 "Stephen Gill"

14 Martin Slavin, UCL Bartlett School of Planning London Planning Seminar Series, 3 November 2011.

15 Antoine Picon, "Anxious Landscapes: From the Ruin to Rust", *Grey Room*, no. 1 (Fall 2000): 64–83.

16 Wray and Higgott, *Camera Constructs*, 28.

17 "Nobody's Bookshop", http://nobodybooks.com/shop/ (accessed 1 December 2011).

18 Correspondence with Stephen Gill, 8 November 2011.

19 Roger Luckhurst, "The Contemporary London Gothic and the Limits of the Spectral Turn", *Textual Practice* 16, no. 3 (2002): 526–45.

20 Luckhurst, "Contemporary London Gothic", 530.

21 Luckhurst, "Contemporary London Gothic", 532.

22 Julian Stallabrass, *High Art Lite: British Art in the 1990s* (London and New York: Verso, 1999). 250.

23 DEME, "Creating Land for the Future", Dredging, Environmental & Marine Engineering , http://www.deme.be/projects/belg_dec_london_olympics.html (accessed 5 December 2011).

24 lifeisland.org, "Gardeners exposed to 2012 Olympics Construction Radiation Hazard", 15 October 2010, http://www.lifeisland.org/ (accessed 3 January 2012).

25 An example of distress aesthetics would be fashion designer Hussein Chalyan's 1993 collection, "The Tangent Flows", in which he buried clothes in his back garden and dug them up again, turning dirt and decomposition into a luxury commodity. See Katherine Townsend, 'The Denim Garment as Canvas: Exploring the Notion of Wear as a Fashion and Textile Narrative", *Textile* 9, no. 1 (2011): 90–107.

26 Mike Raco and Emma Tunney, "Visibilities and Invisibilities in Urban Development: Small Business Communities and the London Olympics 2012", *Urban Studies* 47, no. 10 (2010): 2069–91.

27 Buchli and Lucas, "Absent Present".

28 Griselda Pollock, "The Image in Psychoanalysis and the Archaeological Metaphor", in Griselda Pollock (ed.), *Psychoanalysis and the Image: Transdisciplinary Perspectives* (Oxford: Oxford University Press, 2006), 10.

29 Wray and Higgot, *Camera Constructs*, 5, 19.

Notes to Iles, "The Lower Lea Valley: From Fun Palace to Creative Prison"

1 Joan Littlewood, quoted in Stanley Matthews, *From Agit-Prop to Free Space* (London: Black Dog, 2007), 66.

2 Matthews, *Agit-Prop to Free Space*, 72.

3 Matthews, *Agit-Prop to Free Space*, 81.

4 Reyner Banham, "Flatscape with Containers", *New Society* 10 (1967).

5 Quoted in Andrew Culf, "Olympics Can Help UK Rebrand Itself, Says New Cultural Chief", *Guardian*, 27 April 2007.

6 Bill Morris, "The Cultural Olympiad – be inspired", 11 March 2008, http://www.london2012.com/blog/2008/03/the-cultural-olympiad-be-inspired.php (accessed 22 March 2012)

7 Quoted in Matthews, *Agit-Prop to Free Space*, 69.

8 Joan Littlewood, "Non-Program: A Laboratory of Fun", *Drama Review* 12, no. 3 (Spring, 1968): 127–34.

9 Alexander Trocchi, quoted in Matthews, *From Agit-Prop to Free Space*, 112.

10 Matthews, *Agit-Prop to Free Space*, 69.

11 "New Book on 1972 Class Struggle in Bri tain: Militant Tactics Smash Tory Laws", *Socialist Worker*, no. 1722 (11 November 2000), http://www.socialistworker.co.uk/archive/1722/sw172213.htm (accessed 22 March 2012).

12 "1972 Class Struggle in Britain".

13 "1972 Class Struggle in Britain".

14 Wikipedia, "Port of London Authority", http://en.wikipedia.org/wiki/Port_of_London_Authority (accessed 22 March 2012).

15 London County Council, *Administrative County of London Development Plan 1951 Analysis* (London: London County Council, 1951).

16 Matthews, *Agit-Prop to Free Space*, 195.

17 Letter from Littlewood to Gordon Pask, quoted in Matthews, *Agit-Prop to Free Space*, 121.

18 Similar points are made with regard to a collaborative project by Reyner Banham, Peter Hall and Cedric Price, "Non-Plan an Experiment in Freedom", discussed in Simon Sadler and Johnathon Hughes (eds.), *Non-Plan: Essays on Freedom Participation and Change in Modern Architecture and Urbanism* (Oxford: Architectural Press, 2000).

19 Quoted in Matthews, *Agit-Prop to Free Space*, 195.

20 Brian Holmes, "The Flexible Personality: For a New Cultural Critique", *Transversal*, no. 11 (2006), http://eipcp.net/transversal/1106/holmes/en (accessed 22 March 2012).

21 Tony Blair, "The Greenest Games Ever", *Guardian*, 23 January 2007.

22 Bryan Finoki, "Fantasy Prison", 2 February 2007, http://subtopia.blogspot.com/2007/02/fantasy-prison.html (accessed 22 March 2012).

23 James Heartfield, "Creative London", *Mute*, 6 October 2007, http://www.metamute.org/editorial/articles/creative-london (accessed 22 March 2012).

24 Quoted in Heartfield, "Creative London".

25 Giorgio Agamben, "In Playland: Reflections on History and Play", in Giorgio Agamben, *Infancy and History* (London: Verso, 2004), 79.

26 Randy Martin, "Marxism after Cultural Studies", http://www.generation-online.org/c/fc_rent7.htm (accessed 15 January 2012).

Notes to Gray, "Duck! You Regeneration Sucker"

1 The phrase belongs to Paul Willemens: Paul Willemens, "An Avant-Garde for the '90s", in *Looks and Frictions: Essays in Cultural Studies and Film Theory* (London: British Film Institute, Indiana University Press, 1994), 157.

2 Stewart Home, *Bubonic Plagiarism: Stewart Home on Art, Politics & Appropriation* (London: Sabotage Editions, 2006), 10.

3 Stanley Mitchell, "Introduction", in Walter Benjamin, *Understanding Brecht* (London: Verso, 1998), xiii.

4 William Fowler, "Offshore Speculation: In Conversation: Anja Kirschner, Director of Polly II Plan for a Revolution in Docklands", *Vertigo Magazine* 3, no. 4 (Winter 2004).

5 A device that vividly evokes the cinema of Michael Powell and Emeric B. Pressburger, for instance, *Black Narcissus* (1947) and *Peeping Tom* (1960), and their interest in the irrational frictions lurking beneath the carapace of the rational mind.

6 Walter Benjamin, *Illuminations* (London: Pimlico, 1999), 248.

7 Patricia Nelson Limerick, *The Legacy of Conquest: The Unbroken Past of the American West* (New York: Norton, 1987), 55.

8 Neil Smith, *The New Urban Frontier: Gentrification and the Revanchist City* (London: Routledge, 1996).

9 Smith, *New Urban Frontier*, xiii.

10 Smith, *New Urban Frontier*, xvi.

11 Robert Beauregard, *Voices of Decline: The Postwar Fate of US Cities* (Oxford: Basil Blackwell, 1993).

12 Smith, *New Urban Frontier*, xvii.

13 Loic Wacquant, *Urban Outcasts: A Comparative Sociology of Advanced Marginality* (London: Polity Press, 2008), 2.

14 Michael Hardt and Antonio Negri, *Multitude* (London: Penguin Books, 2004), 231–47.

15 For background, see Anthony Iles and Benedict Seymour, "The Re-Occupation", *Mute*, 5 January 2006, http://www.metamute.org/editorial/articles/re-occupation (accessed 22 March 2012).

16 See Stuart Christie, *Granny Made Me an Anarchist: General Franco, The Angry Brigade and Me* (London: Scribner, 2004), 318–411; and John Barker, "The Angry Brigade", *Transgressions: A Journal of Urban Exploration* 4 (Spring 1998):

101–7, available at http://www.reocities.com/pract_history/barker.html (accessed 22 March 2012).

17 Quoted in Benjamin, *Illuminations*, 251.

Notes to Davis, "From the Blue Fence to the Emerald City"

1 Richard Rogers et al., *Towards an Urban Renaissance: Final Report of the Urban Task Force* (London: Urban Task Force, 1999).

2 Henri Lefebvre, *The Production of Space* (Oxford: Basil Blackwell, 1991), 38–9.

3 Lefebvre, *Production of Space*, 38–9.

4 Edward Soja, *Postmetropolis: Critical Studies of Cities and Regions* (Oxford and Malden MA: Blackwell, 2000).

5 LDA, *London Development Agency (Lower Lea Valley, Olympic and Legacy) CPO 2005: Inspector's Report* (London: London Development Agency, 2006).

6 LDA, *CPO 2005*, 245

7 LDA, *CPO 2005*, 258

8 Eastway Users Group representative, interview by the author, 19 August 2008.

9 Lefebvre, *Production of Space*, 43–4.

10 LDA, *CPO 2005*, 365

11 R. Imrie and H. Thomas. "Law, Legal Struggles and Urban Regeneration: Rethinking the Relationships", *Urban Studies* 34, no. 9 (1997): 1401–18.

12 Lefebvre, *Production of Space*, 44.

13 KCAP Architects and Planners, Allies & Morrison Architects & EDAW, *Legacy Masterplan Framework (LMF) People and Places: a framework for consultation* London (LDA, 2009), 57–9, 78–9.

14 K. Rattenbury, *This Is Not Architecture* (London: Routledge, 2002).

15 Sebastiano Serlio, *Five Books of Architecture* (Mineola, New York: Dover Publications, [1537–51] 1983).

Notes to Hatcher, "Forced Evictions"

1 COHRE, *Hosting the 2012 Olympic Games: London's Olympic Preparations and Housing Rights Concerns* (Geneva: Centre on Housing Rights and Evictions, 2007).

2 COHRE, *Hosting the Games*, 28.

3 Mark Stephens of the law firm Finers Stephens Innocent, which represented a number of businesses evicted from the Olympic site, in J. Prynn and R. Lydall, "Row over Olympic Site", *Evening Standard*, 19 April 2005.

4 W. Blackstone, *Commentaries on the Laws of England* (Chicago: Chicago University Press, [1765–9] 1979).

5 R. P. Malloy and J. C. Smith, "Private Property, Community Development, and Eminent Domain", in R. P. Malloy (ed.), *Private Property, Community Development and Eminent Domain* (Farnham: Ashgate, 2008), 7.

6 See B. Denyer-Green, *Compulsory Purchase and Compensation* (London: Estates Gazette, 2000).

7 European Convention of Human Rights, Art. 1 Protocol 1, my emphasis.

8 T. Allen, "Controls over the Use and Abuse of Eminent Domain in England: A Comparative View", in Malloy, *Private Property, Community Development and Eminent Domain*, 78.

9 *James v United Kingdom* (1998) 98 Eur. Ct. H.R. (ser. A).

10 Allen, "Controls over the Use", 79.

11 G. Poynter, "The 2012 Olympic Games and the reshaping of East London", in R. Imrie, L. Lees and M. Raco (eds.), *Regenerating London: Governance, Sustainability and Community in a Global City* (London: Routledge, 2009), 146.

12 Cited in C. M. Hall, "Imaging, Tourism and Sports Event Fever: The Sydney Olympics and the Need for a Social Charter for Mega-events", in C. Gratton and I. P. Henry (eds.), *Sport in the City: The Role of Sport in Economic and Social Regeneration* (London: Routledge, 2001), 176.

13 Hall, "Imaging, Tourism and Sports".

14 It is not clear what percentage were forcibly evicted, or whether some residents volunteered to move.

15 COHRE, *Fair Play for Housing Rights: Mega-events, Olympic Games and Housing Rights* (Geneva: Centre on Housing Rights and Evictions, 2007).

16 COHRE, *Fair Play for Housing Rights.*

17 COHRE, *Fair Play for Housing Rights.*

18 The London Development Agency [LDA] (Lower Lea Valley, Olympic and Legacy) *Compulsory Purchase Order [CPO] 2005.*

19 LDA, *CPO 2005.*

20 The Government announced that regional development agencies are to close at the end of March 2012.

21 D. Rose, *Report to the Secretary of State for Trade and Industry: Application by the London Development Agency for Confirmation of the London Development Agency (Lower Lea Valley, Olympic Legacy) Compulsory Purchase Order 2005*, Planning Inspectorate, 2006.

22 Rose, *Report to the Secretary*, 308.

23 D. Mitchell, "The Annihilation of Space

by Law: The Roots and Implications of Anti-Homeless Laws in the United States", in N. Blomley, D. Delaney. D. and R. T. Ford (eds.), *The Legal Geographies Reader* (London: Blackwell, 2001), 15.

24 Land Compensation Act 1973.

25 *Savoury and others v Secretary of State for Wales and another* (1976) 31 P. & C.R. 344.

26 Sax, "Do Communities Have Rights?", *University of Pittsburgh Law Review* 45, 1984, 506.

27 Rose, *Report to the Secretary.*

28 Communities and Local Government, *Compulsory Purchase and Compensation: Compulsory Purchase Procedure* (Wetherby: Communities and Local Governments Publications, 2004), 22, my emphasis.

29 Rose, *Report to the Secretary*, 70.

30 LDA 2006, cited in Rose, *Report to the Secretary* , 70.

31 Rose, *Report to the Secretary*, 71.

32 The author was unable to establish contact with any of the residents living on this estate.

Notes to Slavin, "Scenes from Public Consultations"

1 DCMS/Strategy Unit, *Game Plan: a strategy to for delivering Government's sport and physical activity objectives* (London: Cabinet Office, 2002), 66.

2 *Report to the Secretary of State for Trade and Industry: Application by the London Development Agency for Confirmation of the London Development Agency (Lower Lea Valley, Olympic Legacy) Compulsory Purchase Order 2005*, Planning Inspectorate, 359-360.

3 Julian Cheyne, "7 Planners and a Cupboard", 15 Feb 200, http://www.gamesmonitor.org.uk/node/379

Notes to Hay & Hay, "Future Orientations"

1 Sebastian Coe, Olympic bid presentation, Singapore, 6 July 2005.

2 ODA, "Olympic and Paralympic Village", Olympic Delivery Authority, http://www.london2012.com/athletes-village (accessed 4 December 2011).

3 Newham Borough Council, "Westfield Stratford City, Newham's Lasting Legacy", http://www.newham.gov.uk/news/2011/september/westfieldstratfordcitynewhamslastinglegacy.htm (accessed 4 December 2011).

4 ODA, "Olympic Park", Olympic Delivery Authority, http://www.london2012.com/olympic-park (accessed 4 December 2011).

5 Newham Borough Council, "Newham and the 2012 Games", http://www.newham.gov.uk/2012Games/AboutThe2012Games/default.htm (accessed 4 December 2011).

6 ONS, "Indices of Deprivation 2010 for Super Output Areas", Office for National Statistics.

7 Gordon MacLeod and Craig Johnstone, "Stretching Urban Renaissance: Privatizing Space, Civilizing Place", *International Journal of Urban and Regional Research* 36, no. 1 (2012): 1–28.

8 Anna Minton, *What Kind of World Are We Building? The Privatisation of Public Space* (London: Royal Institution of Chartered Surveyors, 2006).

9 Anna Minton, *Ground Control: Fear and Happiness in the Twenty-First Century City* (London: Penguin, 2009).

10 Loic Wacquant, *Urban Outcasts: A Comparative Sociology of Advanced Marginality* (Cambridge: Polity, 2008).

11 Minton, *Ground Control.*

12 Minton, *Ground Control.*

13 MacLeod and Johnstone, "Stretching Urban Renaissance".

14 MacLeod and Johnstone, "Stretching Urban Renaissance".

15 Chris Allen, *Housing Market Renewal and Social Class* (London: Routledge, 2008).

16 Allen, *Housing Market Renewal*

17 Peter Malpass, *Housing Associations and Housing Policy: A Historical Perspective* (Basingstoke: Macmillan, 2000).

18 Peter Hall, "The City of Towers: The Corbusian Radiant City", in *Cities of Tomorrow* (London: Blackwell Publishing: 2002).

19 Alan Murie, "The Social Rented Sector, Housing and the Welfare State in the UK", *Housing Studies* 12, no. 4 (1997): 437–61.

20 Murie, "The Social Rented Sector".

21 Murie, "The Social Rented Sector".

22 Anne Power, *Hovels to High Rise: State Housing in Europe since 1850* (London: Routledge, 1993).

23 Power, *Hovels to High Rise.*

24 Power, *Hovels to High Rise.*

25 Hall, "City of Towers".

26 Power, *Hovels to High Rise.*

27 Rowena Hay, *Guide to Localism, Part 2: Getting Community Engagement Right* (London: Royal Institute of British Architects, 2011).

28 Power, *Hovels to High Rise.*

29 Loretta Lees, "The Urban Injustices of New Labour's 'New Urban Renewal': The Case of the Aylesbury Estate in London", conference paper presented at European Network for Housing Research, 7 July 2011.

Notes to Harding, "Legacy Now"

1 Our landlord, Michael Dalton of Percy Daltons Peanuts, chaired this group until it moved out in 2006.

2 "The Mayor will, and the boroughs should... support the provision and creation of a range of workspaces suitable for new and existing enterprises of all kinds, including a high quality media and creative industry cluster at Hackney Wick that will provide premises and from association with the Games, should be used to effect a positive, sustainable and fully accessible economic, social and environmental transformation for one of the most diverse and most deprived parts." GLA, *The London Plan: Spatial Development Strategy For Greater London* (London: Greater London Authority, 2011), 43–4.

3 DCMS, *Before, During and After: Making the Most of the London 2012 Games* (London: Department for Culture, Media and Sport, 2008).

4 SPACE has contributed to the Hackney Wick Local Development Framework, the Fish Island Conservation Area Characterisation Study, and the 2011 Fish Island Local Development Framework, among others.

5 Anna Minton, *Ground Control: Fear and Happiness in the Twenty-First Century City* (London: Penguin, 2009), 22.

6 All these are under severe threat. Graffiti in January 2012 read "Real Graf lives it won't ever die – Fake graffiti artists boom bye bye".

7 Eric Reynolds of Urban Space Management summed up his frustration at the red tape he was facing working with the BBC building a structure in the Park when he said: "£40,000 to move four trees at the Olympic Park".

Notes to Sprogis, "Stratford Façade"

1 Historically, the court sculptor or artist would be summoned shortly after the death of the monarch or nobleman, and a plaster impression would be taken from their face. The masks were ceremonial in origin; as aids to the production of wax "effigies" of dead monarchs and nobles for state funeral displays. Their function evolved over the centuries, serving as models on which to base posthumous portraits or busts. By the 19th century, the death mask assumed the role of the *memento mori*, becoming the object of memorial and reverence itself. See Ernst Benkard and Margaret Green, *Undying Faces, A Collection of Death Masks* (New York: W.W. Norton & Company, 1927).

2 Ray Clancy, "2012 Olympic Effect Sees Rental Demand Grow and Property Prices Rise Well Above Average in East London", *Property Community*, 27 July 2010, http://www.propertycommunity.com/property-in-the-uk/652-2012-olympic-demand-grow-property.html (accessed 25 March 2012).

3 High Street 2012, "About", http://www.highstreet2012.com/background (accessed 28 February 2012).

Notes to Watt & Kennelly, "Seeing Stratford and the 2012 Olympics through the eyes..."

1 J. Kennelly and P. Watt, "Sanitizing Public Space in Olympic Host Cities: The Spatial Experiences of Marginalized Youth in 2010 Vancouver and 2012 London", *Sociology* 45, no. 5 (2011): 765–81; J. Kennelly and P. Watt, "Seeing Olympic Effects through the Eyes of Marginally Housed Youth: Changing Places and the Gentrification of East London", *Visual Studies* (forthcoming).

2 R. Croghan, C. Griffin, J. Hunter and A. Phoenix, "Young People's Constructions of Self: Notes on the Use and Analysis of the Photo-elicitation Methods", *International Journal of Social Research Methodology* 11, no. 4 (2008): 345–56; P. Mizen and Y. Ofosu-Kusi, "Unofficial Truths and Everyday Insights: Understanding Voice in Visual Research with the Children of Accra's Urban Poor", *Visual Studies* 25, no. 3 (2010): 255–67.

3 Kennelly and Watt, "Sanitizing Public Space"; Kennelly and Watt, "Seeing Olympic Effects".

Notes to Powell, "Structures of Enchantment"

1 Stephen Barber, *Extreme Europe* (London: Reaktion Books, 2001), 29.

2 Part of an AHRC Fellowship in the Creative and Performing Arts at Bartlett School of Architecture, UCL.

3 George Bataille, *The Accursed Share Vol 1* (New York: Zone Books, 1991), 2.

4 Formally Sugar House Lane, now Strand East. Owned and developed by Landprop.

5 Charles–François Viel, *De l'Impuissance des Mathematiques Pour Assurer La Solidité Des Batiments*, quoted in Walter Benjamin, *The Arcades Project* (Cambridge: Harvard University Press, 1999), 95.

6 From "peep show" concertina tunnel books to carousel books and rotating volvelles.

7 This is discussed in Smithson's essay "A tour of the Monuments of Passaic, New Jersey", in *The Collected Writings* (Berkeley: UC Press, 1996).

8 Louis Aragon, *Le Paysan de Paris* (Paris: Gallimard, 1923).

About the Contributors

Juliette Adair is a writer (of fiction mostly). She runs workshops on the Dorset coast which connect writing with walking and landscape, often using the tools of Process-Oriented Psychology to explore these relationships more deeply. writewalkwild.co.uk

Lara Almarcegui is a Spanish artist based in Rotterdam. Her work often explores neglected or overlooked sites, carefully cataloguing and highlighting each location's tendency towards entropy.

Andrew Bailes is a poet, author, and founding member of Dog Chair Press. He used to live in Hackney Wick and now lives on a narrowboat. He belongs to londonboaters.org, helping the community that lives on London's rivers and canals to find lost cats and fight corporate malfeasance and conspiracy.

Benjamin Beach is a political activist and architecture student at Bartlett, UCL. He developed a strong interest in narrative and memory whilst studying at Byam Shaw, which he is attempting to expand within a critique of the city as a factory and a field of struggle.

Monica Biagioli is an artist, writer and academic living in London. In 2008, she began curating the Sound Proof series of exhibitions, a commissioning project bringing together works by artists working with sound components. This evolving cycle of five yearly exhibitions will complete with Sound Proof 5 during London 2012.

Polly Braden's photography explores the relationship between daily life, work and leisure. Her images are acutely observed portraits within a broader assessment of contemporary culture. She has exhibited internationally. Publications include *China Between* (Dewi Lewis, 2010). pollybraden.com

Jessie Brennan's work encompasses drawing within a socially engaged practice. Her works investigate the construction of narrative through meticulous pencil drawings, performative actions and video installations informed by social history and engagement. Jessie studied at the Royal College of Art (2007) and was Second Prize Winner, Jerwood Drawing Prize 2011.

David Campany is a writer, curator and artist. His books include *Photography and Cinema* (2008) and *Jeff Wall: Picture for Women* (2011). He exhibits and publishes his photographic work occasionally. He teaches at the University of Westminster.

Ben Campkin is Lecturer in Architectural History and Theory at the Bartlett School of Architecture, University College London, and Director of the UCL Urban Laboratory. He is co-editor of *Dirt: New Geographies of Cleanliness and Contamination* (2007), and is currently completing a book on London, *The Regeneration Game.*

Man Cheung is a photographer. A common thread in his work explores the theme of community. His interest focuses on the people who live within those communities, how they are affected and relate to their surrounding environment. mancheung.com

Alessandra Chilá is a photographer based in London. She is currently studying a Master in Photographic Studies whilst working professionally in the media industry. Her work has been exhibited in group shows and solo exhibitions in Belgium, Italy and the UK. alessandrachila.com , alessandrachila.blogspot.co.uk

Stephen Cornford is an artist working at the intersection of sculpture and music and is currently a Research Fellow at the Sound Art Research Unit of Oxford Brookes University. He studied sculpture at Slade School before completing a MA in Time-Based Arts Practices at Dartington College of Arts. scrawn.co.uk

Rebecca Court's practice explores political rhetoric through performative interventions, installations and text pieces. She holds a BA in Fine Art from Norwich School of Art and Design in 2008 and graduated from Royal College of Art in 2011 with an MA in Photography. rebeccacourt.co.uk

Juliet Davis is Cities Research Fellow at LSE, where she also completed a PhD in Sociology focused on the politics of envisioning an urban regeneration "Legacy" to the 2012 Olympics. Her current research focuses on urban resilience in terms of the relationship between the design and governance of urban form.

Richard DeDomenici is an artist who uses subversive satire to create uncertainty and possibility. He's preparing six Olympic-related projects, before touring his new show *Popaganda* this autumn.In 2011 he performed in Tokyo, New York, Amsterdam, Berlin and was an Oxford

Samuel Beckett Theatre Trust Award finalist. dedomenici.com

Silke Dettmers is an artist and lecturer who also, occasionally, curates and writes. Originally trained as a Graphic Designer, her practice for the last two decades has been Fine Art. Her work comprises of sculptures, drawings, and bookworks. She is a user (and abuser) of photography.

Chris Dorley-Brown has lived and worked in the east end of London for the last thirty years. Largely self-taught his cultural education was formed in east London in the late seventies, against a backdrop of strongly polarised political conflict and change. modrex.com

Alberto Duman is an artist, lecturer and independent researcher. His work explores the portable and the architectural, the local andinternational and the permanent and the temporary across various media. He is currently running a BA Fine Art module at Middlesex University and is working on a road movie. albertoduman.co.uk

Fantich & Young. Artists Mariana Fantich and Dominic Young have been working together since 2008, and they have lived in Hackney Wick since 2004. The art of Fantich&Young addresses parallels between social evolution and evolution in the natural word; nature as model or nature as threat. fantichandyoung.co.uk

Jem Finer works in experimental and popular music, film, photography and installation. An enduring fascination with deep time and space has been the impetus behind much of his work. elrino.co.uk

David George has been a photographer for over 30 years. He gained a BA in Photography and Fine Art from Derby University and an MA from the Sir John Cass School of Art, London. He is also the co-founder/publisher of the contemporary photography broadsheet "Uncertain States." davidgeorge.eu , uncertainstates.com

Stephen Gill became interested in photography in early childhood thanks to his father and a fascination with the microscopic inspection of pond life and insects. Gill's books in response to Hackney include *Hackney Wick*, *Archaeology in Reverse*, *Hackney Flowers*, *A Series of Disappointments*, *Eton Mission*, and *Off Ground.* stephengill.co.uk

Neil Gray is a writer, researcher and film-maker. He writes frequently for *Variant* magazine which he also co-edits, and regularly on urban issues, cinema and radical politics for magazines and journals. He is a housing activist in Glasgow, where he sometimes practices a form of public walking as critical pedagogy.

Anna Harding is Chief Executive of SPACE.

Craig Hatcher is a PhD candidate in the School of Geography at the University of Zürich. Craig also studied and trained as a lawyer in London. He continues to undertake human rights work and maintains a commitment to integrate his professional experience with his academic research.

Rowena Hay is a social researcher specialising in qualitative and participatory research methods. She is currently working on a PhD on mixed tenure housing in London and Newcastle. She is also a member of Resilient Communities. talesfromthefifteenthfloor.blogspot.co.uk

Duncan Hay is studying for a PhD in English Literature at the University of Manchester, focusing on Iain Sinclair's writings. His research interests include psychogeography, Walter Benjamin, and the relationship between contemporary art and literature. He has worked for Hull Time Based Arts, the Free Word Centre and Cornerhouse. walled-city.net

Sara Heitlinger and Franc Purg have been working together since 2006. *Privileged Tactics* explored creative survival tactics in crisis situations, and won a UNESCO Digital Art Award. Their work has been exhibited extensively in the UK and abroad. privilegedtactics.net, francpurg.net, saraheitlinger.net

Adelita Husni-Bey is an Italian/Lybian artist and researcher. She studied Fine Art at Chelsea School of Arts and Photography & Sociology at Goldsmiths University. Her current research involves autonomy, micro-utopias, pirate-utopias, the "Land Issue", (the production of) collective memory, dissent and control, anarchist pedagogy and free-schools.

Anthony Iles is a writer of criticism, fiction and theory, based in London. He is assistant editor of *Mute* magazine, editor of the books, with Mattin, *Noise & Capitalism* (2009), with Stefan Szczelkun, *Agit Disco* (2011) and co-author of, with Josephine Berry Slater, *No Room to Move: Radical Art and the Regenerate City* (2010).

Jacqueline Kennelly is Adjunct Professor of Sociology at Carleton University in Ottawa, Canada.

Anya Kirshner and David Panos' long-form films and installations collide popular culture references, historical research and literary tropes. Their work often involves amateurs, actors and specialists from other disciplines in the creation of speculative histories and spectacular fantasies that interrogate social reality and the relatin of art to class power.

Victoria Lenzoi Lee is a Trinidadian-born architectural / spatial designer, with experience in international design projects in London, Shanghai, Istanbul and Oslo. A Masters of the Arts was gained at Central Saint Martins, and specialism developed in community engagement for urban design projects.

Helen Jefferson Lenskyj is Professor Emerita at the University of Toronto, Canada, an author, activist, recreational athlete, and Olympic critic. Her books include *Inside the Olympic Industry* (SUNY: 2000), *Best Olympics Ever?* (2002) and *Olympic Industry Resistance* (2008).

Ali MacGilp is an independent curator and writer. She is interested in film, video, performance and installation practices as well as archive materials. She is a founder and editor of artvehicle.com and half of curatorial collective norn.

Isaac Marrero-Guillamón is a post-doctoral research fellow at Birkbeck, University of London. His project "The Militant City" investigates the role of art in the configuration of spaces of dissent in relation to the Olympic mega-event. themilitantcity.wordpress.com

Mimi Mollica has covered assignments across the world, photographing current events and in-depth photo essays for various magazines and newspapers from *The Guardian* to *Granta Magazine*. mimimollica.com

Alyssa Moxley is a writer, musician and sound artist telling stories about music, art, ideas, social issues and characters that capture her imagination and sympathy. alyssamoxley.com

Sally Mumby-Croft is a writer and film maker. She originally met and interviewed Leigh Niland as part of her elegaic 16 minute film *Edgelands* (2009) exploring the deletion of landscape and communities by the Olympic development.

Gustavo Murillo is a photographer. He graduated in Arts and Culture from Pompeu Fabra University in Barcelona and is currently living and working in London. His work has been exhibited in Barcelona and London. gustavomurillophoto.com

Tanya Nagar is a street photographer and blogger based in London. tanya-n.com

Leigh Niland is an American painter/printmaker. Her work deals with themes of human emotional states conveyed through land usage. She currently lives near Boston but was previously based in Hackney Wick. Niland teaches Printmaking at the New Hampshire Institute of Art.

Laura Oldfield Ford, originally from Halifax, West Yorkshire, completed a Fine Art Painting MA at The Royal College of Art in 2007 and has since become well known for her politically active and poetic engagement with London as a site of social antagonism. lauraoldfieldford.blogspot.co.uk

Thomas Pausz studied Philosophy in Paris before gaining a Masters in Design at the RCA in London. Thomas develops participatory projects and researches new formats for design, production and exchange. In 2012-2013 he is a design fellow at the Akademie Schloss Solitude. pausz.org

Hilary Powell is an artist and is currently AHRC Fellow in the Creative and Performing Arts at the Bartlett School of Architecture, UCL working on a three-year project critiquing the utopian narratives of the Games through the appropriation of the traditional techniques of pop-up book production and etching. hilarypowell.com

Giles Price's interest in photography began whilst a Royal Marine Commando during the first Gulf War during which time he created a snapshot diary, *Operation Haven*, now in the Imperial War Museum, London. His current work includes *E20 12 Under Construction*, shot from a helicopter above the Olympic Park. gilesprice.com

Jean-François Prost is a Montreal-based artist with an interest in new urban research territories on the fringe of areas rarely explored by artistic intervention. jean-francoisprost.blogspot.co.uk

Susan Pui San Lok is an artist and writer whose exhibition and publication projects range across installation, moving image, sound, performance and text and evolve out of interests in notions of nostalgia and aspiration, place and migration, translation and diaspora. susanpuisanlok.com

Vicky Richardson is Director of Architecture, Design, Fashion at the British Council. She was previously Editor of Blueprint magazine and Trustee for the Campaign for Drawing.

Jude Rosen is a researcher on urban cultures and citizenship, a translator and poet. The *Reclamations* sequence grew out of an artistic collaboration with WeSellBoxesWeBuyGold, part performed in Hackney Museum in 2007. Her pamphlet *A Small Gateway* was published in 2009 by Hearing Eye.

Benedict Seymour is a writer and film maker based in London. He is currently working on a video essay about dyslexic development and dialectical riots. He is contributing editor of *Mute* magazine and a Lecturer in Fine Art at Goldsmiths.

Alistair Siddons is a Hackney-based writer and artist.

Iain Sinclair has lived in Hackney since 1969. His books include *Downriver*, *Lights out for the Territory*, *London Orbital* and *Edge of the Orison*. His most recent publications are *Hackney, That Rose-Red Empire* and *Ghost Milk*.

Martin Slavin is a photographer and activist and a member of Games Monitor – an activist network dedicated to "debunking Olympic Myths". gamesmonitor.org.uk

Alex Sprogis is a graduate of the Bartlett School of Architecture and has lived in east London for five years. He currently works at Nissen Richards Studio, an architectural practice in Hackney. alexsprogis.com

Jan Stradtmann, born 1976 in Wittenberg (Germany), has an MA in Photographic Studies from the University of Westminster, London. In 2006/2007 he received a one year DAAD (German Academic Exchange Service) postgraduate grant for Great Britain and lives and works in Berlin since 2009. janstradtmann.de

Oliver Wainwright is an architectural writer, critic and designer based in London. He studied at Cambridge and the RCA, and has worked at OMA*AMO, muf architecture/art and Design for London. oliverwainwright.co.uk

Julian Walker is an artist, writer and educator. He has worked with several major galleries and museums in the UK and abroad, and leads workshops at the British Library, on language, literature, art, history and printing. He is the author of a number of books on the English language. julianwalker.net

Cathy Ward and Eric Wright met at The Fine Art residency programme at The Banff Centre, Canada in 1989. Major commisions include *Transromantik* (1997), *Volksgeist* (2002), *Gathering in The May* (2003) and *BeauRoque*. Recent projects include *Destiny Manifest* (2005) and *Tender Vessels* (2009). ward-wright.com

Paul Watt is Senior Lecturer in Urban Studies at Birbeck, University of London.

Mark Wayman has made pieces for locations as diverse as a rotting boat in Deptford, an Occupied square in Amsterdam, street routes in many towns and cities, high walkways and gaps under floors. He studied at Cardiff School of Art and Lancaster University. He now lives and works in London.

Henrietta Williams uses still photography and multimedia to explore man-made and built environments, both within and outside of the city. Her work focuses on ideas around fortress urbanism and change through development. henriettawilliams.com

Jim Woodall is an artist. He has worked and exhibited widely as part of the Cut-Up Collective. He lives and works in London. jimwoodall.co.uk

Gesche Wuerfel is a visual artist primarily engaging with spaces in transition and notions of place through genres of urban, landscape and architectural photography. geschewuerfel.com

John Wynne's work, widely exhibited and broadcast around the world, includes large-scale installations, delicate sculptures, composed documentaries and flying radios. He has a PhD from Goldsmiths College and is a Reader in Sound Art at the University of the Arts London. sensitivebrigade.com

Hackney Wick
June, 2012